100 HISPANICS YOU SHOULD KNOW

100 HISPANICS YOU SHOULD KNOW

Iván A. Castro

LIBRARIES
UNLIMITED
A Member of the Greenwood Publishing Group

Westport, Connecticut • London

Library of Congress Cataloging-in-Publication Data

Castro, Iván.
   100 Hispanics you should know / by Iván Castro.
     p. cm.
   Includes bibliographical references and index.
   Audience: Grades 6-12.
   ISBN 1-59158-327-6 (alk. paper)
    1. Spain—Biography—Dictionaries—Juvenile literature. 2. Latin America—Biography—
Dictionaries—Juvenile literature. 3. Spaniards—Biography—Dictionaries—Juvenile literature.
4. Latin Americans—Biography—Dictionaries—Juvenile literature. 5. Hispanic Americans—
Biography—Dictionaries—Juvenile literature. I. Title. II. Title: One hundred Hispanics you
should know.
  CT1347.C37 2007
  920.009268—dc22   2006030668

British Library Cataloguing in Publication Data is available.

Library of Congress Catalog Card Number: 2006030668
ISBN 10: 1-59158-327-6

First published in 2007

Libraries Unlimited, 88 Post Road West, Westport, CT 06881
A Member of the Greenwood Publishing Group, Inc.
www.lu.com

Printed in the United States of America

The paper used in this book complies with the
Permanent Paper Standard issued by the National
Information Standards Organization (Z39.48–1984).

10 9 8 7 6 5 4 3 2 1

To my wife, Isora, for her help. To my children Bryan, Patrick, and Ashley, for their support.

Contents

Introduction

I have always wanted to write books, but not this one. The idea for this volume came to me in October 2003. I had gone to pick up my daughter Ashley at her middle school when I noticed a board hanging in one of the school's halls displaying biographies written by students. October is Hispanic Heritage Month at Miami-Dade County and the subjects of these biographies were famous Hispanics. To my surprise and chagrin, every single one of the individuals portrayed was either a popular singer or a sports figure.

"We are more than this," I said to myself. I thought right away of José Martí, Cuba's beloved founding father and poet; México's statesman Benito Juárez; Chile's great poets Gabriela Mistral and Pablo Neruda; Hernán Cortés, Francisco Pizarro, and other Spanish conquistadors; Spain and México's celebrated tenor Plácido Domingo; Costa Rica's Nobel Peace Prize winner Oscar Arias Sánchez; Simón Bolivar, Venezuela-born liberator of vast areas of South America; Argentina's statesman and educator Bartolomé Mitre; or even New Mexico's renowned gunfighter Elfego Baca.

Why didn't these students know about Hispanics who, in the larger view of life, were more important than the popular singers and sports heroes? There are several reasons. First, to me there seems to be an inherent bias against Hispanics in the American educational system. Or perhaps it is just a form of ignorance. In very few, if any, books does one find the names of Hispanics who have made great contributions to the sciences, the arts, or many other fields of human endeavor. Second, and in this case I hold Hispanics responsible as much as anybody, there is no real interest among Spanish-speaking historians in keeping the necessary records of Hispanic achievement. Of course, there is some information to be had, but it is usually piecemeal and incomplete. In addition, even in many Spanish-language publications and Web sites, there is more information on English- or German-speaking individuals than Spanish-speaking ones. In more than one Spanish-language Web site that I have visited, I have found more information on William Shakespeare than on Miguel de Cervantes. The lack of books in English about these people is also appalling.

Third, there is an economic factor. It is easier and probably more profitable to write about popular figures. Their biographies are readily available in magazines and on Web sites, and most people tend to be more interested in celebrities than in scientists, composers, statesmen, poets, writers, painters, or revolutionaries.

In any case, I decided a book on these forgotten or overlooked Hispanics was needed, and if no one else would do it, I would write that book.

The process of choosing who would be included in this book and who would be left out was simultaneously simple and complex. Defining the categories was the easy part, but choosing the individuals to include was more challenging. I knew I wanted to include founding fathers. Since all nations claim their own founding fathers, this could have been a very lengthy list. I decided to use those who impacted more than one nation in one way or another. Some of these patriots were military men; others were poets, educators, and intellectuals whose influence is felt all over the Spanish-speaking world.

Next, I wanted the myriad facets of Spanish arts and sciences represented. Therefore, writers, poets, painters, and composers had to be included. At this point I should say that I'm partial to that group of Spanish writers from the end of the nineteenth to the beginning of the twentieth centuries known as the Generation of '98. Never before, or after, has a group of authors had such influence in the communal psyches of Spain, Central America, and South America. Many a reader might think that the group is over-represented. I believe that I did not include enough of them.

Then there were those who definitely were the best in their respective fields. Authors, artists, and scientists who won Nobel Prizes for their achievements can be found in this category, and are represented in this guide. A few who did not win the coveted prize but made remarkable contributions to their fields are also included. Explorers and conquerors of the New World are also included. Whether the imposition of European customs, values, and ideas in the Americas was for better or for worse, the importance of these people cannot be denied.

Individuals who were part of, or made contributions to, the history of the United States are also part of this book. For too long the contributions of Hispanics to the development of this great nation have been underexposed.

Finally, a couple of Wild West individuals are profiled. The role of Hispanics (and other minorities) in the settling of the West has for too long been ignored in history books as well as Western fiction. The way I see it, if the exploits of Wyatt Earp, Bat Masterson, and Kit Carson are the stuff of legend, well, read on and find out about Juan Cortina and Elfego Baca.

Recent political figures will not be found in this book. History still has to pass judgment, and the author's purpose is not to create controversy, but to demonstrate the influence that a particular group has had on history.

The result of my work is a collection of 100 short biographies of men and women from around the world and throughout history who have made significant achievements. They are also all Hispanics. The profiles are arranged alphabetically by name, and each includes birth and death dates, a list of that individual's achievements, and a short biography. Resources for further information are given at the end of each profile.

It is hoped that this collection will inform readers of all cultural backgrounds, and inspire young people of Hispanic descent. Students may wish to use this guide for research and reports. Educators may wish to use it as a ready reference and teaching resource.

This work is neither all encompassing nor absolute. I know that there are many other Hispanics who deserve recognition, and that if somebody else had authored the biographies, the list would have been different. Furthermore, the life histories presented here are brief—less than 1,000 words—and that was done intentionally. This book is meant only as a primer, an introduction to the many contributions made by the people of an ancient and noble lineage to the United States, the Western Hemisphere, and, indeed, the world.

There will be many, I'm sure, that would wonder why this book is written in English and not in Spanish. The answer is simple: reach. Today English is an international language, and I want this volume to be read and understood by as many people as possible around the world.

Finally, I would like to invite the reader to turn the page and begin reading about men and women of, to paraphrase Winston Churchill, the "Spanish Speaking Peoples," and those of Hispanic heritage whom everybody should know about.

100 HISPANICS YOU SHOULD KNOW

Ciro Alegría

Indianizing Literature

Novelist,
Politician

- ❖ Born in Sartinbamba, Perú.
- ❖ Birth date: November 4, 1909.
- ❖ Death date: February 17, 1967.

Career Highlights

- Joined APRA, *Alianza Popular Revolucionaria Americana* (The Popular Revolutionary American Alliance), a Peruvian populist party.
- Published his first novel, *La Serpiente de Oro* (*The Golden Serpent*), in 1935.
- Published *El Mundo es Ancho y Ajeno* (*Broad and Alien is the World*) in 1941 and won the Latin American Prize Novel Contest.
- Became a member of the Peruvian Language Academy in 1960.
- Elected to the Peruvian Chamber of Deputies (House of Representatives) in 1963.

Important Contributions

Ciro Alegría is one of the first writers in Spanish-speaking America who rejected the European form and subject in the novel and infused it with a New-World style. Through his works the world knew and understood the misery faced by the native population of South America. As a member of APRA (Alianza Popular Revolucionaria Americana), he was committed to better the lives of the Peruvian Indians, the country's majority population.

Career Path

When Ciro Alegría was born in 1909, his native province of Huamachuco in the northern Peruvian Andes was an unqualified school for political radicalism. Living conditions for the isolated, poor, uneducated, and overworked Indian population were appalling. They lived in shacks, food was almost non-existent, and there were no warm blankets to protect them from the highlands cold. Alegría, the son of a *mestizo* (of Spanish/Indian ancestry) father and a Spanish-Irish mother, saw at an early age the oppression of the Indians that would become the inspiration for all of his future novels. These conditions also colored his political outlook. He would later join APRA, a party committed to social and economic reforms. Its main goal was to improve the fortunes of Native Americans, who form the majority in Perú. At the beginning, the *apristas* (members of APRA) promoted changes through violence, but eventually evolved into promoting changes through democratic means.

After receiving his primary education in his hometown, Alegría attended the National College of San Juan in Trujillo, where he graduated from secondary school. Through the next decade he worked at a variety of jobs and became involved in politics. He became an *aprista* in 1930, and the same year went to work for the newspaper *El Norte* (*The North*) and enrolled at the University of Trujillo. By 1933 his political commitments landed him in jail. Due to the humid conditions, lack of food, and torture, Alegría's health deteriorated to the point that friends and relatives believed he would not make it out alive. When the government decreed an amnesty and he was freed from jail, he went into exile in Chile.

During the following decade, he published his most important works: *Los Perros Hambrientos* (*Hungry Dogs*) in 1939, and two years later, his much-honored masterpiece, *Broad and Alien is the World*, about the difficult lives of the Peruvian Indians abandoned by their government and facing exploitation by white European landowners. *Broad and Alien is the World* was widely translated, and its English version caused quite an uproar in the United States and England. The plot presented an Indian village as the oppressed hero, and the white landowners, the army, and the government as villains serving the United States' interests. This was one of the first Latin American novels to obtain recognition in the United States. It was called *indigenista* (indigenous) because the subject dealt with the Peruvian Indians—heady stuff for 1941.

He then moved to New York, where he lived for eight years, earning his living as a foreign correspondent for various Spanish-language papers and teaching at different universities. From New York he relocated to Puerto Rico, where he taught at the University of Puerto Rico, and then to Cuba, again working as a journalist.

Alegría returned to his native Perú in 1957, joined the *Partido Acción Popular* (Popular Action Party), and was elected to the Chamber of Deputies in 1963. He died suddenly in the Peruvian capital of Lima in 1967. His legacy as a thematic innovator established him in the annals of Hispanic literature. In addition, many of today's most radical Latin American revolutionary movements consider him one of their intellectual ancestors.

Bibliography

Escajadillo, Tomás G. *Mariátegui y la Literatura Peruana*. Lima, Perú: Amaru Editores, 2004.

Flores, Angel. *Spanish American Authors: The Twentieth Century*. New York: H. W. Wilson, 1992.

Foster, David William, and Foster, Virginia Ramos, eds. *Modern Latin American Literature*. New York: Frederick Ungan Publishing Co., 1975.

Tocilovac, Goran. *La comunidad indígena y Ciro Alegría: un estudio de El mundo es ancho y ageno*. Lima, Perú: Ediciones de la Biblioteca Universitaria, 1975.

Varona, Dora. *La sombra del cóndor: biografía ilustrada de Ciro Alegría*. Lima, Perú: Diselpesa, 1993.

Luis Alvarez

Of Atomic Bombs and Dinosaurs

Physicist

- ❖ Born in San Francisco, California.
- ❖ Birth date: June 13, 1911.
- ❖ Death date: September 1, 1988.

Career Highlights

- Designed detonators for atomic bombs.
- Invented three types of radar.
- Awarded the Albert Einstein Medal in 1961.
- Awarded the Nobel Prize in Physics in 1968.
- Co-proposed the theory that the death of the dinosaurs resulted from a meteor impacting Earth.

Important Contributions

Luis Alvarez was more than a physicist. He was also an archaeologist, college professor, dinosaur hunter, and a bit of an adventurer. As a physicist, he discovered more than seventy new atomic particles, designed detonators for the atomic bombs dropped on the Japanese cities of Hiroshima and Nagasaki, and was responsible for developing three types of radar. He taught at the University of California, Berkeley. His adventurous spirit, as well as his professional relevance, landed him a seat as an observer in a second B-29 that trailed the plane that bombed Hiroshima. Later he accompanied his son, Walter, during an excavation campaign that produced their much-debated theory that postulated that a cloud of dust created by a meteor impact caused the extinction of the dinosaurs.

Career Path

Luis Walter Alvarez, an unassuming scholar, had an enormous impact on the modern world. His inventions have helped destroy and save millions of lives. His theories have assisted us in understanding not only the evolution of life on earth but also political assassinations.

Alvarez's grandfather on his father's side emigrated from Spain to Cuba, from Cuba to Los Angeles, from Los Angeles to Hawaii, and finally to San Francisco, all the while amassing a considerable fortune. His ancestors on his mother's side traveled from Ireland to the City by the Bay via a much more direct route.

Alvarez attended elementary school and the first few years of high school in his hometown of San Francisco. But when his father, a medical doctor and researcher, accepted a position at the world-famous Mayo Clinic in Rochester, Minnesota, the family moved, and Alvarez graduated from Rochester High School.

In 1928 he enrolled at the University of Chicago, majoring in chemistry, but the subject bored him. Alvarez had an epiphany in his junior year when he took a course called "Advanced Experimental Physics: Light." He changed his major to physics, earned his bachelor's of science degree in 1932, his master's degree in 1934, and his doctorate degree two years later. Upon graduation, he accepted a faculty and research position at the University of California, Berkeley.

At Berkeley, Alvarez made his first big research breakthrough. He is credited as co-discoverer of the cosmic rays' "East-West effect." In a nutshell, this theory states that the quantity of cosmic rays reaching the earth's atmosphere hinges on the direction from which they are coming. However, with the outbreak of World War II, the world of scientific research was turned upside down. For the next five years, all research would have to be applied to defense matters. In 1940 the military moved Alvarez to the Massachusetts Institute of Technology (MIT), where he worked on radar systems. While the official name of his research division at MIT was Special Systems, everybody knew it as Luis's Gadgets. His contributions to radar improvements were three-pronged. The following systems were developed under his leadership: the microwave early warning system, which assembles images of airplanes in cloudy skies; the high-altitude bombing system code-named "Eagle," which was used to find ground targets when they could not be seen; and GAC, or Ground-Controlled Approach, a narrow-beam radar that allows controllers on the ground to guide airplanes landing in zero visibility. Modern versions of GAC are still used today in most airports around the world.

In 1943 he was assigned to the Manhattan Project. His job was to build detonators for atomic bombs. He developed the detonators for the first atomic bomb set off at Trinity Site near Alamogordo, New Mexico, and for "Fat Man," the bomb dropped on Nagasaki. His expertise and sense of adventure earned him a place on the observation plane during the first explosion of a nuclear device on July 16, 1945, and on the B-29 that trailed the *Enola Gay* on the August 6 bombing of Hiroshima. On August 9, Fat Man was dropped on Nagasaki, leading the Japanese to surrender on August 14, 1945.

With World War II over, Alvarez returned to Berkeley. There he directed the design and construction of the world's first forty-foot linear accelerator, which enabled him to discover seventy new atomic particles. His knowledge of physics also led him to explain how President John F. Kennedy's head could have jolted backward if Lee Harvey Oswald shot him from behind, therefore debunking some of the myths created around the president's assassination. He also worked on big liquid hydrogen bubble chambers, which help with density calculations of objects. In 1965 he used his equipment on an archaeological mission to Egypt to look for hidden compartments on the Great Pyramid of Khufu, but didn't find any. The Nobel foundation recognized his work with the 1968 Nobel Prize in Physics.

In 1980 he developed his most controversial idea, and it had nothing to do with physics. While on an archaeological trip to Italy with his son Walter, an archaeologist at Berkeley, they came up with geological proof that a meteor might have hit the earth some 66.4 million years ago. The cloud of dust, they hypothesized, could have killed most of the planet's life-forms, including the dinosaurs. While more evidence has been found to prop up the theory, it is still being hotly contested today.

Luis Alvarez died of cancer at Berkeley. His legacy includes twenty-two patents and one dinosaurian controversy.

Bibliography

Allison, Amy. *Luis Alvarez and the Development of the Bubble Chamber.* Bear, DE: Mitchell Lane Publishers, 2003.

Alvarez, Luis. *Alvarez: Adventures of a Scientist.* Berkeley: University of California Press, 1987.

Greenstein, George. *Portraits of Discovery: Profiles in Scientific Genius.* New York: John Wiley, 1998.

"Luis Walter Alvarez." Earth Sciences. Macmillan Reference USA, 1999. Reproduced in Biography Resource Center. Farmington Hills, MI: Thomson Gale, 2005.

Sherby, Louise S., ed. *The Who's Who of Nobel Prize Winners 1901–2000.* Westport, CT: Oryx Press, 2002.

Trower, W. Peter, ed. *Discovering Alvarez: Selected works of Luis W. Alvarez, with commentary by his students and colleagues.* Chicago: University of Chicago Press, 1987.

Oscar Arias Sánchez

A Peace Plan for Central America

Statesman

❖ Born in Heredia, Costa Rica.
❖ Birth date: September 13, 1941.

Career Highlights

- Appointed Costa Rica's Minister of National Planning and Political Economy in 1972.
- Elected president of Costa Rica in 1986.
- Awarded the Nobel Peace Prize in 1987.

Important Contributions

Arias' doctoral thesis, *¿Quién Gobierna en Costa Rica?* (*Who Rules Costa Rica?*), stirred political controversy not only in his homeland, but all over Latin America by bringing people face to face with the social inequalities that plague the region. Even though his plans for a ceasefire, the freeing of political prisoners, the withdrawal of all foreign forces, and free and democratic elections in all Central American nations did not all come about, he was awarded the 1987 Nobel Peace Prize.

Career Path

Oscar Rafael de Jesús Arias Sánchez, his full name in the Spanish tradition of using both the father's and mother's last names, did not have to get into politics to exercise power. As the scion of a wealthy, politically powerful family, he could have been one of the powers behind the throne in his native Costa Rica. But a genuine desire to improve his countrymen's lives and a good dose of self-esteem prevented him from just staying in the background. He wanted to wield power, and he had the resources to achieve his goal.

Arias was educated in his hometown of Heredia at the best private schools and eventually in the United States. He received his law degree from the University of Costa Rica, where he became involved with the *Partido de Liberación Nacional* (National Liberation Party), better known by its Spanish initials, PLN. Legendary PLN leader José Figueres, a three-term president, established the party's dual objectives of social equality and antimilitarism. Arias embraced both principles with a passion, working on various PLN campaigns.

Arias went to England in 1966 to study at the University of Essex and the London School of Economics. The British ingredient in his education was primordial in the development of his democratic beliefs. Back in Costa Rica with a PhD in economics, Arias published a provocative book, *Grupos de Presión en Costa Rica* (*Pressure Groups in Costa Rica*) and held a chair of political science at the university. His doctoral thesis was published under the name of *Who Rules Costa Rica?* in 1971. The following year he resigned his post at the university to become Minister of National Planning and Political Economy in Figueres' third-term cabinet.

In 1975 Arias became the PLN International Secretary, and one year later was elected to the Costa Rican legislature. It took him only four years to achieve the top party post, that of General Secretary. Arias served in the legislature until 1981 and as General Secretary of the PLN until 1984. He was ready to campaign for the presidency. However, his popular slogan of *Techo, Trabajo, y Paz* (Roofs, Jobs, and Peace), along with his hard work, did not prove a strong mandate, winning him only 52.3 percent of the votes. But it was enough for Arias to become the youngest president in the history of Costa Rica, and enabled him to tackle an economic recession and violence in the region. Arias's domestic efforts for a more equitable society were only partially successful and his foreign initiatives not altogether great. But nobody could deny his convictions, efforts, and good intentions.

On August 7, 1987, the presidents of Nicaragua, Costa Rica, Guatemala, Honduras, and El Salvador signed the Central American Peace Agreement, which was also referred to as the Arias peace plan. Not all of its objectives were met, but it brought some peace and stability to the region. The same year, the Nobel Foundation awarded Arias the Peace Prize.

He is the president of the Arias Foundation, an organization promoting equality, political participation, and demilitarization in Central America, and he is active with the Carter Center's Council of Freely

Elected Heads of Government. Arias has received honorary degrees from Harvard and Dartmouth universities and many other institutions of higher learning.

On February 5, 2006, the voters of Costa Rica elected Oscar Arias to a new presidential term.

Bibliography

Arias Sánchez, Oscar. Selección y Prólogo de Manuel E. Araya Incera. *El camino de la paz*. San José, Costa Rica: Editorial Costa Rica, 1989.

Keene, Ann T. *Peacemakers: Winners of the Nobel Peace Prize*. New York: Oxford University Press, 1998.

LeMoyne, James. "Arias: Whom can he trust?" *The New York Times Magazine*. January 10, 1988, p. 32.

Rolbein, Seth. *Nobel Costa Rica: A Timely Report on our Peaceful Pro-Yankee Central American Neighbor*. New York: St. Martin's Press, 1989.

Sherby, Louise S., ed. *The Who's Who of Nobel Prize Winners 1901–2000*. Westport, CT: Oryx Press, 2002.

Desi Arnaz

"Lucy, I'm Home!"   Singer, Actor, and
Television Pioneer

❖ Born in Santiago de Cuba, Cuba.
❖ Birth date: March 2, 1917.
❖ Death date: December 2, 1986.

Career Highlights

- Musical director of the Bob Hope radio show.
- Television producer.
- Co-star of *I Love Lucy.*

Important Contributions

After arriving in the United States, Arnaz was one of the chief promoters of Latin American music, mainly the Cuban rumba, in the 1930s and 1940s. Early on, he understood the impact that a new medium, television, would have on society, and recognized its potential as an industry. Arnaz was half of the duo that created one of the most enduring, universal television comedies of all times: *I Love Lucy.* The show, done with his wife Lucille Ball, began its run on American television more than half a century ago, and is still broadcast in hundreds of cities around the world, dubbed in more than twenty languages and dialects.

Career Path

Desiderio Alberto Arnaz y de Archa III was not the happy-go-lucky individual projected by his public persona. He was a driven, shrewd, visionary businessman whose understanding of the technological features of television allowed him to create many of the filming techniques and business practices still widely used in the industry. Aware of the problems created by the four time zones in the United States, Arnaz pushed to have the show filmed. At the time, television shows were broadcast live on the East Coast to cater to the largest possible audience. In order to get the audience feedback that live shows had, *I Love Lucy* was staged as a play that was filmed by various set cameras. Afterwards, the material was edited and sent to CBS studios in New York for later broadcast. To this day, that is generally the way most situation comedies are taped.

Monetary quibbles with CBS over production costs led Arnaz to propose a radical new way of compensating the actors. Arnaz and Ball would work for less money if, after the shows were broadcast, CBS would revert the rights to them. Arnaz was already thinking of re-runs.

Desi Arnaz was born into a family of prosperous landowners in what was then Cuba's Oriente province. He received his elementary education at *Colegio Dolores* (Dolores School) and then attended the Jesuit Preparatory School, both in Santiago. By 1933, life had become difficult for his family. Cuba at the time was still reeling from the fall of strongman Gerardo Machado. The Arnaz family ran into political trouble, and his father sent his son and wife to the United States. Arnaz survived the next four years by performing with various groups. In 1937 Xavier Cugat signed him as a singer and guitar player. A year later, at the height of the conga craze in the United States, Arnaz formed his own band at the Conga Club in Miami, Florida. In 1939 Arnaz got a part in the Broadway show *Too Many Girls*. The following year he went to Hollywood to act in the movie version, met Lucille Ball on the set, and married her soon after.

Ball continued her movie and radio career while Arnaz pursued his in music, but the constant separation, and Arnaz's affinity for other women, caused problems almost from the beginning. By 1946, Ball's movie career was shaky and Arnaz was the musical director for the Bob Hope radio show. Ball got a break when CBS cast her in *My Favorite Husband*, a radio program about a banker's wife. It was a hit and the network wanted Ball to do the show on television. The couple, hoping that working together might save their marriage, pitched the idea of having Arnaz play the husband. CBS balked. The network was concerned about how American audiences would react to a Cuban husband, thick accent and all. Undaunted, the couple did a stage tour in 1950, getting positive responses from audiences. CBS was still not completely swayed, so Arnaz persuaded his wife to use their $5,000 savings to produce the show. The rest is history. The show was a success, Desilu, the first major television-producing studio was born, and Ricky and Lucy Ricardo became American icons.

But the success of the show did not change Arnaz's wayward ways, and the couple divorced in 1960. Arnaz, always a drinker, began having problems with alcohol after the split. He spent most of his time at either his horse-breeding ranch at Corona or his hideaway in Del Mar, both in California. He became a best-selling author when his autobiography, titled simply *A Book*, was published in 1976. With the help of Desi Jr., Arnaz finally gave up drinking, but soon after died at his home in Del Mar. He was sixty-nine. His famous line, "Lucy, I'm home" is still uttered by many a man upon his return home from work.

Bibliography

Arnaz, Desi. *A Book*. New York: Morrow, 1976.

Carlson, Lorie Marie, ed. *Barrio Street, Carnival Dreams: Three Generations of Latino Artistry*. New York: St. Martin's Press, 1999.

Cierco, Salvador Clotas, et al, eds. *Enciclopedia Ilustrada del Cine*. Barcelona: Editorial Labor S. A., 1970.

Kanfer, Stefan. *Ball of Fire: The Tumultuous Life and Comic Art of Lucille Ball*. New York: Alfred A. Knopf, 2003.

Reyes, Luis & Rubie, Peter. *Los Hispanos en Hollywood*. New York: Random House Español, 2002.

Sanders, Coyne Steve, and Gilbert, Tom. *Desilu: The Story of Lucille Ball and Desi Arnaz*. New York: Morrow, 1993.

Elfego Baca

One Tough Hombre

Peace Officer, Publisher, and Politician

❖ Born in Socorro, New Mexico Territory.
❖ Birth date: February 10, 1865.
❖ Death date: August 27, 1945.

Career Highlights

- Fought off eighty cowboys for thirty-six hours when he was nineteen years old.
- Admitted to the bar in 1894.
- Elected sheriff of Socorro County in 1919.
- Published *La Opinión Pública* (*Public Opinion*), a Spanish-language newspaper.

Important Contributions

Gunfighter, lawman, lawyer, publisher, politician, and businessman are a few of the labels that can be applied to Elfego Baca. As a young peace officer, he became the hero of the Southwest Spanish-speaking population, and a gun-fighting legend, after he battled eighty Anglo cowboys upset because he had arrested one of their friends.

Career Path

All that Elfego Baca wanted was to be a lawman, and he got his chance while he was still a teenager. In October 1894 some of the local Anglo cowhands at the town of Frisco in southwestern New Mexico decided to have fun at the expense of Mexicans by shooting at their feet, making them "dance," and manhandling some women. Baca, a swaggering, self-appointed lawman, arrested one of them. Other cowboys showed up and wanted their friend released. Baca shot one in the knee and the gunfire scared the horse of another one. The animal reared and fell on top of the rider, killing him. Baca spent the night at the jail with his prisoner. In the morning, a justice of the peace fined the cowboy $5, which satisfied Baca. As he was leaving the building, eighty men confronted him, including the owner of the ranch where the hands involved in the previous evening's events worked. Bullets began flying, and Baca plunged into a small house nearby. Baca was in trouble, or so it appeared. For the next thirty-six hours Baca held off the throng of cowhands trying to kill him. He killed four and eight more were wounded as a result of his marksmanship. It is said that more than 4,000 rounds were fired. Finally, the justice of the peace and various other authorities put an end to the battle that became known as the "Frisco War." Baca came out of the hut to the cheers of the town's Spanish-speaking population, with not a scratch on him, and agreed to go to Socorro. Accompanied by the cowboys and elected officials, and with the prisoner, Elfego Baca rode at the back, pistols drawn, and into Southwestern folklore.

Baca was born in the New Mexico Territory, his family moved to Kansas when he was still a child, and he did not come back to New Mexico until he was a teenager. It was then that he began fancying himself a peace officer. At around eighteen years of age, he ordered a badge by mail and began to wear it and carry two revolvers around town. Just the year before, his father had been sent to jail for killing a pair of cowhands in a gunfight, and Baca also wanted to be as tough as his dad. It did not take long for Elfego Baca to get both of his wishes. Within a year he was known as a mean hombre.

With the Frisco War over, Baca began to study law on his own in 1888. Many thought his wild ways were over, but they were wrong. Even though he did become a lawyer, he was accused of murder twice and exonerated both times. Legend has it that as a lawyer, he always carried his six-shooters into the courtroom and only lost one case.

At some point in the Mexican Revolution, Baca got in trouble with Pancho Villa, the revolutionary and guerrilla leader. It is not quite clear what it was about, but most historians believe it had to do with either an illegal weapons' deal gone sour, or the stealing of one of Villa's prized revolvers. In any case, Villa sent a hired gun after Baca. In the ensuing gunfight, Baca was wounded in the leg, but he killed the gunfighter. From then on, Baca had to walk with the help of a cane.

After serving as a deputy U.S. marshall, he became mayor of Socorro and later sheriff of Socorro County. He also published *La*

Opinión Pública and was involved in various business enterprises. Eventually Baca moved to Albuquerque, where he ran a private detective agency until his death. Elfego Baca, indomitable to the last, passed away quietly in his hometown of Socorro.

Bibliography

Ball. Larry D. *Elfego Baca in Life and Legend.* El Paso, TX: Texas Western Press, 1992.

Bryan, Howard. *Incredible Elfego Baca: Good Man, Bad Man of the Old West.* Santa Fe, NM: Clear Light Publishers, 1993.

"John Wayne in Spanish—Latino heroes: Latinos discover a hero." *The Economist* (US). March 10, 2001, p. 5.

La Follette, Robert Hoath. *Eight Notches: "Lawlessness and Disorder Unlimited" and Other Stories.* Albuquerque, NM: Valliant Print Co., 1950.

Lamar, Howard R., ed. *The Reader's Encyclopedia of the American West.* New York: Thomas Y. Crowell Company, 1977.

Pío Baroja

Anarchist with a Pen   Writer

- ❖ Born in San Sebastián, Spain.
- ❖ Birth date: December 28, 1872.
- ❖ Death date: October 30, 1956.

Career Highlights

- Journalist, poet, essayist, and play-wright.
- Wrote more than sixty novels.
- Wrote a twenty-two-volume family history that is considered a narrative classic.
- Admitted to the Royal Academy of the Spanish Language in 1934.

Important Contributions

Pío Baroja was perhaps the most accomplished Spanish writer of his generation. His anarchist, anti-clerical views still permeate the attitudes and outlook of much of modern Spain.

Career Path

Pío Baroja y Nessi considered himself a hypersensitive, mentally unbalanced person. Since he never went to a psychoanalyst, we will never know. What we do know is that he was timid, independent, and a misogynist, all of which lead him to believe that mankind was cruel, brutal, and not to be trusted. Therefore, the church, government, marriage, and just about anything created by humans was not to be trusted.

Born in the province of Guipuzcoa in the Basque Region of Spain, Baroja was the son of an engineer caught up in the cultural life of the city. The Barojas had been involved in the book-publishing business since the Napoleonic Wars. The family moved around for a while, but in 1886, Baroja began his university studies in Madrid, where he finished his doctorate in medicine. Baroja worked at the town of Cetsona for a year, but this job did not agree with him. While there, he wrote his first book, *Vidas Sombrías* (*Gloomy Lives*).

Back in Madrid in 1887, Baroja and one of his brothers took over as managers of an aunt's bakery. The bakery did not do well, and neither did Baroja's career as a doctor. In what may be considered fits of depression, he would close himself up in the attic of his house to write. A few years later, in 1902, he published one of his best-known novels, *Aventuras, inventos, y mixtificaciones de Silvestre Paradox* (*The Adventures, Inventions, and Hoaxes of Silvester Paradox*). In 1903 he worked as a war correspondent for the daily newspaper *El Globo* (*The Globe*) in Tangiers. Finishing his stint in Tangiers, Baroja traveled to England, France, Switzerland, and Italy, where he wondered about his ancestors on his mother's side, the Lombards. To him, the Lombards were people of light; his Basque side represented darkness.

Between 1904 and 1910, Baroja wrote numerous novels, many in a trilogy format still popular today. In 1911 he published *El árbol de la ciencia* (*The Science Tree*), about triumph and defeat. After hearing the stories of one of his ancestors during the Carlist uprising, when Don Carlos, brother of Ferdinand VII, fought princess Isabella over the right of succession, he began writing the twenty-two-volume *Memorias de un hombre de acción* (*Memories of a Man of Action*) in 1911. It took him twenty-four years to complete.

When the Spanish Republic came into being in 1931, Baroja publicly voiced his dislike for both the church and the state, bringing about a minor disagreement with many of the other writers of the Generación del 98 (the Generation of '98 was a group of Spanish intellectuals who improved the cultural life of Spain and dealt with the loss of empire and decadence in the country after 1898), who supported the new government. When the Spanish Civil War broke out, Baroja, unhappy with both sides, moved to Paris. He made a living by writing newspaper articles, mostly for Argentina's *La Nación* (*The Nation*). After the end of the war, Baroja returned to Spain and wrote the first volume of his memoirs, *Desde la última vuelta del camino* (*From the Road's Last Turn*), completing it in 1948.

Pío Baroja y Nessi died in Madrid. His works, full of anti-heroes, anti-church, and anti-government characters, are representative of a large segment of Spanish society.

❖   ❖   ❖

Bibliography

Aldahola, Adrián D. *En torno a Don Pío Baroja con motivo de un centenario*. San Sebastián: Imp. Offset Navarro, 1972.

Andújar, Manuel, et al. *Encuentros con Don Pío: homenaje a Baroja*. Madrid: Al-Borak, 1972.

Baroja, Ricardo. *Arte, cine y ametralladora*. Madrid: Cátedra, 1989.

Benet, Paloma, et al. *Pío Baroja*. Madrid: Ediciones Rueda, 2000.

Gil Bena, Eduardo. *Baroja o El miedo: biografía no autorizada*. Barcelona: Ediciones Península, 2001.

Patt, Beatrice P. Shapiro. *Pío Baroja*. New York: Twayne Publisher, 1971.

Romero, Marina. *Paisaje y Literatura de España; antología de los escritores del 98*. Madrid: Editorial Tecnos, 1957.

Gustavo Adolfo Bécquer

Romantic without Peer   Poet

- ❖ Born in Seville, Spain.
- ❖ Birth date: February 17, 1836.
- ❖ Death date: December 22, 1870.

Career Highlights

- Spain's official censor.
- Wrote sixty-six different poems, eventually published as *Rimas* (*Rhymes*).
- Unappreciated during his lifetime, his work signals the beginning of modern Spanish poetry.

Important Contributions

Bécquer fused popular Spanish literary currents with Germanic influences, creating a new, Romantic style. His poems, full of fantasy, love, loneliness, and disillusionment, remain popular among young lovers.

Career Path

Gustavo Adolfo Domínguez Bastida was born into a well-to-do Andalusian family of painters. His father, uncle, and brother were all artists. He would later drop the family name and adopt that of his Flemish ancestors, Becker—Bécquer in Spanish. His affluent lifestyle changed in 1841 when his father died and he was compelled to enter a naval school for poor nobles. After Bécquer's mother died six years later, he came under the care of an uncle and his godmother. Bécquer studied art and humanities, but by 1848, he showed his true inclination by writing *Oda a la Muerte de Don Alberto Lista* (*Ode to the Death of Don Alberto Lista*).

By 1853 Bécquer had published many works in small, obscure publications, but had made little money. The next year, swept away by the Romantic current, a literary movement that rejected rationalism and stressed strong emotions, he moved to Madrid. There he wrote light operettas and comedies such as *La Novia y el Pantalón* (*The Bride and the Trousers*) in 1856, and *La Historia de los Templos de España* (*History of Spanish Temples*), a lengthy essay on the relationship between religion, architecture, and history, in 1857. His finances, however, showed no improvement. Around this time he met and fell in love with Julia Espín. She liked him too, but wanted to marry money. Bécquer was heartbroken. Around the same time, he contracted a serious illness that would trouble him for the rest of his life. Most historians believe that it was the "Romantic illness," tuberculosis.

In 1861 he married Casta Esteban y Navarro, the daughter of his doctor. His economic difficulties disappeared for a while. In 1864 the Spanish Crown appointed Bécquer censor of novels, and paid him an excellent salary of 24,000 reales. His personal life, however, soon took a downward turn. Never really happy in his marriage, he found solace by writing many of his *Rimas* (*Rhymes*), which appeared in different publications. Matters got worse in 1868 when Bécquer lost his job, his health deteriorated, most of his *Rimas* were lost when a mob ransacked the house of the government official was to finance their publication, and he found out that Casta was unfaithful. They separated. He moved with his children and brother, Valeriano, to the Veruela Monastery and resided in a monk's cell. There he rewrote and copied some of his old *Rimas*, which were published in *El Libro de los Gorriones* (*The Book of Sparrows*). He also began a series of articles called *Cartas desde mi celda* (*Letters from my cell*).

Early in 1870 he returned to Madrid with his brother. Valeriano died on September 23, and, distraught, Bécquer died almost three months later of tuberculosis. He was thirty-four years old. All of his *Rhymes* were finally published in one volume after his death. They are a seminal work of Spanish poetry.

Bibliography

Alonso, Dámaso. *Poetas españoles contemporáneos*. Madrid: Editorial Gredos, 1978.

Barbachano, Carlos J. *Bécquer*. Madrid: E.P.E.S.A., 1970.

Baruj Benacerraf

Never, Never Quit

Medical Researcher

❖ Born in Caracas, Venezuela.
❖ Birth date: October 29, 1920.

Career Highlights

- Became a U.S. citizen in 1943.
- Commissioned first lieutenant in U.S. Army Medical Corps in 1945.
- Elected president of the American Association of Immunologists in 1973.
- Received the 1980 Waterford Biomedical Science Award.
- Awarded one-third of Nobel Prize for Physiology or Medicine in 1980.

Important Contributions

Benacerraf will not only be remembered for his immunological research on how humans create antibodies, but as a shining example of the struggle against ignorance, prejudice, politics, and economic pressures faced by many of the world's greatest minds as they toil to improve lives.

Career Path

If he had been a quitter, Baruj Benacerraf would have allowed prejudice and financial pressures to prevent him from winning the 1980 Nobel Price in Physiology or Medicine. As it was, discrimination proved to be only a small hurdle in his life. Benacerraf was born in Venezuela to parents of Spanish and Jewish extraction. The family, having French lineage on his mother's side, moved to France when he was five years old. Benacerraf attended elementary and secondary school in Paris, but at the beginning of World War II in 1939, the family moved back to Caracas. Later they moved to the United States, where young Benacerraf could pursue his education. He enrolled at Columbia University in 1940 and received his bachelor's of science two years later.

Eager to attend medical school, Benacerraf applied for admission at several universities, but prejudice reared its ugly head. Even though he had excellent grades, no college would accept him because he was Jewish and not a U.S. citizen. However, one of his friend's fathers who had connections at the Medical College of Virginia got him an interview and he was accepted. Benacerraf started his medical studies in July 1942. The following year he was drafted, became a naturalized U.S. citizen, and married Annette Dreyfus, whom he had dated while at Columbia University. Commissioned as a second lieutenant, he was sent to France by the Army. His wife joined him and they stayed there until his discharge in 1947.

Back in the United States, Benacerraf, motivated by suffering from asthma as a child, turned to research in immunology. He began his work at Columbia's Neurological Institute in February 1948. Due to family issues, he moved back to Paris in the next year and accepted an appointment at the Bernard Halpern laboratory in the Broussais Hospital. He carried out his experiments in Paris for six years, but anti-Semitism and anti-foreign attitudes in France prevented him from establishing his own laboratory, which he needed to further his career. Benacerraf decided to return to the United States in 1956. Back in the States, he was appointed as an assistant professor of pathology at New York University School of Medicine, and continued his research in immunology. In time he rose to the position of professor of pathology.

In 1968, he became director of the Laboratory of Immunology of the National Institute of Allergy and Infectious Diseases in Bethesda, Maryland, and in 1970 accepted the chair of pathology at Harvard, where he continued his research. Finally, his work on the genetic regulation of the immunological system, and the different reactions of each organism to producing antibodies against the same foreign bodies, earned him the 1980 Nobel Prize in Physiology or Medicine. Benacerraf's work led to the understanding of the immune system's ability to respond to antigens (infectious agents or foreign materials in the body). His findings also revealed the mechanisms underlying autoimmune diseases, in which the immune system attacks its own tissues.

Today Benacerraf is a fellow of the American Academy of Science and the American Academy of Arts and Sciences. In addition, he is a president emeritus of the Dana-Farber Cancer Institute, which is part of Harvard Medical School. Baruj Benacerraf is a true example that prejudice is no match for intelligence, study, and hard work.

Bibliography

Benacerraf, Baruj. *From Caracas to Stockholm: A Life in Medical Science.* Amherst, New York: Prometheus Books, 1998.

Kurian, George Thomas. *The Nobel Scientists: A Biographical Encyclopedia.* Amherst, New York: Prometheus Books, 2002.

Magill, Frank N., ed. *All the Nobel Prize Winners: Physiology and Medicine.* Pasadena, CA: Salem Press, 1991.

Sherby, Louise S., ed. *The Who's Who of Nobel Prize Winners, 1901–2000.* Westport, CT: Oryx Press, 2002.

Strongin, Jeanne. "Baruj Benacerraf" (interview). *Omni.* July 1983, pp. 78–88.

Jacinto Benavente

The Playwright as Social Critic

Playwright, Poet

- ❖ Born in Madrid, Spain.
- ❖ Birth date: August 12, 1866.
- ❖ Death date: July 14, 1954.

Career Highlights

- Established himself as a gifted stylist with the book *Cartas de Mujeres* (*Women's Letters*).
- His most famous play, *Los intereses creados* (translated as *The Bonds of Interest*, but closer to *The Establishment*), debuted in 1907.
- Wrote more than 170 plays, plus numerous books and poems.
- Awarded the Nobel Prize in Literature in 1922.

Important Contributions

Unlike most of his contemporaries, Jacinto Benavente wrote numerous plays about women, usually set in rural areas. He moved away from modern drama to write about life in Spain in a most traditional way. Also, contrary to the ideology of most writers of his time, he supported the uprising of Francisco Franco against the Republicans during the Spanish civil war.

Career Path

It seems that from the day he was born, Jacinto Benavente wanted to be a playwright. His father, a renowned pediatrician, had a large library, and from the time Benavente could read, possibly as early as four years of age, he gravitated to plays and books about the theater. He also put on productions for his friends and house servants. Benavente would grow up to write plays about the lives of Spanish women, a subject largely ignored at the time. In addition, his plays poked fun at the bourgeoisie.

By the time Benavente enrolled at the University of Madrid in 1882, he already spoke several languages, most learned before he was fifteen years old. He intended to become a lawyer, but when his father died two years later and left him a considerable fortune, the young man decided to travel. He visited Russia, France, and England before returning to Spain. Back in his homeland, Benavente began his writing career. He collaborated with important newspapers and became editor of the publication *Vida Literaria* (*Literary Life*).

Benavente, a certified member of the Generation of 98, achieved minor fame in 1892, when he published a collection of poems and a book based on women's letters, which he probably wrote himself. Later that year, he was recognized as a dramatist for a series of plays published under the title *El teatro fantástico* (*The Fantastic Theater*).

El nido ajeno (*Another's Nest*), performed in 1894, did not get good reviews, but was popular nonetheless. It was *Gente conocida*, usually translated as *High Society*, but closer to *Celebrities*, that sealed his fame in 1896.

Even though he continued to write plays for the next five years, his best work appeared early in the twentieth century. His plays *La gobernadora* (*The Governor's Wife*) in 1901, and *Rosas de otoño* (*Autumn Roses*) in 1905, were both extremely popular. *Los intereses creados*, about the reason why evil has to exist, is considered Benavente's masterpiece. Two other famous plays, *Señora ama* (*The House Mistress*) and *La malquerida* (*The Wrongly Loved*) appeared in 1908 and 1913, respectively. In 1913, Benavente, whose works encompass just about everything from high comedy to rural-themed plays, was elected to the Spanish Academy.

Benavente's importance as a dramatist was recognized worldwide in 1922 when he received the Nobel Prize in Literature. Like other Spanish intellectuals of his time, Benavente suffered dearly during his country's 1933–1936 civil war, and his aristocratic background and conservative views positioned him on the side of Francisco Franco's Nationalists. The Republicans placed him under house arrest for a few months. After the war, Benavente wrote again, completing thirty more plays in the next twenty years.

Jacinto Benavente died on July 14, 1954, at the age of eighty-seven in his hometown of Madrid.

Bibliography

Frenz, Horst, ed. *Nobel Lectures, Literature 1901–1967*. Amsterdam: Elsevier Publishing Company, 1969.

González del Valle, Luis. *El canon: reflexiones sobre la recepción literaria—teatral: Pérez de Ayala ante Benavente*. Madrid: Huerga y Fierro, 1993.

Pérez-Embid, Florentino, ed. *Forjadores del Mundo Contemporáneo*. Barcelona: Editorial Planeta, 1960.

Sheehan, Robert Louis. *Benavente and the Spanish Panorama*. Chapel Hill, NC: Estudios de Hispanófila, 1976.

Tzitsikas, Helene. *La supervivencia existencial de la mujer en la obra de Benavente*. Barcelona: Puvill Libros, 1982.

Santos Benavides

Southern Tejano

Confederate
Officer

❖ Born in Laredo, Texas.
❖ Birth date: November 1, 1823.
❖ Death date: November 9, 1891.

Career Highlights

- Mayor of his hometown of Laredo.
- Turned down an appointment as a general in the Union army in 1861.
- Defeated Mexican American insurgent Juan Cortina.
- Prevented much larger Union forces from taking Laredo in 1864.

Important Contributions

Santos Benavides, a colonel, was the highest-ranking Hispanic officer in the Confederate army. There is some evidence that he was promoted to the rank of general just before the war ended, but the promotion never took place. His exploits are textbook cases of the effectiveness of a small, mobile military unit defending its home terrain against much larger military forces.

Career Path

Whether north or south of the border, Santos Benavides stood for states' rights and risked his life to fight for what he believed. Benavides' ideals grew from the remoteness of Texas and Mexico City to Washington, D.C. When the Federalist-Centralist wars of the 1830s and 1840s swept México, Benavides, very much a regionalist, supported the side whose principles were closer to his ideology, the Federalists. Later, when Texas joined the Confederacy during the American Civil War, Benavides wore the gray uniform of the South. Son of an old and respected *Tejano* (Texans of Spanish ancestry) family, Santos Benavides became the highest-ranking Mexican American to serve in the Confederate Army.

Benavides' great-grandfather was Tomás Sánchez de la Barrera y Garza, the founder of Laredo. Nothing is known of his formal education, if he even had any. Eventually Benavides became one of the most prominent merchants and ranchers in the area around Laredo. His commercial accomplishments were in no small part due to his uncle, Basilio Benavides, who was mayor of Laredo four times, three under Mexican rule, and who also served as a state representative. Benavides' prominence led to his elections as mayor of Laredo in 1856, and to chief justice of Webb County three years later. He also gained additional notoriety as an Indian fighter.

When Texas seceded in March 1861, Benavides was offered a Union generalship. Instead he became a captain of the 33rd Texas Cavalry, which became known as the Benavides' Regiment. The unit, made up mostly of *Tejanos* like himself, defeated Juan Cortina on May 22nd, 1861, at the Battle of Carrizo, and put down other uprisings against Confederate rule. He was elevated to the rank of colonel in November 1863 and allowed to create his own regiment. In 1864 Benavides won his two most important victories for the South. The first was the defense of Laredo in March 19, 1864. With only forty-two men he prevented the Union First Texas cavalry, with about 200 troops, from taking the city and destroying over 5,000 bales of cotton that were to be shipped to the Mexican town of Matamoros, the only outlet for the South's most precious commodity. The Confederates did not lose a single man. His second accomplishment was the skill with which he passed cotton down the Rio Grande to Matamoros when northern troops occupied Brownsville.

After the Civil War he went back to business, politics, and international intrigue. His ranching enterprises continued to flourish, and he was elected to the Texas legislature three times. He made the Democratic Party a powerhouse among Hispanics in his region, and even supported military incursions from Texas into México against Dictator Porfirio Díaz. Nonetheless, in 1880, Díaz chose him as an emissary to the United States.

Benavides died quietly in his hometown on November 9, 1891.

❖   ❖   ❖

Bibliography

Collier, Christopher, and Collier, James Lincoln. *Hispanic America, Texas, and the Mexican War.* Tarrytown, NY: Benchmark Books, 1999.

"Colonel Santos Benavides—Confederate Freedom Fighter." http://georgiaheritagecouncil.org/site2/news/Benavides_flyer.pdf (September 18, 2006).

Kelley, Michael. "Col. Santos Benavides." 37th Texas. http://www.37thtexas.org/html/Santosbio.html (January 7, 2005).

"Tejano Soldados for the Union and Confederacy." http://www.nps.gov/archive/shil/Documents/Tejanoweb.pdf (September 18, 2006).

Thompson, Jerry. "Benavides, Santos (1823–1891)." *The Handbook of Texas Online.* http://www.tsha.utexas.edu/handbook/online/articles/view/BB/fbe47.html (January 7, 2005).

Simón Bolívar

El Libertador

Revolutionary
Hero, Statesman

❖ Born in Caracas, Venezuela.
❖ Birth date: July 24, 1783.
❖ Death date: December 17, 1830.

Career Highlights

- Liberated Venezuela from Spain the first time, entering Caracas on October 1813.
- Liberated Colombia in 1819, and established *La Gran Colombia* (Greater Colombia).
- Liberated Venezuela and Ecuador and annexed their territories into Greater Colombia.
- Became dictator of Perú in 1824.

Important Contributions

Under Simón Bolívar's leadership, the Spanish rulers of South America were forever defeated, and five modern-day countries gained independence. In Greater Colombia he established a large country that rivaled any world power in land mass and population. But, alas, his dictatorial powers and regionalist sentiments splintered the region into what are today the nations of Colombia, Panama, Venezuela, and Ecuador.

Career Path

Bolívar was known as *El Libertador* (The Liberator), and the moniker is well deserved. As a military and political leader, he defeated the

Spaniards in a series of battles, securing Greater Colombia's independence from Spain. Bolívar also established Bolivia, named in his honor, in the region known as *Alto Perú* (Upper Perú). He was also a first-rate public speaker and writer.

Simón José Antonio de la Santísima Trinidad Bolívar was born into an aristocratic family. He was orphaned at an early age, but his parents left him a wealthy boy. Young Bolívar was tutored, well-traveled, and became familiar with the Enlightenment Period and the writings of French philosopher Jean-Jacques Rousseau. His financial means allowed him to travel widely throughout Europe and to live in Spain, where he married María Teresa Rodríguez del Toro, a noble lady, in 1802. They moved back to Caracas, and she died of yellow fever soon after. Bolívar returned to Europe in 1804. During this trip he witnessed Napoleon's coronation and saw Spain weakened after the French invasion. While in Rome, he took a vow to liberate his homeland. It is said that he did so in front of the ruins of the Roman Senate chambers. Returning to Caracas, he joined the revolutionary movement of 1810 that expelled Venezuela's Spanish governor and declared the nation's independence in 1811. One of Bolívar's main assignments at this time was as envoy to Great Britain. He failed in his assignment when the British promised only neutrality, but not the aid the revolutionaries needed. By 1814 the Spaniards had re-conquered Venezuela. Bolívar fled to Curacao, organized an army, landed in Venezuela's northern coast, and reclaimed his beloved Caracas from Spain.

New difficulties forced Bolívar to flee to Jamaica where, again, he raised an army, returned to Venezuela, captured the city of Angostura (now Ciudad Bolívar) in 1816, and set up a dictatorship.

With the defeat of the Spanish troops at the Battle of Boyacá in 1819, Bolívar liberated the territory of Colombia and established the nation of Greater Colombia. Two years later, he routed another Spanish army at the Battle of Carabobo in Venezuela, and then moved on to Ecuador, incorporating that country into Greater Colombia. In 1824 he ended Spanish hegemony in South America when his chief lieutenant, Antonio José de Sucre, trampled the Spaniards at the celebrated battle of Ayacucho, Perú. Bolívar became dictator of Perú. It was this penchant for setting himself up as dictator that would be Bolívar's undoing. By 1829 the political and business leaders of the nations of Greater Colombia were so distraught with his authoritarianism that a rebellion took place. Bolívar's dream of a united South America came to an end the next year with the split of Greater Colombia into the present nations of Colombia, Panama, Ecuador, and Venezuela. Bolivar himself narrowly escaped an assassination attempt on September 25, 1828. Disappointed and bitter, Bolívar withdrew to the city of Santa

Marta, Colombia, where the news of Antonio José de Sucre's assassination hastened his own death from tuberculosis on December 17, 1830.

Bibliography

Bushnell, David. *Simón Bolívar: hombre de Caracas, proyecto de América: una biografía.* Buenos Aires: Editorial Biblos, 2002.

Conway, Christopher B. *The Cult of Bolívar in Latin American Literature.* Gainesville, FL: University of Florida Press, 2003.

Díaz-Trechuelo, Sínola María Lourdes. *Bolívar, Miranda, O'Higgins, San Martín: cuatro vidas cruzadas.* Madrid: Ediciones Encuentro, 1999.

Greene, Carol. *Simón Bolívar: South American Liberator.* Chicago: Children Press, 1989.

Harvey, Robert. *Liberators—Latin America's Struggle for Independence.* London: John Murray, 2000.

Vázquez, Germán, y Martínez Díaz, Nelson. *Historia de América Latina.* Madrid: Ediproyectos, S.A., 1990.

Alvar Núñez Cabeza de Vaca

Wandering into History   Explorer

❖ Born in Jerez de la Frontera, Spain.
❖ Birth date: Circa 1490.
❖ Death date: Mid-1550s.

Career Highlights

- Joined Pánfilo de Narváez's Florida expedition in 1527.

- Explored the American Southwest or México's north from 1528 to 1536.

- Kept records of people, animals, and fauna he encountered.

- Appointed governor of La Plata (today's Argentina) in 1541.

Important Contributions

While the area of the North American continent he explored is open to discussion, there is no doubt that Cabeza de Vaca's keen eye for the many new things he encountered has proven invaluable to historical, environmental, sociological, botanical, and zoological researchers. In a way, he also proved that Europeans could live in peace with the native people of the region.

Career Path

Alvar Núñez Cabeza de Vaca is the mystery man of the Spanish exploration of the New World. We don't know precisely when he was born or when he died, and his given name probably doesn't match the one we know him by. We are not even sure of the exact path of his

North American exploration! Of course, we don't even know what kind of education, if any, he had as a young man. When he was old enough, he took the Alvar Núñez name from his mother's side of the family. While his father's last name was de Vera, he also took his mother's last name, Cabeza de Vaca.

During the reign of Charles V, Cabeza de Vaca joined the military and served in Italy. He had a good reputation and was able to become the treasurer in Narváez's proposed voyage to explore Florida. The expedition left Spain in June 1527 and reached Florida ten months later. After landing on the peninsula's west coast, Narváez, who had leadership problems during the conquests of Cuba and México, had problems again. He divided his forces, sending 300 men into the interior. Soon, they were isolated, without food, and under attack by natives. As their numbers dwindled, Narváez decided to build rafts and travel down the Florida coast. That worked for a while, but in 1532, a hurricane destroyed the small flotilla, and all but eighty died. Eventually seventy-six would die, and only Cabeza de Vaca, Alonso Castillo Maldonado, Andrés Dorantes de Carranza, and Estevanico, a Moorish slave, endured.

Somehow they made their way to Texas, where Cabeza de Vaca was separated from the others, and survived by becoming a medicine man around the area of modern-day Galveston. Using his limited knowledge of medicine, a bit of faith healing, and some native herbs, Cabeza de Vaca managed to cure enough sick natives to have them spare his life. He also became something of a businessman, trading shells and other items to the native people for furs.

One way or another, he got back together with the other three survivors and they began to move west. A number of historians believe they traveled through the American Southwest, while others think they went through northern México. Only one thing about the trip is certain: After nine years of travel, in 1536 they made it to the Pacific coast near the Mexican town of Culiacán. The written reports of the first Europeans to trek across most of North America are full of precious information about the fauna, climate, geography, and native people they encountered. Cabeza de Vaca claimed to have been the first European to see the American bison. In 1536 Cabeza de Vaca arrived in Mexico City and returned to Spain by 1537. The report of his odyssey he wrote for Charles V was published in 1542 under the title *La Relación*. Eventually he was appointed Governor of the La Plata region of South America, but, mostly due to his incompetence, the colonists revolted, put him in chains, and shipped him back to Spain. The Crown, upset with his ineptitude, expelled him to North Africa. Later he was allowed to return under a form of house arrest. Although his personal liberties where limited, Cabeza de Vaca became somewhat of a wealthy trader and died in Seville.

Bibliography

Chipman, Donald E., and Joseph, Harriett Denise. *Explorers and Settlers of Spanish Texas: Men and Women of Spanish Texas*. Austin, TX: University of Texas Press, 2001.

Howard, David A. *Conquistador in Chains: Cabeza de Vaca and the Indians of the Americas*. Tuscaloosa, AL: University of Alabama Press, 1996.

Kerby, Elizabeth Poe. *The Conquistadors*. New York: G. P. Putnam's Sons, 1969.

Krieger, Alex D., Hester, Thomas R., and Kriege, Margery H. *We Came Naked and Barefoot: The Journey of Cabeza de Vaca across North America*. Austin, TX: University of Texas Press, 2002.

Maestro, Betsy, and Maestro, Giulio. *Exploration and Conquest: The Americas After Columbus: 1500–1620*. New York: HarperTrophy, 1997.

Wood, Michael. *Conquistadors*. Berkeley, CA: University of California Press, 2002.

José Capablanca

Conquering the World of Chess

Chess Player

- ❖ Born in Havana, Cuba.
- ❖ Birth date: November 19, 1888.
- ❖ Death date: March 8, 1942.

Career Highlights

- Became Cuban chess champion in 1901.
- Beat the U.S. champion in 1909.
- Became World Champion in 1921.
- Proposed the addition of two new pieces to the chessboard.

Important Contributions

Capablanca is arguably one of the greatest chess players of all time. American Bobby Fischer (World Champion 1972–1975) said that "Capablanca was possibly the greatest player in the entire history of chess." Germany's Emanuel Lasker (World Champion 1894–1921) said: "I have known great masters, but only one genius: Capablanca." His imaginative moves are still a source of amazement to students of the game. Capablanca authored three books on chess.

Career Path

The most gifted chess player of his time, José Raúl Capablanca y Graupera was only the third-ever world champion, holding the title from 1921 to 1927.

By the time Capablanca was four years old, he knew how to play chess. He learned the complications and permutations of chess from watching his father play. The senior Capablanca was not a very good player, but made up for his lack of skills with enthusiasm. After José had beaten his father a few times, the elder Capablanca took the boy to the Havana Chess Club so he could see "real" players and maybe play a game or two. It didn't take long before the club was abuzz. Although not yet ready to beat the best players, the boy was a tough opponent, and good enough for everybody to see that they were in the presence of a genius. When he was just twelve years old, Capablanca turned Cuba on its ear by beating the island nation's national champion, Juan Corzo.

Most of Capablanca's formal education took place in the United States, where he first attended private school and then Columbia University in New York City. While at Columbia, Capablanca became a regular at the Manhattan Chess Club, where at the age of twenty, he trounced U.S. champion Frank Marshall. Marshall became a fan. Two years after his astonishing win over Marshall, Capablanca entered one of the toughest competitions ever, the 1911 tournament in San Sebastian, in Spain. It was Marshall who goaded Capablanca into taking part. To most every expert's surprise, Capablanca won first place ahead of all the great masters in the competition.

At this point, Capablanca felt he could face the reigning world champion, Emanuel Lasker of Germany. World War I prevented the match from taking place, but Capablanca continued playing in various tournaments and lost only one match in ten years.

Aside from his earnings as a chess player, Capablanca made a living as an official of the Cuban Foreign Service. He had the bombastic title of Ambassador Extraordinary and Plenipotentiary General from the Government of Cuba to the World at Large.

By the end of World War I, Lasker did not really feel up to competing and even though a match had been set for 1920, he resigned his title in favor of Capablanca. But the chess community wanted a competition, and after Capablanca found financial backers in Cuba, a match was set up in Havana. Alleging failing health, Lasker resigned when Capablanca was leading four games to zero with ten draws. That made Capablanca the world's *Número Uno*.

In 1921 Capablanca also married Gloria S. Betancourt. The couple had two children, a boy named after his father and a girl named after her mother.

It was at this time that Capablanca proposed adding two pieces to the game and playing on a ten-by-ten grid. The two pieces were the chancellor, which could move like both a rook and a knight, and the archbishop, which could move like both a bishop and a knight.

In the 1920s the chess world was in a state of anarchy due to finances and the conditions Capablanca imposed for a championship match. Nonetheless, Capablanca continued his mastery of the chessboard, winning tournaments in London in 1922 and in New York in 1927. In time, the Soviet Union's Alexander Alekhine obtained the backing of Argentina's president and other business interests and more or less forced Capablanca into a championship match. It took place in Buenos Aires in 1927. It was the longest World Championship match up to that time, lasting seventy-three days and thirty-four games. At last, Alekhine took the crown when he won the required sixth game to Capablanca's three.

The two chess titans had grown to dislike each other so much that Alekhine refused to play in any tournaments that included Capablanca. Capablanca continued playing in tournaments, winning in 1928 in Berlin, and in 1936 in Moscow and Nottingham, England. It was in Nottingham that Alekhine and Capablanca finally faced each other again, and the Cuban won.

Capablanca died of a stroke in New York City on March 8, 1942. As it turned out, his most bitter opponent was among his foremost admirers. When Alekhine passed away in 1946, a compilation of Capablanca's greatest games was found among the Russian's belongings. He meant to have them published, and in the introduction Alekhine had written that with the Cuban's death, "we have lost a very great chess genius whose like we shall never see again."

Bibliography

Alekhine, Alexander. *107 Great Chess Battles, 1939–1945.* Mineola, NY: Dover Publications, Inc., 1992.

Bjelina, Dimitrije, traducción Zorita Stamencic. *José Raúl Capablanca.* Madrid: Zugarto Ediciones, 1993.

Chernev, Irving. *The Golden Dozen: The Twelve Greatest Chess Players of All Time.* New York: Oxford University Press, 1976.

Lerner, Peter Morris. *Famous Chess Players.* Minneapolis, MN: Lerner Publications Co., 1973.

Reinfeld, Fred. *The Immortal Games of Capablanca.* Mineola, NY: Dover Publications, Inc., 1990.

Winter, Edward. *Capablanca: A Compendium of Games, Notes, Articles, Correspondence, Illustrations, and Other Rare Archival Materials on the Cuban Chess Genius José Raúl Capablanca, 1888–1942.* Jefferson, NC: McFarland & Company, Inc., 1989.

José Carreras

Tenor,
Humanitarian

- ❖ Born in Barcelona, Spain.
- ❖ Birth date: December 5, 1946.

Career Highlights

- Won Grammy Award in 1991 for Best Classical Vocal Performance.
- Musical director of the Barcelona Olympic Games in 1992.
- Goodwill Ambassador of UNESCO (United Nations Educational, Scientific, and Cultural Organization).
- Received the Albert Schweitzer Music Award in 1996.
- Received the 1996 St. Boniface General Hospital Research Foundation International Award.

Important Contributions

Together with his Three Tenors partners, José Carreras has propelled opera to new heights of popularity. His rich, clear tenor voice, which is among the best of the last 200 years, has won fans the world over for himself and his art form. After suffering from, and being cured of leukemia, Carreras has become quite a humanitarian. His worldwide leukemia foundation raises millions of dollars each year for research.

Career Path

It is difficult to be the world's third best-known tenor. Not the third best, mind you, but the third best known. If one were to ask José

Carreras, he might not tell you he is the best, but will declare that he is as good as his two partners in the Three Tenors. Many critics agree. Some would even say that, because Carreras is younger than Plácido Domingo and Luciano Pavarotti, he might be at the full height of his career, while the other two are beginning to slip. But as unknown as he might be to the general public, Carreras is a colossal figure in the world of opera.

He was born Josep (the Catalonian version of his name) Carreras. His father, a teacher whose career had been wrecked because he fought for the Republicans during the Spanish civil war, took the family to Argentina when Carreras was four years old. The journey proved unsuccessful and they returned to Spain in 1952, where Carreras's father became a policeman and his mother opened a hair dressing shop.

Carreras took to singing from the time he was about five years old. It is said that he sang all the way from Argentina back to Spain on the steamship. He started taking singing classes after school when he was six, joined the Barcelona Conservatory by eight, and at eleven sang "*La Donna e Mobile*," a song he had loved since he heard Mario Lanza's recording of *The Great Caruso* on Spanish National Radio.

Soon he was singing soprano with the players of the *Gran Teatro del Liceo*, Barcelona's opera house. By the time he reached adulthood, Carreras's voice had changed into the tenor he is today. At the urging of his voice tutor, Carreras took a crack at the part of Flavio in Norma, which was an up-and-coming production of the *Gran Teatro*. Even though Flavio is a minor character, the critics, and better still Montserrat Caballé, the star of the show, were impressed. Caballé requested Carreras for the part of Gennaro in Gaetano Donizetti's *Lucrezia Borgia*. The producers agreed, and in 1970 Carreras had what he regards as his debut as a tenor. The next year his career took off after singing the lead role to Maria Stuarda in London.

In 1974 Carreras made his first appearances in three of the four greatest opera houses: he played Vienna's Staatsoper, London's Royal Opera House, and the New York Metropolitan Opera. He played the fourth, Milan's La Scala, in 1975. He had achieved stardom at the tender age of twenty-nine.

Carreras' career was in high gear for the next twelve years. He was doing about seventy shows yearly the world over. But in 1987, everything came crashing down when he was diagnosed with leukemia. He was told his chances of survival were no better than 10 percent. However, his treatment proved successful, and Carreras survived. In 1998 he established the José Carreras International Leukemia Foundation in Barcelona to raise funds to fight the illness. He also began a ten-year relationship with Austrian director Herbert Von Karajan, who produced some of the tenor's best work.

In 1992 Carreras divorced his wife. It seems the long separations created by his career took its toll on the marriage. He has not remarried.

The first Three Tenors concert was a fundraiser for his foundation. Today Carreras splits his time between doing a few performances a year and working for the foundation, which now has branches in Germany, Switzerland, and the United States.

Bibliography

Carreras, José. *Singing from the Soul: An Autobiography*. Seattle, WA: YCP Publications, 1991.

Lewis, Marcia, trans. Anibal Leal. *Los Tres Tenores: la vida de Plácido Domingo, Luciano Pavarotti y José Carreras*. Buenos Aires: Javier Vergara, 1997.

Peccel, Jean. "Bioraphy of José Carreras." José Carreras. http://www.jcarreras.com/biohome.htm (March 16, 2004).

Pérez Sens, J. *El Placer de Cantar—Un Retrato Autobiográfico*. Barcelona: Ediciones de Nuevo Arte Thor, 1988.

Pablo Casals

Master Musician

Cellist,
Conductor, and
Composer

❖ Born in Vendrell, Spain.
❖ Birth date: December 29, 1876.
❖ Death date: October 22, 1973.

Career Highlights

- Performed for Queen Victoria in 1899.
- First toured the United States in 1901–1902.
- Played at the White House for President John F. Kennedy in 1961.

Important Contributions

Casals was a musical revolutionary. He used new techniques and expanded the repertoire for the cello. Before him the cello was considered merely an ensemble instrument; he made it into a solo instrument. Among Casals' best works were his interpretations of the cello suites of Johann Sebastian Bach. Despite his fame as a musician, Casals wanted to be remembered as a humanitarian. During his lifetime he contributed generously to education programs and peace organizations all over the world.

Career Path

Pablo Casals, committed humanitarian, eminent composer, illustrious conductor, gifted pianist, and considered by many the greatest cellist of the twentieth century, loved his homeland of Spain.

Even though he spent many years away from Spain, his beloved Barcelona, and his hometown of Vendrell, he always tried to return. He loved the land, the people, the architecture, the music, but most of all, he loved the traditions. He was so impacted by the Fascist takeover of his country that the last thirty-three years of his life, which he lived in exile, where desperate ones. Sorrow eroded his mental and physical talents.

He was born as Pau Carlos Salvador Defilló in the Spanish province of Catalonia. His father, the parish organist and choir director, started Casals' musical career by instructing him in piano, violin, and organ. He was eleven years old when he first saw a cello performance and decided that was his instrument. The following year his Puerto Rican-born mother took Casals to Barcelona's prestigious *Escuela Municipal de Música* (the City Music School) and enrolled him in piano and cello classes. It took Casals only three years to begin his mastery of the instrument. He gave a solo recital in Barcelona on February 23, 1891, when he was only fourteen. Two years later he graduated with honors.

At this point, his life could have taken a turn for the worse. Casals was drafted to serve in the Spanish army. Most likely he would have been sent to Cuba or Puerto Rico, which at the time were involved in wars of liberation against Spain. But there was no way his mother would allow him to serve in the army that sustained foreign dominance of her homeland. Casals did not want to serve in a colonial force, either. So he bought his way out of it. This was legal and widespread among those who could afford it. He never regretted it.

For the next three years Casals played in various ensembles in Paris and Madrid. He became known as a virtuoso innovator whose skills, expressiveness, and musicality were beyond compare. After a performance with the Madrid Symphony Orchestra in 1897, the Queen of Spain decorated him with the Order of Carlos III. Now that he was an established cello maestro, Casals toured the world and played for many heads of state, including Queen Victoria and President Theodore Roosevelt.

He fulfilled one of his lifelong dreams of directing his first performance in 1919. He established the *Orquesta Pau Casals* in Barcelona, and with him as conductor, it became a notable artistic organization. The orchestra ceased performing in 1936 with the beginning of the Spanish civil war. Casals, a dedicated advocate of Spanish republicanism, exiled himself to France. When the Nationalist and Fascist forces of General Francisco Franco claimed victory, Casals vowed not to return to his homeland until democracy was restored. During World War II he played a few concerts in Switzerland and Vichy France. His inability to return to his homeland and participate in Spain's many music festivals began to wear him down, but he swore not to play in any country that recognized the Franco regime. With a sole exception, he did not. That exception took place on November 13, 1961, when Casals played in a concert at the White House. He was a great admirer of John F. Kennedy and could not turn down the invitation of the American president.

Casals's refusal to play in many countries did not hinder his career. One of his main projects was the commemoration of the bicentennial of Johann Sebastian Bach's death. Among Casals' many compositions are *El pesebre* (*The Manger*) and *Himno a las Naciones Unidas* (*Hymn to the United Nations*). He conducted the first performance of *Himno* just two months before he turned ninety-five. Casals moved to San Juan, Puerto Rico, in 1956, and died there on October 22, 1973. He did not survive the Franco regime in Spain, but his music did.

Bibliography

Alavedra, Joan. *Pablo Casals*. Madrid: Publicaciones Españolas, 1976.

Baldock, Robert. *Pablo Casals*. Boston: Northeastern University Press, 1993.

Blum, David. *Casals and the Art of Interpretation*. Berkeley, CA: University of California Press, 1980.

Corredor, José María. *Pablo Casals Cuenta su Vida: Conversaciones con el Maestro*. Barcelona: Editorial Juventud, 1975.

Garza, Hedda. *Pablo Casals*. New York: Chelsea House Publishers, 1992.

Goodnough, David. *Pablo Casals: Cellist for the World*. Springfield, NJ: Enslow Publishers, 1997.

Fray Bartolomé de las Casas

The Protector of the Indians

Missionary, Human Rights Activist

- ❖ Born in Seville, Spain.
- ❖ Birth date: Either 1474 or 1482.
- ❖ Death date: July 31, 1566.

Career Highlights

- First priest ordained in the Western Hemisphere.
- Convinced Charles V to use peaceful means for the conversion of the Indians in 1520.
- Obtained papal protection of the Indians.
- Obtained royal decree to end slavery in Perú.
- Appointed Bishop of Chiapas, México, in 1544.

Important Contributions

After accepting slaves for his service during the conquest of Spanish territories in the Americas, Bartolomé de las Casas had a change of heart and became the first European to campaign for a humane treatment of the native peoples of the New World. In a sense, he was a precursor to the human rights movement. Confronted by colonists and facing an unconcerned Europe, las Casas's efforts produced few results. In places such as Cuba and Argentina, the Indian population was totally eradicated. In the rest of the Americas, the Indians continued to be second-class citizens. But las Casas's actions may have taken away some of the shame Spain and the other European powers brought upon themselves with their treatment of the native people of the Western Hemisphere.

Career Path

El defensor de los indios (Protector of the Indians) was the mocking title given to Fray Bartolomé de las Casas by the Spanish colonists of the New World. But at the time, the Dominican priest was certainly the protector, and maybe the only one, of the indigenous people of the Americas.

Las Casas was born to a middle-class merchant family. When he was eleven or thirteen, his father enrolled him at the Cathedral of Seville school to study Latin. He then attended the University of Salamanca to study theology and humanities.

Like other youths of his time, las Casas, not yet a priest, embarked for the island of Hispaniola in 1502. There he earned an *encomienda*, land and a group of natives to work it, for his involvement in the colonization process. But even then he was different. He tried to evangelize the natives placed under his tutelage. Four years later he returned to Spain. He went to Rome where he was ordained a deacon. In 1511, after listening to a sermon by a Dominican priest condemning the abuse of the Indians, he freed all of his Indian servants. Back in Hispaniola the next year, he was ordained as the first priest in the New World.

In 1513 las Casas left Hispaniola with Diego Velázquez as expedition chaplain, and first witnessed the brutal annihilation of Indians during the Spanish conquest of Cuba. From 1515 to 1520 he traveled back and forth to Spain, campaigning for better treatment for the Indians. On his last trip, Emperor Charles V approved his starting a colony in what is today's Venezuela where Spanish settlers and free Indians would live together. Other local colonists who owned Indian slaves did not take kindly to the experiment and harassed las Casas and the settlement. Finally, in January 1522, the integrated village had to be abandoned. Saddened by this failure, las Casas returned to Hispaniola in 1523, joined the Dominican Order, and turned to writing. Among the works he produced during this period are *La Historia General o Apologética de las Indias* (*General History or Apologetic of the Indies*) and the unfinished *Historia de la Indias* (*History of the Indies*).

In 1530 las Casas was in Spain, where he convinced the king to do away with the encomiendas in Perú. The Spanish pioneers opposed the plan, and the Crown retracted. But las Casas would not give up. He returned to the court in 1544 and induced Charles V to sign *Las leyes nuevas* (The New Laws), legally abolishing the encomiendas. While in Spain he wrote *Brevísima relación de la destrucción de las Indias* (*A Brief Report on the Destruction of the Indies*), his most famous and important defense of the Indians. Unfortunately, in his zeal to protect the Native American people, las Casas was also an advocate of the slavery of Africans who would take the place of the Indians at the colonists' farms, mines, and houses.

To make sure the new laws were enforced, las Casas was selected Bishop of Chiapas, in present-day México, and he left Spain in July 1544. Needless to say, his welcome was less than warm. The Spanish immediately opposed him, and within a year the king repealed portions of the laws. Although disappointed, las Casas once again returned to Spain, gave up his bishopric, and continued to speak out and write books condemning the poor treatment of the New World native peoples. Las Casas, *el defensor de los indios* indeed, died in Madrid on July 31, 1566. His incomplete *History of the Indies* was first published the following year, 1567.

Bibliography

Arias, Santa. *Retórica, historia y polémica: Bartolomé de las Casas y la tradición intelectual renacentista.* Lanham, MD: University Press of America, 2002.

Báez, Vicente, ed. *La Enciclopedia de Cuba.* Madrid: Enciclopedia y Clásicos Cubanos, Inc., 1973.

Freitas Neto, José Alvarez. *Bartolomé de las Casas.* São Paulo: Annablume, 2003.

Menéndez Pidal, Ramón. *El Padre las Casas: su doble personalidad.* Madrid: Espasa Calpe, S.A., 1963.

Pérez, Fernández, Isacio. *Bartolomé de las Casas, viajero por dos mundos: su figura, su biografía sincera, su personalidad.* Cuzco, Perú: Centro de Estudio Regional Andino Bartolomé de las Casas, 1998.

Sanderlin, George, ed. *Witness: Writings of Bartolomé de las Casas.* New York: Orbis Books, 1992.

Richard E. Cavazos

Rising to the Top

Army Officer

❖ Born in Kingsville, Texas.
❖ Birth date: January 31, 1929.

Career Highlights

- Commissioned a second lieutenant in the U.S. Army in 1951.
- Received more than twelve decorations for gallantry and valor.
- Served as the defense attaché to the U.S. Embassy in México.
- Received the National Infantry Association Doughboy Award in 1991.
- Became the U.S. Army's first Hispanic general.

Important Contributions

The U.S. Army has had difficulties accepting and promoting minorities. While the U.S. Navy was fully integrated by the time of the Civil War, the Army would not achieve the same distinction until the 1950s. Richard Cavazos, who joined in the early 1950s, would prove that those with talent, courage, hard work, and honor can achieve just about anything, including rising in the ranks of the U.S. Army to become a full four-star general.

Career Path

For a young Mexican-American second lieutenant who started as a platoon leader in a Puerto Rican regiment, Richard Cavazos didn't do badly at all. He went on to become the first Hispanic general in the U.S. Army.

Cavazos was born outside a small city in southern Texas. As any boy growing up on a ranch, he went to school and did chores. Upon graduation from high school, he attended Texas Technological University at Lubbock, where he joined the ROTC (Reserve Officers' Training Corps). After earning his bachelor's degree in geology, Cavazos was commissioned a second lieutenant. Before being shipped to Korea, Cavazos finished his officer basic training at Fort Benning, Georgia, and then completed airborne school. In Korea, he joined the 65th Infantry Regiment's Company E as a platoon leader. The 65th, deactivated in 1956, was known as *Los Borinqueños* (the Borinqueneers, after Puerto Rico's Indian name, Borinquen).

Cavazos did not take long to distinguish himself and his actions, securing the capture of an enemy soldier during battle on February 25th, 1953. For his actions, Cavazos was awarded a Silver Star, one of the military's highest honors. Five months later, his valor would earn him a Distinguished Service Cross for a battle fought on June 14, 1953.

After Korea, Cavazos became an ROTC instructor at his alma mater. His next posting was as an operations officer at the U.S. Army's European headquarters in West Germany. He also continued learning. He furthered his training at the U.S. Army Command and General Staff College, the British Army Staff College, and the U.S. Armed Forces Staff College. In February 1967, Cavazos, then a lieutenant colonel, was appointed commander of the 1st Battalion of the 18th Infantry Division.

By then, the Vietnam War was raging. Once again, Cavazos did not waste time in distinguishing himself. In October 1967 he led his unit during the two-day Battle of Lo Ninh, near the Cambodian border, causing more than 100 casualties to the enemy, while losing only five of his men. His individual acts earned him his second Distinguished Service Cross.

After completing his tour of Vietnam, Cavazos became Director of Concept Studies at the Army's Combat Development Command Institute; Chief of the Offense Section in the Department of Division Operations at the Army Command and General Staff College; and defense attaché at the U.S. Embassy in México. In 1976 he was promoted to brigadier general, the first Hispanic to reach such rank. The following year Cavazos became commander of the 9th Infantry Division; one of his subordinate officers was H. Norman Schwarzkopf, who later became famous as the chief of coalition forces during Desert Shield and Desert Storm in Iraq. Cavazos was promoted to major general in 1978. His last two commands were with the III Group, at Fort Lewis, Washington, as a lieutenant general, and as a full four-star general overseeing the U.S. Army Forces Command. Again, he was the first Hispanic to hold such ranks in the U.S. Army. Cavazos retired from the military on June 17, 1984, and moved back to Texas with his wife and four children.

In addition to his Silver Star and two Distinguished Service Crosses, Cavazos received two Legion of Merit awards, five Bronze Stars for Valor, and a Purple Heart. Retirement has not meant downtime for Cavazos. President Ronald Reagan appointed him to the Chemical Warfare Review Commission in 1985, and later he served on the board of regents of Texas Technological University. He still advises the military on many matters.

Bibliography

"General Richard E. Cavazos." Rangers Hall of Fame. http://www.benning. army.mil/rtb/Hall_of_fame/Halloffame_ inaugural/general_cavazos.htm. (March 17, 2005).

"Hispanic-Americans and the U.S. Military in the Korean War." Neta.com http:// www.neta.com/~1stbooks/korea6.htm (April 12, 2003).

"Richard E. Cavazos." Thomson/Gale. http:// www.galegroup.com/free_resources/chh/ bio/cavazos_r.htm (November 30, 2004).

Miguel de Cervantes

Fighting Windmills

Writer,
Adventurer

- ❖ Born in Alcalá de Henares, Madrid, Spain.
- ❖ Birth date: September 29, 1547.
- ❖ Death date: April 23, 1616.

Career Highlights

- Joined various military expeditions, including the Spanish Armada.
- Published his first work *La Galatea* (*Galatea*) in 1585.
- Published a tragedy in verse titled *Numancia*.
- Published the first part of *Don Quixote* in 1605 and the second part in 1615.

Important Contributions

Cervantes, playwright and novelist, is best known for his main contribution to Spanish and world literature, *Don Quixote*. The book is considered the first major work in Spanish as a totally distinct language from Latin. The main character, Alonso Quijano el Bueno, aka Don Quixote de la Mancha, is a universal character that appeals to all cultures and languages.

Career Path

If he had never written one line, Miguel de Cervantes Saavedra, known as *el Manco de Lepanto* (the one-armed man from Lepanto), might have been just as celebrated for his adventures. He fought at the famous Battle of Lepanto against the Turks in 1751, where he lost the use of his left hand. Later, fighting against the Moslems in North Africa, Cervantes was captured by Barbary pirates and held captive in Algiers for five years. He served in the Spanish Armada, was excommunicated, jailed, and finally, became a favorite in the court of Phillip II.

The years of confinement in Algiers were crucial for Cervantes' development as a writer. It was not just the impact that prison life had on him; it was also the city itself. Blessed with a wonderful Mediterranean climate, Algiers was, at the time, a thriving center of commerce, art, and science. Such was the energy of Algiers, that even a prisoner could experience it. In addition, it was a remarkably tolerant place where Christians, Jews, and Muslims lived in harmony. Cervantes also took on a new appreciation of Muslim civilization. He had been familiar with some Muslim art and architecture, as Spain had been occupied by the Moors (the Moors were members of the Spanish Muslim population and were of mixed Arab, European, and Berber origins). In Algiers he came to learn that there was nothing inferior about Muslim culture, architecture, or artwork. He understood that Muslims were as advanced as Western Europeans, and in many fields, such as medicine and astronomy, more so.

Cervantes was born near Madrid. Most of his early instruction was at a Catholic school there; there are no records of his attending any institution of higher learning. Through the auspices of an Italian bishop he went to Rome in the midst of the Renaissance and familiarized himself with most of the ideas that were taking root at that time. It was during his return to Spain that the Barbary pirates imprisoned him.

Back in Spain after five years, the thirty-seven-year-old Cervantes married nineteen-year-old Catalina de Salazar y Palacios in Esquivias, in the Spanish province of Toledo. There Cervantes tried his hand at writing for the first time and published *Galatea*. He also made an unsuccessful attempt at playwriting.

In 1588 he joined the Spanish Armada as a supply officer, but alleged irregularities landed him in jail. His three excommunications followed soon after, all derived from his attempts as a tax collector in Granada to make the church pay assessments as required by law.

Finally, he decided to give writing another try, and in 1605 published the first part of *El Ingenioso Hidalgo Don Quixote de la Mancha* (*The Ingenious Peer Don Quixote of la Mancha*) about an elderly man who, influenced by tales of chivalry, believes himself to be a knight–errant (a knight who travels in search of adventures). In *Don Quixote*, Cervantes explores reality and pokes fun at the Spanish society of his time. The book's success was overwhelming, to the point that a second story was published by a bogus writer. This forced Cervantes to write a subsequent part, which was available ten years after the first.

Cervantes' work also includes sonnets, pastoral poems, and other minor poems. Some of his tragedies and comedies were produced for the theater. His other major works include the novels *Novelas Ejemplares* (*Exemplary Novels*) and the play *Ocho comedias y ocho entremeses* (*Eight Comedies and Eight One-act Farces*), which was produced for the theater in 1615. *Los trabajos de Pérsiles y Segismundo* (*The Works of Persiles and Seguismund*), his final novel, was published in 1617, one year after he died in Madrid.

Don Quixote is considered one of the masterpieces of world literature and ranks with the Bible and *The Three Musketeers* as one of the most translated books on the planet.

Bibliography

Branston, Julian. *The Eternal Quest*. London: Sceptre, 2003.

Durán, Manuel. *Cervantes*. Boston: Twayne Publishers, 1974.

Garcés, María Antonia. *Cervantes in Algiers: A Captive's Tale*. Nashville: Vanderbilt University, 2005.

García López, José. *Resumen de Historia de las Literaturas Hispánicas*. Barcelona: Editorial Teide, S.A., 1979.

McCrory, Donald. *No Ordinary Man: The Life and Times of Miguel de Cervantes*. London: Peter Owen Publishers, 2002.

Parker, Mary, ed. *Spanish Dramatists of the Golden Age: A Bio-Bibliographical Sourcebook*. Westport, CT: Greenwood Press, 1998.

Franklin Chang-Díaz

Spaceman

Astronaut,
Physicist

❖ Born in San José, Costa Rica.
❖ Birth date: April 5, 1950.

Career Highlights

- Became a NASA astronaut in 1981.
- Helped develop propulsion systems for future spaceflights.
- Veteran of seven spaceflights.
- Received three doctorates *honoris causa* from universities in North, Central, and South America.

Important Contributions

Franklin Chang-Díaz logged more hours in space—1,600 plus—than any other Hispanic. He was part of the last joint American-Soviet mission in space when the Space Shuttle *Discovery* docked with the Mir Space Station. The work he has done in plasma fusion and rocket propulsion based on magnetism will help propel other explorers through space on future missions.

Career Path

Franklin Chang-Díaz is a unique individual. While not the first Hispanic to go into outer space, he has flown more missions that any other Spanish-speaking person. Born in the small Central American nation of Costa Rica, Chang-Díaz eventually became a U.S. citizen. After his space adventures, he was honored with the highest award Costa Rica presents a foreign national, the title of Honorary Citizen. Needless to say, he is the only Honorary Citizen of that nation who was actually born in Costa Rica.

Chang-Díaz's parents named him in honor of Franklin Delano Roosevelt, who remains one of the most popular American presidents among residents of Latin America. His early education took place at the prestigious *Colegio De La Salle* (La Salle School), which he attended until 1967. When he moved alone to the United States, he had only $50, and didn't even speak English. Nonetheless, he graduated from Hartford High School in Connecticut in 1969. He studied mechanical engineering at the University of Connecticut and worked as a research assistant in the physics department. After earning his bachelor of science degree in 1973, he was accepted into a physics doctorate program at the Massachusetts Institute of Technology (MIT). He received his PhD in applied plasma physics in 1977.

Soon after graduating he went to work for the Charles Stark Draper Laboratory and applied for NASA's astronaut program. He was chosen in 1980, the same year he became a U.S. citizen, and earned his astronaut wings within twelve months. However, it would be five years before Chang-Díaz went into space. During that time he participated in design studies for the space station; started the Astronaut Science Colloquium Program, a program to bring together astronauts and scientists; and led the Astronaut Science Support Group at Cape Canaveral.

Finally, on January 12, 1986, Chang-Díaz joined the crew that blasted off from the Kennedy Space Center in the Space Shuttle *Columbia* on a six-day mission to deploy a communications satellite and conduct astrophysics experiments. Six more trips into space followed. Of those, the *Atlantis* flight that deployed the Galileo probe on its trip to Jupiter (October 18–23, 1989), and the *Discovery* mission to the Mir Space Station (June 2–12, 1998) were particularly important. He is still director of the Advance Space Propulsion Laboratory at Houston's Johnson Space Center, a position to which he was appointed in 1993. He is also an adjunct professor of physics at Rice University and at the University of Houston, and is involved with the development of a Latin-American space agency.

More than a scientist and a space explorer, Chang-Díaz is also concerned about earthbound issues, volunteering at a facility for mental patients and in a rehabilitation program for Hispanic drug users.

To this day he travels regularly to his homeland to visit his mother, brothers, and sisters. In Costa Rica, Franklin Chang-Díaz, the boy who in 1957 sat atop a mango tree to try to see *Sputnik*, is a national hero.

❖ ❖ ❖

Bibliography

"Award-Winning Astronaut Franklin Chang-Díaz Follows Dream." Space Explorers Web site, *Planetary Times*, October 22, 2003. http://news.space-explorers.com/display.asp?v = 1&I = 15&a = 5 (March 3, 2005).

"Franklin Chang-Díaz (Astronaut)." Info-COSTARICA.com. http://www.infocostarica.com/people/franklin.html (April 4, 2004).

Ianiszewski, Jorge. "Latinoamericanos en el espacio orbital." *Circuloastro.* http://www.circuloastronomico.cl/noticias/chile.html (January 20, 2005).

Peña, Silvia Novo. "The Next Frontier: Hispanics in the Space Program." *Hispanic.* January–February 1989, p. 28.

César Chávez

- ❖ Born near Yuma, Arizona.
- ❖ Birth date: March 31, 1927.
- ❖ Death date: April 23, 1993.

Career Highlights

- Acquired philosophy of non-violence from reading about St. Francis of Assisi, Mohandas Gandhi, and Martin Luther King, Jr.
- Founded the National Farm Workers Union (NFWA) in 1962.
- Led the grape and lettuce boycotts of the late 1960s and early 1970s.
- Awarded *El Aguila Azteca* (the Aztec Eagle), México's highest civilian decoration, given to persons of Mexican ancestry for contributions abroad.

Important Contributions

A legendary figure of the American labor movement, César Chávez almost single-handedly organized the first successful farm workers union in the United States. Under his leadership, farm workers, an underpaid and ill-treated segment of labor, gained many benefits and improved their standard of living.

Career Path

César Chávez, the second child of Mexican immigrants, knew what it was like to be poor, helpless, and hungry. For ten years he and his five brothers and sisters lived on a small farm in Arizona, where his family strained to make a living. When the Chávez family lost the farm in 1937, he embarked on the life of the migrant worker—toiling long hours to help other poverty-stricken farmers.

Chávez first became a migrant worker at the age of ten. The Great Depression was in full swing when the family lost its little farm. The Chávez's were forced to look for work anywhere they could find it, usually picking crops. The next year they moved to California. Like most of the 300,000 migrant workers at the time, the Chávez's made very little money. They earned a total of $300 in 1938.

The constant moving hampered César's education and the fact that he spoke only Spanish, which was prohibited in the schools, didn't help. He finally graduated from the eighth grade in 1942, when he was fifteen years old. Chávez had left school when his father was injured in an accident; he had gone to work in the fields to spare his mother from it. Chávez saw right away the injustices committed against migrant farm workers and spoke out with little success.

During World War II Chávez joined the U.S. Navy and fought in the Pacific. Once discharged, he went back to California and his job. Chávez married Helen Fabela in 1948, six years after they had met. Like him, she was bothered by the way farm workers were treated.

It was early in his married life that Chávez began to develop his beliefs in non-violence. In 1952 he went to work as an organizer with the Community Service Organization (CSO) in Oxnard, California. He led his first battle for migrant workers' rights, and won. Against government regulations, the local farm owners refused to hire community farm workers, and instead brought in recruits from México. Chávez took the case to the federal government. Eventually, the laws were enforced, and the farm owners had to hire local workers.

Six years later Chávez became the CSO's national director. However, since the organization was not interested in organizing a farm workers union, Chávez gave up his job and founded the NFWA (National Farm Workers Association). The union's motto was *Viva la Causa* (Long Live the Cause). His experience as an organizer paid off, and by 1964 the NFWA had 1,000 members, each paying monthly dues of $3.50.

The NFWA and Chávez became nationally known in 1965, when the union joined a strike of Filipino workers against grape growers for better pay and living conditions. Under Chávez, NFWA members picketed, boycotted, fasted, and, in 1966, marched to Sacramento. Even though only seventy-five people had started the march, there were 10,000 at the rally at the California capital. In the end, Schenley Vineyards Corporation signed the first-ever contract with farm workers in the United States.

During the next twenty-five years Chávez led many other strikes, marches, and boycotts. Two of his most famous campaigns were the 1967–1969 grape boycott against the Guimarra Vineyards Corporation and the 1970 lettuce strike.

Chávez died at age sixty-six in San Luis, Arizona. His union, now called the United Farm Workers and part of the Change to Win Federation, continues his crusade.

Bibliography

Ada, Alma Flor, and Campoy, F. Isabel. *Caminos*. Miami, FL: Santillana USA Publishing, 2000.

Dalton, Frederick John. *The Moral Vision of César Chávez*. Maryknoll, NY: Orbis Books, 2003.

Griswold del Castillo, Richard. *César Chávez: A Triumph of the Spirit*. Norman, OK: University of Oklahoma Press, 1997.

Krull, Kathleen. *Harvesting Hope: The Story of César Chávez*. San Diego, CA: Harcourt Children's Books, 2003.

Seidman, David. *César Chávez: Labor Leader*. New York: Franklin Watts, 2000.

Yinger, Winthrop. *César Chávez: The Rhetoric of Nonviolence*. Hicksville, NY: Exposition Press, 1975.

Dennis Chávez

Transforming New Mexico   Statesman

❖ Born in Los Chávez, New Mexico.
❖ Birth date: April 8, 1888.
❖ Death date: November 18, 1962.

Career Highlights

- Received law degree in 1920.
- First elected to the U.S. House of Representatives in 1930.
- Appointed to fill a vacancy in the U.S. Senate in 1935.
- Elected to the U.S Senate in 1936.
- Served as chairman of the Senate's Committee on Post Office and Post Roads and the Committee on Public Works.

Important Contributions

Dennis Chávez believed that elected officials are servants of the citizens who elect them. During the Depression he was instrumental in establishing the Home Owners' Loan Corporation, which helped countless homeowners avoid repossession of their properties. Once in the Senate, he was influential in the development of the Interstate Highway System and the construction of federal office buildings. He guided many defense and technological contracts that are still producing dividends to his home state of New Mexico.

Career Path

As a member of Congress for almost forty years, Dennis Chávez was one of the most influential and well-known politicians in the history of New Mexico. He was the main force in attaining the important projects that shaped the economic, social, and historical development of the forty-seventh state.

Dionisio Chávez was born in a small community in Valencia County just south of Albuquerque. He attended public and Catholic schools in Albuquerque after his family moved there when he was seven. While he was in the seventh grade, the family's lack of finances forced Chávez to leave school. He worked at a grocery store for the next eleven years. However, being out of school did not mean that the young man had forgotten his education. Chávez spent countless hours at the Albuquerque Public Library reading everything he could, mostly biographies and books about U.S. history.

In 1906 Chávez took a job with the city's engineering department, joined the Democratic Party, and began his political activism. He supported the unsuccessful Octaviano Larrazolo's bid for territorial delegate to Congress in 1908, and was Governor William D. MacDonald's interpreter four years later.

Chávez failed the first time he ran for public office in the 1916 election for Bernalillo County Clerk. But that year wasn't all bad for Chávez. He campaigned for the successful Democratic Senate candidate, Andieus A. Jones. Chávez's bilingualism proved key to Jones' election, and he was rewarded with a clerkship at the office of the secretary of the United States Senate. While working as the senator's clerk, Chávez attended Georgetown University at night, eventually receiving his law degree in 1920. After being admitted to the bar the same year, he opened a law practice in Albuquerque.

Chávez was elected to the state House of Representatives, where he served eight years. There he began his lifelong effort in support of education. He was appointed to committees that were of interest to his constituency: Public Land, Veterans, War Claims, Public Building, Indian Affairs, and Irrigation and Reclamation. During his second term, he became chairman of the Committee for Irrigation and Reclamation.

He lost his 1934 senate race to incumbent Republican Bronson Cutting; however, Cutting died in a plane crash on his way back to the nation's capital, and the governor appointed Chávez to fill the vacancy. He took office on May 11, 1935, and would never lose an election again, being elected to the position on November 3, 1936. From the time he arrived in Washington, D.C., Chávez was a supporter of President Franklin Delano Roosevelt's New Deal. The New Deal transformed government, business, agriculture, banking, industry, and most important to Chávez, education. The program lifted the nation out of the Depression and restored the people's faith in democracy.

As a committee or subcommittee chairman, Chávez used his power to secure federal programs that would benefit the economy and the people of New Mexico. Senator Chávez was also an early advocate of civil rights. A Southern filibuster in 1948 vanquished his four-year campaign to create a Fair Employment Practices Commission with vast powers to stop employment discrimination due to race, creed, national origin, or ancestry.

Chávez died in Washington, D.C., on November 18, 1962, far from his beloved home state.

Bibliography

"Chávez, Dennis." *World Book Encyclopedia 1990 Edition.* Chicago: World Book, Inc., 1990.

Etulain, Richard W., ed. *New Mexican Lives: Profiles and Historical Stories.* Albuquerque, NM: University of New Mexico Center for the American West, 2002.

Lamar, Howard R., ed. *The Reader's Encyclopedia of the American West.* New York: Thomas Y. Crowell Company, 1977.

Meier, Matt S., ed. *Mexican American Biographies: A Historical Dictionary: 1836–1987.* Westport, CT: Greenwood Press, 1988.

Stein, R. Conrad. *New Mexico.* Chicago: Children's Press, 1998.

Vigil, Maurilio E. "Senator Dennis Chávez: His Legacy Lives on." *Las Vegas Optic*, April 2, 1991, p. 1.

Hernán Cortés

The Conqueror of México   Explorer

❖ Born in Medellín, Spain.
❖ Birth date: Circa 1485.
❖ Death date: December 2, 1547.

Career Highlights

- Participated in conquest of Cuba in 1511.
- Left Cuba for México in 1519.
- Completed conquest of México in 1521.
- Explored parts of lower California in 1535.

Important Contributions

With the conquest of México's rich Aztec Empire, Cortés began the enrichment of the Spanish Crown, which led to Spain's rise to the position of the world's greatest power. His expeditions also provided Madrid with its most important foothold in the New World's mainland.

Career Path

The most famous of the Spanish *conquistadores* (conquistadors), Hernán Cortés was proud and arrogant. He was also a man of courage, genius, and few principles.

He was born to a noble but poor family in the province of Extremadura. His exact date of birth is unknown. When he was fourteen the family sent him to Salamanca to study law. Lack of interest in academics, restlessness, and numerous love affairs caused him to put away his books soon after and take up a life of adventure.

He served as a soldier in Europe and in 1504 sailed for Hispaniola, which lies between Cuba and Puerto Rico (today Haiti occupies the western third of the island; the eastern two-thirds are the Dominican Republic). While there, he acted as a scribe for Governor Nicolás de Ovando, and helped Diego Velázquez put down an Indian uprising. When Velázquez undertook the conquest of Cuba, Cortés went along. In Cuba he became now-Governor Velázquez's secretary, and eventually mayor of Santiago.

By 1518 Velázquez had sent two unsuccessful expeditions to the area of modern-day México to investigate a rich Indian empire on the mainland. Trusting Cortés to succeed, the governor of Cuba chose him to lead a third journey. So thorough was Cortés in his preparations that Velázquez became suspicious and removed him from the command. But that did not bother Cortés. On February 18, 1519, Cortés left Cuba for the mainland. Cortés did not realize how powerful México's Aztec Empire was, so he took only eleven ships and 600 men, 100 sailors among them. But in all fairness, had he known, it would not have mattered. The often-told story of the conquest of México is well known. On Good Friday Cortés established Veracruz on the coast of Campeche Bay and was appointed captain-general. This made him directly responsible to the king, and led to a total split with Velázquez. In Veracruz the Spaniards first came in contact with the Aztec's dreadful religious practices. A small number of Aztec messengers arrived to force twenty local Indians into being human sacrifices during a ceremony. Cortés took advantage of the situation. The Spaniards allowed two of the Aztecs to escape to demonstrate support for Moctezuma, the Aztec emperor. On the other hand, Cortés told the local Indians, afraid of the emperor's retribution, that he would defend them. Those who hated the Aztecs became Cortés' allies. Moctezuma sent gifts of gold, silver, and jewels in an attempt to placate the man he considered the god, Quetzalcatl, but to no avail. The horses and guns used by the Spaniards, which the Aztec had never seen, led Moctezuma to believe that the leader, Cortés, was the powerful god.

Before marching on Tenochtitlán, the Aztec capital, Cortés had all his ships burned, and told his soldiers that there would be no retreat, only victory. On the way, while in the city of Cholula, there was an attempt on the Spaniards' lives. Some historians say Indians were the perpetrators; others believe that discontented Spaniards were behind it. In any case, Cortés' response ended in a massacre of natives.

Partly assisted by the natives' belief that he was the god Quetzalcoatl, Cortés and his men walked into Tenochtitlán on November 8, 1519, and took the emperor prisoner. In May of the following year, Spanish troops under Pánfilo de Narváez arrived from Cuba to take

Cortés prisoner. Cortés defeated Narváez, whose soldiers then came under his command. Upon his return to Tenochtitlán, Cortés found the city in chaos. Moctezuma was killed, and Cortés and his men had to flee. They would not return until May 1521, when they laid siege to the city with thousands of Indian allies. Tenochtitlán finally fell on August 13.

Cortés continued his exploration of the mainland, going as far south as Honduras. In due course, he fell out of favor with the king, now King Charles I of Spain, who had become Holy Roman Emperor Charles V. In 1528 Cortés went to Spain looking for redress. He received many honors, but no power, and so returned to México (then New Spain) to further explore the north. In 1540 he returned to Spain. The following year on a disastrous expedition to Algiers, he managed to uphold his fame as a man of arms.

Cortés died on December 2, 1547, in Castilleja de la Cuesta, near Seville.

Bibliography

Chrisp, Peter. *The Spanish Conquest of the New World.* New York: Thomson Learning, 1993.

Lilley, Stephen R. *The Importance of Hernando Cortés.* San Diego, CA: Lucent Books, 1996.

Maestro, Betsy, and Maestro, Giulio. *Exploration and Conquest: The Americas After Columbus: 1500–1620.* New York: HarperTrophy, 1997.

Marks, Richard Lee. *Cortés: The Great Adventurer and the Fate of Aztec México.* New York: Alfred A. Knopf, 1993.

Martínez, Paula. *El drama de México: Cuauhtémoc o Cortés?* México City: Edamex, 2001.

Ruiz, Ramón Eduardo. *Triumphs and Tragedy: A History of the Mexican People.* New York: W.W. Norton & Company, 1992.

Thomas, Hugh. *Conquest: Cortés, Montezuma, and the Fall of Old México.* New York: Simon & Schuster, 1995.

Juan Cortina

Hero or Ruffian

Revolutionary

- ❖ Born in Camargo, México.
- ❖ Birth date: May 16, 1824.
- ❖ Death date: October 30, 1894.

Career Highlights

- Notable member of the South Texas Democratic Party in the 1850s.
- Proclaimed an independent republic of the Río Grande in 1859.
- Defeated by Confederate troops under Santos Benavides in 1861.
- Appointed general of the Mexican army in 1863.

Important Contributions

Juan Cortina demonstrated that from the time Texas joined the Union there would be Mexican Americans who would demand equal treatment under the laws of the United States. In many ways, Cortina was a forerunner of the civil-rights activists who emerged in the United States during the 1960s. Today, many Mexican Americans, while disagreeing with his violent ways, see him as a hero.

Career Path

If you were one of the Mexican Americans whose rights Juan Cortina defended, he was your champion. If you were an Anglo American settler whose property and lives he threatened, he was a thug.

Juan Nepomuceno Cortina was born into wealth. His family had sizeable holdings of land on both sides of the Río Grande, including a large cattle ranch close to Brownsville, Texas. Even though the family had moved from the state of Tamaulipas to north of the Río Grande when Cortina was a teenager, he fought on the Mexican side during the Mexican-American War. Once the conflict ended with the 1848 Treaty of Guadalupe Hidalgo, he returned north again.

Cortina became a notable political boss for the Democratic Party in southern Texas. Although he lost many acres of land due to cancellation of Spanish land grants by the U.S. government, he continued to be wealthy and powerful. His standing in the community kept him from being arrested when he was indicted twice for cattle rustling. However, by the mid-1850s Cortina had become a thorn in the side of attorneys and judges in the Brownsville region. He accused them of taking advantage of Mexicans who did not comprehend the American legal system. On July 13, 1859, the events that started the first "Cortina War" were set in motion. That day marshal Robert Shears pistol-whipped a Mexican cowhand who had worked for Cortina. Furious, Cortina demanded that Shears stop beating the *vaquero* (cowboy). When the marshal refused, Cortina shot him in the shoulder and rode away with his former employee.

Brownsville had not seen the last of Cortina. On September 28 he returned with some sixty men. He took the town, released Mexicans whom he believed were unjustly arrested, killed five Anglos, and, with shouts of "Death to the gringos," proclaimed the area the Republic of the Río Grande. Some of the town's prominent citizens got the Mexican authorities in Matamoros, just across the border, to intervene. They persuaded Cortina to leave. Back at his ranch, Cortina released a declaration condemning discrimination against Mexicans and upholding their right to self-preservation.

Later a group of Brownsville residents calling themselves the Brownsville Tigers, along with some Mexican militias, attacked Cortina's ranch, but were defeated. The Texas government then sent in the Texas Rangers, a statewide law enforcement agency, to put down Cortina's uprising. The Rangers didn't do any better than the Tigers. Cortina appealed to Governor Sam Houston to stand up for the rights of Mexicans in Texas. Houston's answer was to send a second, larger, and more disciplined unit of the Rangers. This time the Rangers won, defeating Cortina at the Battle of Río Grande City on December 27, 1859. Cortina retreated into México.

Texas' secession from the Union on March 1861 enabled Cortina's easy return. In May of that year Cortina invaded Zapata County in southern Texas. But the second Cortina War was short-lived. Confederate troops under the command of Captain Santos Benavides, himself a Mexican American, defeated Cortina, who again retreated to México.

Cortina remained in México fighting at Puebla against an intervention by the French in 1862. The following year he declared himself governor of Tamaulipas. President Benito Juárez appointed him to a position as a general of the Mexican Army of the North in 1863. In 1870 he once again showed up on the border. Although there was popular support for his return, the U.S. government pressured México to have him arrested. Cortina was jailed in the Mexican capital from 1875 until 1890. Eventually freed, he died in Azcapotzalco, a borough of México City, on October 30, 1894.

Was Cortina Robin Hood, or just a regular hood? It depends on who writes history.

Bibliography

Castillo, Pedro. *Furia y muerte: los bandidos chicanos*. Los Angeles: Aztlán Publications, 1973.

"Juan Cortina." *The West*. http://www.pbs.org/weta/thewest/people/a_c/cortina.htm (November 24, 2004).

Lamar, Howard R., ed. *The Reader's Encyclopedia of the American West*. New York: Thomas Y. Crowell Company, 1977.

Thompson, Jerry, D., ed. *Juan Cortina and the Texas-México Frontier, 1859–1877*. El Paso, TX: Texas Western Press, University of Texas at El Paso, 1994.

Woodman, Lyman L. *Cortina: Rogue of the Río Grande*. San Antonio, TX: Naylor, 1950.

Salvador Dalí

Mad Genius   Artist

- ❖ Born in Figueres, Spain.
- ❖ Birth date: May 11, 1904.
- ❖ Death date: January 23, 1989.

Career Highlights

- Held first exhibition in 1918.
- Became a surrealist in 1929.
- Collaborated with director Luís Buñuel in the surrealistic film *Un Perro Andaluz* (*An Andalusian Dog*) in 1929.
- Kicked out of the surrealist movement in 1934.

Important Contributions

To most people, Salvador Dalí *is* surrealism. Like no other artist before or since, Dalí found inspiration in his dreams (some say nightmares), paranoia, and his most private experiences. Furthermore, he had the audacity to put them on canvas. Dalí redefined art.

Career Path

As the unquestionable master of surrealism, Salvador Dalí was an ostentatious painter, graphic artist, sculptor, writer, and filmmaker. But most of all, he was a shameless self-promoter. His image of a mad genius was all-important. When his sister described his childhood as "normal" and "happy" in a book, Dalí's revenge was to create a crude painting of her.

The future artist was born into a prosperous family in the northeastern Spanish province of Catalonia, and was baptized Salvador Felip

Jacinto Dalí Domènech, his name in Catalan. He was the second son his parents named Salvador. Their first son Salvador died before his second birthday, and the newborn inherited his name. His parents, perhaps to diminish any psychological problem the child may have had for being named after his dead brother, pandered to his every desire.

Dalí was a precocious artist, taking his first lessons in his hometown when he was just ten, and having his first exhibition at fourteen. Between 1921 and 1925 Dalí attended the Royal Academy of Art in Madrid, but was expelled a couple of times for contending that he was a better artist than his teachers and for refusing to take his final exams. The same year he left school, Dalí had his first show in Barcelona, where he exhibited realist, cubist, and futuristic works.

His first experiments in surrealism took place in 1926, when he created *La Cesta de Pan* (*The Breadbasket*). Dalí traveled to Paris in 1928 and established himself as the foremost surrealist painter in France. While in the City of Lights, he met André Breton, the recognized founder of surrealism, an artistic movement based on the liberation of the mind and the theories of the noted psychoanalyst Sigmund Freud. In 1929 Dalí met Gala, a married Russian émigré ten years his senior. She became his lover, model, and business manager. At this point Dalí came into his own as an artist, depicting the fantastic images of his dreams in an almost photographic style. His most famous work, *La Persistencia de la Memoria* (*The Persistence of Memory*), appeared in 1931.

Three years later, due to his continued bickering with Breton and other surrealists, as well as his support of Francisco Franco during the Spanish civil war, Dalí was officially booted from the surrealist movement. The Spanish painter did not care; he was making a lot of money in Europe and the United States, where his works had become enormously popular. Breton began to call Dalí *Avida Dollar*, meaning "greedy for dollars." At this time Dalí began what is called his paranoid-critic era. *Metamófosis de Narciso* (*Metamorphosis of Narcissus*), painted in 1937, is the most important work of this time. He moved to Italy in 1937, and there his paintings became more conventional.

In order to avoid the miseries of World War II Dalí moved to the United States in 1940. He promoted himself brazenly and began a period of religious paintings such as 1954's *Corpus Crucificíon* (*Crucifixion*) and *La Ultima Cena* (*The Sacrament of the Last Supper*) a year later. The beginning of the Cold War in 1945 brought new spiritual factors into Dalí's work. He was acutely upset over the detonation of the first nuclear bomb and from then on was fearful that the world would end in a nuclear holocaust.

In 1958–1959 he painted another masterpiece, the huge *El Sueño de Cristobal Colón,* (Christopher Columbus' Dream), also known in English as *The Discovery of America by Christopher Columbus*. By the 1980s palsy forced Dalí to retire from painting. Unable to work, he plunged into a deep depression made even worse when, in 1984, he got news that Gala, from whom he had separated, had died. He became a recluse, living in the tower of the museum opened in his honor in his hometown. There he died of heart failure on January 23, 1989. Dalí is the only known artist to have two museums dedicated to his work: the Dalí Theatre-Museum in Figueres, Spain, and the Salvador Dalí Museum in St. Petersburg, Florida.

Bibliography

Ades, Dawn. *Dalí*. New York: Thames and Hudson, 1982.

Dalí, Salvador. *Diario de un genio*. Barcelona: Tuquet Editores, 2004.

Gaillemin, Jean-Louis. *Dalí: Master of Fantasies*. New York: Harry N. Abrams, 2004.

Krull, Kathleen. *Lives of the Artists: Masterpieces, Messes (and What the Neighbors Thought)*. New York: Harcourt Children's Books, 1995.

Montagu, Jemima. *The Surrealists: Revolutionaries in Art and Writing, 1919–1935*. London: Tate Publishing, 2002.

Raeburn, Michael, ed. *Salvador Dalí: The Early Years*. London: Thames and Hudson, 1994.

Rubén Darío

❖ Born in Metapa, now Ciudad Darío, Nicaragua.
❖ Birth date: January 18, 1867.
❖ Death date: February 6, 1916.

Career Highlights

- Wrote his first poems at age fifteen.
- Wrote his first novel at age eighteen.
- *Azul* (*Blue*), one of his earliest masterpieces, appeared in 1888.
- Published *Prosas Profanas* (*Profane Poems*) in a definite Modernist style in 1896.

Important Contributions

In his short life, Nicaraguan poet Rubén Darío revolutionized Spanish poetry, turning it from a complex, intricate manifestation of thoughts, feelings, and ideas, into an uncomplicated, forthright expression of the poet's words. He was also the greatest exponent of a style of Spanish literature known as *Modernismo* (Modernism).

Career Path

Without Rubén Darío, there might not have been any Modernism in Latin American literature. The movement's impact on Spain was minor, and although it was highly criticized for using outlandish language, it was greatly influential in the first half of the twentieth century. Modernism was based on three other literary movements: Symbolism, Romanticism, and the Parnassian movement. Symbolists wrote poetry full of symbols instead of simply saying what they meant. The Romantics based their work on medieval verse, full of chivalrous deeds and damsels in distress. The Parnassians—the name coming from a periodical called *The Contemporary Parnassus*—were French poets who believed in writing for the sake of writing. All three movements promoted a highly personal style. Works in the Modernist style, however, tended to be simply written. Darío's *Profane Poems* masterfully fused all elements of the movement, making it the pinnacle of Modernist expression.

Born Félix Rubén García Sarmiento, he assumed the name Darío, the last name of some ancestors, because he liked it better than his own. His parents divorced when he was very young and his godfather raised him. Darío was a precocious child; it is said that he began reading at age three. In 1879, when he was only twelve, he published his first poems: *La Fe* (*Faith*), *Una Lágrima* (*One Teardrop*), and *El Desengaño* (*Disenchantment*).

The year 1882 was eventful. Striving to obtain a scholarship in Europe, Darío read his work *El Libro* (*The Book*), a markedly antireligious poem, in the presence of conservative Nicaraguan president Joaquín Zavala and Congress. He was denied a scholarship as a result of the poem's content. Another notable event that year was his courting of Rosario Emelina Murillo. It seems that she was somewhat notorious, and his friends, fearing an upcoming marriage, dispatched Darío to El Salvador. While there, he met Francisco Gavidia, a famous Salvadoran writer who influenced Darío's later work. Back in Nicaragua, Darío worked on the staff of President Adán Cárdenas.

Encouraged by an army general, he traveled to Chile in 1886. He wrote his first novel, *Emelina*, which was a failure, but his poetry caught the fancy of Chileans. However, there was a problem. Darío's dark skin drew the prejudice of the Chilean upper classes, who considered themselves of European lineage. While his work was admired, he failed to gain any social status as a result. Undaunted, Darío continued writing. He won first prize in a literary contest with the poem *Canto Epico a las Glorias de Chile* (*Epic Poem to the Glories of Chile*) and later published *Blue*. He returned to Nicaragua in 1889 and later traveled to El Salvador, where he married Rafaela Contreras. They moved to Costa Rica, where they had a son, Rubén Darío Contreras.

In 1892 Darío traveled to Spain as part of the Nicaraguan delegation to the festivities of the fourth centenary of the discovery of America. Spanish intellectuals welcomed him with open arms.

His wife Rafaela died in Nicaragua in 1893. Despondent, Darío took to drinking, and in one of his stupors, he was tricked into marrying old flame Rosario Murillo. Soon after, he was appointed

Colombian consul and visited Panama and Buenos Aires. He also visited New York, where he met Cuban patriot and poet José Martí, whom Darío would call *maestro* (teacher) from then on.

Los Raros (*The Rare Ones*), Darío's book about authors such as Edgar Allan Poe, Henrik Ibsen, and José Martí, whom he saw as his "twin soul," was published in 1896. *Profane Poems* was also published that year. Two years later, the Argentinian newspaper *La Nación* (*The Nation*) sent him to Spain to write about the impact of the Spanish-American War. Darío spent the next few years traveling through Europe and publishing compilations of his many articles for *La Nación*. In 1910 he published one of his seminal works, *Poema de Otoño y Otros Poemas* (*Fall Poems and Other Verses*). Darío returned to Nicaragua, where he died at the age of forty-nine on February 6, 1916.

Bibliography

Darío Rubén. *Autobiografía*. Managua, Nicaragua: Ediciones Distribuidora Cultural, 2000.

Foster, David William and Foster, Virginia Ramos, eds. *Modern Latin American Literature*. New York: Frederick Ungan Publishing Co., 1975.

García Marruz, Fina. *Darío, Martí y lo germinal Americano*. El Vedado, Ciudad de La Habana: Ediciones UNION, Unión de Escritores y Autores de Cuba, 2001.

Matamoros, Blas. *Rubén Darío*. Madrid: Espasa Calpe, 2002.

Ortega, Julio. *Rubén Darío*. Barcelona: Ediciones Omega, 2003.

Ruiz Barrionuevo, Carmen. *Rubén Darío*. Madrid: Editorial Síntesis, 2002.

Rodrigo Díaz de Vivar (El Cid Campeador)

Good Vassal to a Bad Lord

Medieval Knight

- ❖ Born in Vivar, Spain.
- ❖ Birth date: Circa 1043.
- ❖ Death date: July 10, 1099.

Career Highlights

- Became top military advisor to King Sancho II of Castile in about 1065.
- Publicly humiliated King Alfonso VI of Castile in 1073.
- Exiled to Saragossa and served Moor and Christian kings alike for six years.
- Took the city of Valencia in June 1094 and defended it against a greater Moorish force two years later.

Important Contributions

El Cid led the early *Reconquista* (the Christian re-conquest of Spanish territory) against the Moors, a Berber-Arab people of northern Africa. Far ahead of his time, El Cid also established friendships, and at times, alliances with Moors based on mutual respect and equality.

Career Path

Better known as *El Cid* or *Sid* (the Lord), the title his Moorish adversaries and friends gave him, Rodrigo Díaz de Vivar's legend has grown for almost a millennium. The great Castilian knight is to the Spanish what King Arthur is to the British; the origin and embodiment of all that is fair, good, and noble in society.

Rodrigo Díaz was born in a hamlet close to the city of Burgos in north-central Spain. At the time, the town was on the border between the kingdoms of Castile and Navarre. His father was a knight under the king of Castile and died when Rodrigo was fifteen years old. As a result, Rodrigo was raised in the royal court of King Ferdinand I, who not only ruled Castile, but also León and three other minor territories. One of the monarch's five children, Sancho, who was about the same age as young Rodrigo, became his close friend. While at court, Rodrigo was given military training and studied law and literature.

After Ferdinand's death in 1065 the kingdom was divided among his children, with Castile going to Sancho. For the next ten years or so, Rodrigo was Sancho's most-trusted lieutenant. After winning battles at Saragossa, Coimbra, and Zamora against the Moors, who occupied a good part of Spain, Rodrigo was knighted and appointed *alférez*, commander in chief of the king's forces. Today *alférez* refers to junior naval officers.

At about 1065, Sancho and the King of Navarre were in dispute over the town of Panzuegos in northeastern Spain. Following the customs of the times, and to prevent bloodshed, each of the two monarchs designated a champion to fight for their claims. Sancho, of course, selected Rodrigo, who won the combat and acquired the title *Campeador*, he who defends justice on the field of battle. Soon after he was called El Cid, more a title of admiration and affection than of submission.

In 1072, Sancho II was murdered, and Alfonso, the king of León and also Sancho's brother, took the Castilian crown. The new sovereign and El Cid did not get along from the beginning, since the knight placed responsibility for his friend's assassination squarely on Alfonso's shoulders. Furthermore, El Cid humiliated the king by making him swear his innocence publicly. El Cid met one of Alfonso's nieces, Jimena, whom he married in 1074. Shortly after the wedding the king appointed El Cid as his ambassador to Seville. This appears to have been a strategy on the part of Alfonso, who soon accused the knight of keeping part of the funds that belonged to the Crown. El Cid was exiled in 1081. About 300 of the best Castilian knights decided to expatriate themselves with El Cid.

Penniless, El Cid fought for diverse sovereigns, both Christian and Muslim. His best-known campaigns were those he undertook for the Muslim ruler Al-Cádir, caliph of Valencia. El Cid won him the townships of Albarracín and Apuente, as well as the contiguous territories nearby. Two years later, a large force of Moors crossed the Straits of

Gibraltar, and Alfonso asked for El Cid's help. That reunion did not last, and the distinguished Castilian knight was exiled again. It took El Cid less than a year to conquer the Muslim territories in and around Lérida, Tortosa, Denia, Albarracín, and Apuente, and, most important of all, Valencia.

Sometime in 1092 or early 1093, Al-Cádir, who had been El Cid's surrogate ruler in Valencia, was murdered, and hostile Moors took over the city. El Cid laid siege to Valencia. He fought from nineteen months to two years, but he entered the city a conqueror. Loyal subject that he had always been, El Cid offered the city to Alfonso, who responded by appointing the knight Lord of Valencia.

But El Cid's biggest—and last—battle was yet to come. In about 1096, a force of more than 150,000 Moorish horsemen with many more foot soldiers attacked Valencia. El Cid and his men defended the city and prevailed. Tired and old for his age at fifty-six, Rodrigo Díaz de Vivar died in Valencia on July 10, 1099. But the legend of El Cid Campeador had just begun.

Bibliography

Corral Lafuente, José Luis. *El Cid*. Barcelona: Edhasa, 2003.

Fletcher, Richard, trans. Javier Sánchez García Gutierrez. *El Cid*. Madrid: Nerea Editoria, 1999.

Koslow, Philip. *El Cid*. New York: Chelsea House, 1993.

Nicolle, David. *El Cid and the Reconquista, 1000–1492*. London: Osprey, 1988.

Olaizola José Luís. *El Cid: El Ultimo Héroe*. Barcelona: Planeta, 1989.

Plácido Domingo

The Greatest Tenor Ever?   Tenor

❖ Born in Madrid, Spain.
❖ Birth date: January 21, 1941.

Career Highlights

- Debuted at the Met in 1968.
- Released an album of *zarzuelas* (Spanish operettas) in 1988.
- Received the Spanish General Society of Composers' Best Lyric Singer of the Year award and the Association of Argentinian Music Critics' award for Best Male Singer, both in 1997.
- Awarded the 2002 Presidential Medal of Freedom.
- Awarded an honorary doctorate from Oxford University in 2003.

Important Contributions

Not even the great Luciano Pavarotti is as important to the opera world as Plácido Domingo. The Spaniard is, by many accounts, the greatest tenor of all time. But it is not only his talent: His personality makes Domingo a vital part of the music world. He has proven to be a great ambassador of "good music," captivating nearly everyone he meets. Domingo has also made a name for himself in popular music by recording traditional songs that other artists could never resurrect such as *El Jinete* (The Horse Rider) and *Asi Como te Buscaba* (The Way I Looked for You).

Career Path

Newsweek magazine dubbed Plácido Domingo the "king of opera," and the Italian newspaper *Corriere della Sera* said he was "a true Renaissance man of music." Both characterizations might fall short of the mark. Better known to American audiences as the mischievous, smiling member of the Three Tenors, José Plácido Domingo Embil was born to parents who were *zarzuela* performers (zarzuela is a form of Spanish operetta). When he was eight he traveled on a tour with his parents. They performed in many Spanish-speaking countries, including Cuba and México, where they decided to settle.

Interestingly enough, Domingo studied conducting and piano, not voice, at México City's Conservatory of Music. He began his career singing in small roles, but with hard work—Domingo has said, "If I rest, I rust"—and supreme talent, he soon rose to the top of the opera world. In the late 1950s he played a part in *Rigoletto* with the National Opera of México. The following year, he got his first starring role, playing Alfredo in *La Traviata* in the northern Mexican city of Monterrey.

In 1962 the still little-known Domingo married Marta Ornelas, also an opera singer whom he met at the conservatory. He began a two-year engagement with the Israel National Opera. Marta became his main advisor and singing coach. Once his commitment to the Israeli opera was finished, Domingo was free to pursue other opportunities. He went to New York, where he starred in *Madame Butterfly* with the New York City Opera in 1965. His breakthrough role came when he sang Maurizio in *Adriana Lecouvreur* for the Metropolitan Opera in 1968. In 1969 Domingo had more successes, first appearing at the world-famous La Scala Opera House in Milan, Italy, and then at the Royal Opera House at Covent Garden in London.

In his career, Domingo has sung ninety operas, thirty of which he can perform from memory, and has made more than 100 recordings. His eighteenth opening-night performance with New York's Metropolitan Opera during the 1999–2000 season surpassed Enrico Caruso's tally of seventeen. He also performed for what is believed to be the largest audience ever to listen to a complete live opera when he sang Giuseppe Verde's *Othello* in front of 35,000 at Madrid's soccer stadium. He also received an eighty-minute ovation and had 101 curtain calls on June 30, 1991, in Vienna.

The press caught wind of a Plácido Domingo-Luciano Pavarotti grudge in the late 1970s. Even though both had nothing but praise for each other, there was a certain degree of tension over who was the best singer. Throughout the 1980s it seemed they tried to outdo each other for the most media exposure, endorsement contracts, recordings with pop singers, and television shows. While the extent of the feud is unknown, they put feelings aside to appear together as the Three Tenors with José Carreras in Rome on July 7, 1990. The Three Tenors have since performed together many times, and recorded several popular albums.

Domingo has performed at all of the world's great opera houses, from Vienna to San Francisco, Tokyo to Hamburg, Paris to London, Barcelona to Madrid, and Buenos Aires to Chicago. He is also a renowned conductor, having directed performances all over the globe. But his impact on the world exceeds his music career. He is also a committed humanitarian, raising millions of dollars for AIDS research, for the victims of earthquakes in México and Armenia, and for the victims of Hurricane Katrina in New Orleans. He also sponsors an annual contest, Operalia, which awards $175,000 in prizes to promising young singers. The competition may ultimately answer the question opera lovers of the world often ask themselves: "After Domingo, who?"

Bibliography

Domingo, Plácido. *My First Forty Years.* New York: Penguin, 1984.

Goodnough, David. *Plácido Domingo: Opera Superstar.* Springfield, NJ: Enslow Publishers, 1997.

Lewis, Marcia, trans. Aníbal Leal. *Los Tres Tenores: La Vida de Plácido Domingo, Luciano Pavarotti y José Carreras.* Buenos Aires: Javier Vergara, 1997.

Reyes, Luis, and Rubie, Peter. *Los Hispanos en Hollywood.* New York: Random House Español, 2002.

Schnauber, Cornelius. *Plácido Domingo.* Boston: Northeastern University Press, 1997.

Juan Pablo Duarte

If at First You Don't Succeed . . .

Statesman

❖ Born in Santo Domingo, Dominican Republic.
❖ Birth date: January 26, 1813.
❖ Death date: July 15, 1876.

Career Highlights

- Established the secret society *La Trinitaria* (The Trinitarian) to fight for independence from Haiti.
- Led struggle for independence from Spain between 1864 and 1865.
- Served his country as a diplomat until his death.

Important Contributions

Juan Pablo Duarte has the singular honor of leading his country, the Dominican Republic, to independence twice, once from Haiti and the second time from Spain.

Career Path

If not for the fact that he truly encompassed the virtues of a nation's founding father, Dominican patriot Juan Pablo Duarte would be a caricature. He was an intelligent, industrious student, a charming, hard-working individual, honorable to the extreme, and an astute politician with an almost fanatical love for his homeland.

Juan Pablo Duarte y Diez's father was a Spaniard and his mother Dominican, the daughter of a Spanish father and a Dominican mother.

Duarte's early education took place in the Dominican Republic, but he was sent to Spain when he was sixteen to continue his studies. Before arriving in Spain he visited the United States, England, and France. Duarte experienced firsthand the effects of the Industrial Revolution and the liberal political ideas in those countries, and his travels had a tremendous impact on his mindset. Little is known of his stay in Spain except that he studied law and was admitted to the bar. Duarte returned to his homeland in 1831 or 1832. By then, the entire island of Hispaniola, including what is today the Dominican Republic, had been under Haitian rule since 1821. Duarte partook of the social life to get an impression of how the majority of the Dominican people, mostly of Spanish lineage, felt about the regime of Haitian strongman Jean Paul Boyer. The outrage and discontent he heard prompted Duarte to work for the independence of his country. On July 16, 1838, he established *La Trinitaria*, a dissident organization whose name came from its motto, *Dios, Patria, y Libertad* (God, Motherland, and Freedom). Duarte jotted down concepts for a liberal constitution that would unite all Dominicans. He became the revolution's leader in Santo Domingo when an insurgency began against Boyer. The insurrection was unsuccessful and Duarte was compelled to leave the country for Venezuela. Some of his coconspirators continued the fight, and on February 27, 1844, they finally declared independence. Upon his return shortly after, Duarte received a hero's welcome and was immediately elected to the provisional government.

Infighting soon broke out between Duarte's liberals and reactionary forces that wanted to return to colonial rule. Under the leadership of wealthy entrepreneur Pedro Santana, the reactionaries won, and Duarte went into exile. In 1861 Santana offered the country as a colony to the United States, France, and Spain. His only taker was Spain. Three years later, Duarte surfaced again in the Dominican Republic and was one of the leaders of an uprising against Santana and Spanish rule. The struggle ended in 1865 with the re-establishment of the republic. Duarte became a diplomat and served his country overseas. He did not return to the Dominican Republic during his lifetime and died in Caracas, Venezuela, on July 15, 1876, at the age of sixty-three. His remains were finally brought to Santo Domingo on February 27, 1884, and buried in the *Altar a la Patria* (Altar to the Motherland) to great public display.

Bibliography

Casa, Roberto. *Juan Pablo Duarte: El Padre de la Patria*. Santo Domingo: Tobogán, 2001.

Estenger, Rafael. *La Vida Gloriosa y Triste de Juan Pablo Duarte—Biografía para Estudiantes*. Santo Domingo: Editorial UNPHU, 1981.

Franco, F., et al. *Duarte y la independencia nacional*. Santo Domingo: Ediciones INTEC, 1976.

Lebrón Saviñón, Mariano. *Heroismo e identidad: Duarte, Libertador, romántico y poeta*. Santo Domingo: Instituto Duartino, 1999.

Troncoso Sánchez, Pedro. *Vida de Juan Pablo Duarte*. Santo Domingo: Editorial Taller, 1980.

Tomás Estrada Palma

Cuba's First President Statesman

- ❖ Born in Bayamo, Cuba.
- ❖ Birth date: July 9, 1832 or 1835.
- ❖ Death date: November 4, 1908.

Career Highlights

- Joined fight for Cuban independence in 1868.
- Expelled from Cuba by the Spanish authorities in 1877.
- Became political leader of Cuba's independence struggle in 1895.
- Took office as first president of Cuba in 1902.

Important Contributions

Estrada Palma was a quiet, unassuming bureaucrat who, as second to Cuba's most honored hero, José Martí, in the *Partido Revolucionario Cubano* (Cuban Revolutionary Party), brilliantly united the Cuban factions fighting for independence against Spain. Although many Cubans considered him a U.S. puppet, Estrada Palma stood up to Washington, D.C., in matters relating to Cuban sovereignty.

Career Path

Overshadowed by other founding fathers and much maligned by his own countrymen, Tomás Estrada Palma, Cuba's first president, was the right man at the right time for Cuban independence. He was an able administrator, skillful negotiator, and a true, albeit realistic, patriot. Most historians assert that Estrada Palma was born in Bayamo, Oriente Province, on July 9, 1835, but others think it was in 1832. It is also unknown where he attended elementary and secondary school, but it is assumed that it was in Havana. However, it is clear that in 1852, Estrada Palma traveled to Seville, Spain, to study law. When his father died in 1865, he returned to Cuba to take care of family affairs, and did not complete his studies.

Cuba in 1865 was a colony in upheaval, divided between *reforma y revolución* (reform and revolution). When no reforms came about, Carlos Manuel de Céspedes, a sugar mill owner, freed his slaves and declared an independent Cuba on October 10, 1868, starting what was to be known as *La Guerra de los Diez Años*, the Ten Years' War. The following day, Estrada Palma was part of a delegation sent by the government to persuade the rebels to lay down their arms; instead, Estrada Palma joined the revolution. He rose to the rank of general and was appointed foreign minister of the provisional government. As such, he obtained diplomatic recognition for the rebellion from Perú, México, Chile, Bolivia, Colombia, and Guatemala. In 1876 Estrada Palma became president of the Republic in Arms, the civilian authority that directed the uprising. He did not last long, but was captured by Spanish troops and exiled to Madrid the following year.

Over the next few years Estrada Palma more or less forgot about the independence of his homeland. In 1884 he met José Martí, twenty-five years his junior, who took Estrada Palma to New York, a center of Cuban revolutionary activity at the time. Estrada Palma traveled widely, searching for support for a revolution. While in Honduras, he met and married Genoveva Guardiola, daughter of Santos Guardiola, Honduras' president. Estrada Palma served as director of that country's postal service.

By the time the Cuban War of Independence began on February 24, 1895, Estrada Palma was second only to Martí in the Cuban Revolutionary Party. When Martí died in combat on May 19, 1895, Estrada Palma became the political leader of the revolution. He moved to Washington and went to work in getting U.S. backing for the island's insurgents. On April 19, 1898, the U.S. Congress passed a joint resolution calling for independence for Cuba and passing the Teller Amendment on April 19, 1898, promising the U.S. would not assert permanent control over Cuba. This led to serious strains in U.S.-Spanish relations. When the USS *Maine* exploded in Havana's harbor, the U.S. blamed Spain. That was the spark that started the Spanish-American War, known in Cuba as the Cuban-Spanish-American War. When the Spaniards were defeated, American forces occupied Cuba, and Estrada Palma remained in the United States. However, after much political maneuvering, Estrada Palma was elected as Cuba's first president on December 31, 1901. Many historians believe that there was considerable arm-twisting on the part of Washington officials to have the Cuban political organizations consent to back Estrada Palma. But Estrada Palma proved to be a good administrator, emphasizing sensible financial policies and improvements in education. He also faced down Washington officials who wanted four naval stations on the island. The United States had to settle for only one, at Guantánamo. Estrada Palma governed well and was re-elected in 1906. Trouble arose over the Platt Amendment to the Cuban Constitution, which gave the United States the right to intervene in Cuban affairs. In addition, there were accusations from the opposition that Estrada Palma had rigged the elections. A revolt was imminent. Rather than face a civil war, Estrada Palma resigned the presidency on September 28, 1906, and American forces moved into the island. Don Tomás Estrada Palma, the first president of Cuba, died on November 4, 1908, near his hometown of Bayamo.

Bibliography

Báez, Vicente, ed. *La Enciclopedia de Cuba.* Madrid: Enciclopedia y Clásicos Cubanos, Inc., 1973.

Márquez Sterling, Carlos, et al. *Presidentes de Cuba 1868–1933.* Miami: Editorial Cubana, 1987.

Santovenia y Echaide, Emeterio Santiago. *Los presidentes de Cuba libre.* La Habana: Editorial Trópico, 1943.

"Tomás Estrada Palma." *The Cuban Experience.* http://library.thinkquest.org/18355/tomas_estrada_palma.html (February 23, 2005).

David Glasgow Farragut

The First American Admiral Naval Officer

- ❖ Born near Knoxville, Tennessee.
- ❖ Birth date: July 5, 1801.
- ❖ Death date: August 14, 1870.

Career Highlights

- Appointed midshipman in 1811.
- Promoted to rear admiral in 1862, the first-ever in the U.S. Navy.
- Won the Battle of Mobile Bay in 1864.
- First to obtain the rank of admiral in the U.S. Navy, in 1866.
- Returned to the United States in 1868 from a yearlong goodwill tour of Europe.

Important Contributions

Not only was David Farragut an exceptional naval tactician who won many battles for the U.S. Navy during the Civil War, he was also an accomplished diplomat who won friends for the United States everywhere he went.

Career Path

The first man promoted to the rank of admiral in the U.S. Navy, David Glasgow Farragut was the son of a Spanish father, War of Independence hero George Farragut, and an American mother, Elizabeth Shine, from North Carolina. He was baptized as George Farragut. Even though he is most famous for his Civil War exploits, Farragut had an illustrious career that lasted nearly six decades.

Farragut first went to sea at age ten as an appointed midshipman aboard the frigate *Essex*. He was adopted by Commodore David Porter, a friend of the family and commander of the New Orleans naval station. Porter had promised the Farragut family, which was struggling financially, that he would take care of the boy and enlist him in the navy. It was in Porter's honor that young George Farragut changed his first name to David. Two years later, during the War of 1812, Farragut distinguished himself when the *Essex* captured several British ships just off the port of Valparaiso, Chile. He put down a prisoners' mutiny and commanded one of the vessels taken. In March 1814 he was taken prisoner in the same vicinity and remained in the custody of the British until November of the same year, when he was shipped to New York after a prisoner swap.

Most of the next ten years were spent on various ships fighting Cuba-based pirates, and on semi-diplomatic trips to Europe and Latin America, where he met many of the world's rulers. His fluency in Spanish and multicultural demeanor made him a popular and influential personality everywhere he went.

Farragut gained his fame during the Civil War, but this was not quite the case at the beginning. He left Norfolk, Virginia, when the state seceded from the Union. His northern sympathies made him, at the very least, unwelcome in the Confederate state. He was committed to the Union Navy, but things did not get much better in the North. His southern birth made him suspect, so his first assignments were shore duties. Finally, he became chief officer of the fleet-blocking southern ports. Already a captain, Farragut guided the task force that bombarded New Orleans for five days until it fell to Union forces on April 28, 1862. He then steered his ships up the Mississippi River to Vicksburg, Mississippi. President Lincoln was impressed, and so was Congress. It approved the president's promotion of Farragut to rear admiral, the first ever in the U.S. Navy.

Afterward, the Union Navy and Army worked together to take Vicksburg and Port Hudson, Louisiana. In 1864, Farragut led the attack on Mobile, Alabama, where he uttered his famous words, "Damn the torpedoes! Full speed ahead!" He defeated the Confederate flotilla in August. In December 1864 he was promoted to vice admiral, and two years later to the rank of admiral. No one had previously held those ranks in the U.S. Navy.

After the end of the Civil War, Farragut was chosen to head the U.S. Navy's European Squadron. For two years he traveled throughout Europe on diplomatic and "show the flag" missions, and was wined and dined by European monarchs. There was even talk of making him king of Spain.

Farragut died on August 14, 1870, while visiting the Portsmouth naval shipyards in New Hampshire. He had made his country and his people proud.

❖ ❖ ❖

Bibliography

Chrisman Abbott. *David Farragut*. Austin, TX: Raintree Steck-Vaughn Publishers, 1999.

Coombe, Jack D. *Thunder Along the Mississippi: The River Battles That Split The Confederacy*. New York: Bantam Books, 1998.

Duffy, James P. *Lincoln's Admiral: The Civil War Campaigns of David Farragut*. New York: Wiley, 1997

Reynolds, Clark G. *Famous American Admirals*. Annapolis, MD: Naval Institute Press, 2002.

Shorto, Russell. *David Farragut and the Great Naval Blockade*. Englewood Cliffs, NJ: Silver Burdett Press, 1991.

Tucker, Spencer C. *A Short History of the Civil War at Sea*. Wilmington, DE: Scholarly Resources, Inc., 2002.

Varona, Frank de, ed. *Hispanic Presence in the United States*. Miami: Mnemosyne Publishing Company, 1993.

Ferdinand of Aragón

The Prince   Monarch

- ❖ Born in Sos, Spain.
- ❖ Birth date: March 10, 1452.
- ❖ Death date: June 23, 1516.

Career Highlights

- In conjunction with Queen Isabella, established the Inquisition in 1478.
- Ended agrarian feudalism in the territories under his rule in 1486.
- Led conquest of Granada in 1492.
- Continued unification of Spain by annexing Navarre in 1512.
- Limited powers of the nobility.

Important Contributions

While his wife, Isabella, concentrated on expanding Spanish frontiers in the New World, Ferdinand made Spain a European power. Under his leadership, most of Spain was united and the territory of Naples was added to the Sicilian crown. His keen political sense did much to create the Spanish empire that dominated the world for the better part of the sixteenth century.

Career Path

Much maligned by Hollywood, the popular media, and even some English-speaking scholars, *Fernando* (Ferdinand) II of Aragón, V of Castile, II of Sicily, and III of Naples, was neither dim-witted nor particularly superstitious. An able general, he directed the military operations that expelled the Moors (a Berber-Arab people of northern Africa) from Spain and defeated France. Ferdinand had the best education a noble could have and was well versed in all the latest ideas, including that of the world being round. He was also an astute, courageous, calculating statesman and prince, so much so that a number of historians consider Ferdinand the inspiration for *The Prince*, Niccolo Machiavelli's renowned book of princely obligations, deportment, and political intrigue.

His father, *Juan* (John) II of Aragón, bestowed the kingdom of Sicily on him when Ferdinand was only sixteen years old. After marrying Isabella in 1469, he became the king of Castile and León. After his father's death, Ferdinand also inherited the crown of Aragón. He and Isabella set out to conquer all the lands in the southern Iberian Peninsula, which were controlled by the Moors.

In 1478, more for political than religious reasons, the monarchs established the Spanish Inquisition. Under the Inquisition, officials of the Church and the government investigated and persecuted Jews and all others suspected of not conforming to a strict interpretation of the Catholic faith. The Inquisition, which lasted for almost four centuries, was also used as a political repression force to squelch opposition and bring about national unity among the quarreling Spanish regions. Ferdinand and Isabella became known as the Catholic Monarchs.

The year 1492 proved to be particularly important in Ferdinand and Isabella's lives, the history of Spain and, indeed, the history of the world. Granada, a Moorish kingdom in Spain, fell to the couple's forces. Ferdinand agreed to the queen's support of Columbus's trip of exploration and discovery. Finally, all Jews were expelled from Spain. Ten years later the remaining Moors would also be expelled. However, Spain was left socially and intellectually the poorer for the expulsion of both of these groups.

After Isabella died in 1504, Ferdinand became regent of Castile for his daughter Joanna. Two years later Joanna's husband, Philip I, became king, but he died of typhus in September 1506. Ferdinand resumed his regency, which continued when Joanna was declared insane. He then served as regent for his grandson Charles, who grew to be the Holy Roman Emperor Charles V. In 1506 Ferdinand married Germaine de Foix, a niece of the king of France. The marriage served two purposes: it sealed a lasting peace between Spain and France, and brought the territories of Navarre and Andorra under Ferdinand's rule.

When Ferdinand became king, Spain was a divided, poor, backward nation. When he died at Madrigalejo in the province of Cáceres, Spain was the most powerful nation in the world.

❖ ❖ ❖

Bibliography

Belenquer, Ernest. *Fernando el Católico: Un Monarca Decisivo en las Encrucijadas de su Epoca*. Barcelona: Ediciones Península, 1999.

Edwards, John. *The Spain of the Catholic Monarchs, 1474–1520*. Boston: Blackwell Publishing, 2001.

Harvey, L. P. *Muslims in Spain, 1500 to 1614*. Chicago: University of Chicago Press, 2005.

Kamen, Henry. *Empire: How Spain Became a World Power, 1492–1763*. New York: HarperCollins, 2003.

Walsh, William Thomas. *Isabella of Spain: The Last Crusader (1451–1504)*. Rockford, IL: Tan Books and Publishers, 1987.

Wilkinson, Philip, and Dineen, Jacqueline. *Statesmen Who Changed the World*. New York: Chelsea House, 1994.

José Ferrer

❖ Born in Santurce, Puerto Rico.
❖ Birth date: January 8, 1909.
❖ Death date: January 29, 1992.

Career Highlights

- Broadway debut in 1935.
- Won a Tony in 1946 and an Oscar in 1950 for his portrayal of Cyrano de Bergerac.
- Director on Broadway and in Hollywood.
- Awarded the National Medal of Arts by President Ronald Reagan in 1985.

Important Contributions

José Ferrer was the first Puerto Rican actor to succeed in Hollywood. His impeccable English and acting talent allowed him to stay away from stereotypical "Latin" roles.

Career Path

Academy Award-winner José Vicente Ferrer de Otero y Cintrón's early education took place in his home island of Puerto Rico. Little is known about his youth, but his family could not have been too poor since he enrolled at Princeton University in 1930, graduating in 1934. It was at Princeton that he took to acting and became a member of the university's Triangle Club, a musical theater group. From Princeton he went to New York, where he soon became a Broadway favorite of both critics and audiences. He played comedy and drama with the same ease. The role of his life came in 1946, when he took over the role of the romantic, big-nosed swordsman Cyrano de Bergerac. Ferrer won the Tony award for best actor for this role.

Hollywood soon called, and Ferrer made his film debut in Ingrid Berman's *Joan of Arc* in 1948. He played the part of the weak, treacherous Dauphin and was nominated for an Oscar as best supporting actor. The next year, it was back to Cyrano, this time in an early television production. But Cyrano would not go away. Ferrer starred in the movie version of the play, and this time won the 1950 Oscar for best actor. He was nominated again for best actor two years later for his portrayal of pint-sized French painter Henry Toulouse-Lautrec in *Moulin Rouge*.

After two failed marriages, and to nearly everybody's surprise, Ferrer eloped with singer Rosemary Clooney in 1953. They were married eight years and had five children: Miguel, María, Gabriel, Monsita, and Rafael.

In 1954 Ferrer played two excellent roles, first as the navy lawyer who defends Humphrey Bogart in *The Caine Mutiny*, and then as an operetta composer in the musical *Deep in My Heart*. The critics loved both efforts.

Having experience as a Broadway director, Ferrer wanted to do the same in Tinseltown. He directed himself in four movies, the best being 1958's *I Accuse*, based on the story of Alfred Dreyfus, a French army general staff officer whose trial for treason rocked France between 1894 and 1906.

Rosemary Clooney and Ferrer divorced in 1961. The next year he appeared in a small but key role in the epic film *Lawrence of Arabia*. He remarried Clooney in 1964, appeared in *The Greatest Story Ever Told* in 1965, and then divorced her again in 1967.

Ferrer always maintained that he played his best parts in the 1950s and that afterward his career was mediocre. Neverthless, he had a half-century career in theater, and a forty-year movie and television career. He was in thirty Broadway plays, in hundreds of performances, and in sixty-plus movies and television programs. Ferrer died in Coral Gables, Florida, of colon cancer at the age of eighty-three.

Bibliography

"About Jose Ferrer." Movieactors.com. http://movieactors.com/winm/ m50.htm (November 29, 2004).

Brown, Dennis. *Actors Talk: Profiles and Stories from the Acting Trade*. New York: Limelight Editions, 1999.

Cierco, Salvador Clotas, et al. eds. *Enciclopedia Ilustrada del Cine*. Barcelona: Editorial Labor S.A., 1970.

Reyes, Luis, and Rubie, Peter. *Los Hispanos en Hollywood*. New York: Random House Español, 2002.

Carlos J. Finlay

The Mosquito Doctor   Medical Doctor

- ❖ Born in Puerto Príncipe, Cuba.
- ❖ Birth date: December 3, 1833.
- ❖ Death date: August 20, 1915.

Career Highlights

- Began to practice medicine in 1857.
- First theorized in the 1860s how yellow fever spreads.
- Awarded France's Legion of Honor Cross in 1901.
- Served as chief health officer of Cuba from 1902 to 1909.

Important Contributions

Not only did Carlos Finlay discover how yellow fever is transmitted, but he also proposed a method of controlling it: spraying oil over ponds where mosquitoes breed. In addition, controlling the disease had an unrelated, but tremendous impact: It made possible the construction of the Panama Canal.

Career Path

Juan Carlos Finlay y de Barré was the son of a Scottish father and a French mother. He was a bright child who was always asking questions. After elementary school in Cuba, he was sent to Germany in 1847, then to Rouen, France, where his father had studied medicine. While in Rouen, he became seriously ill. He developed a stutter due to the sickness. A year of speech therapy eased the impediment, but he was left with a certain slowness that people took for mental deficiency.

His speech would be a hindrance in his struggle to convince others how yellow fever was transmitted.

Back in Cuba, he legally changed his name to Carlos Juan, as it seemed more Cuban. He studied medicine at Jefferson Medical College in Philadelphia, Pennsylvania, receiving his MD in 1855 and opening a practice in Havana. He developed his interest in an exceptionally deadly sickness that turned patients' skin yellow. The illness became known as yellow fever, and nobody knew how it was transmitted. After recognizing that most cases occurred in the summer when ponds held large mosquito colonies, Finlay theorized that there was a connection. Finally, he realized that mosquitoes spread the infection. He wrote papers about it, but no one paid attention.

In 1868, when the Ten Years' War began, Finlay, a well-known advocate of independence, had to move to the island of Trinidad for two years. In 1871, a year after returning to Cuba, he presented his theories on the transmission of the illness at medical conferences in Washington, D.C., and Havana. The medical establishment ridiculed him. They tagged him "the mosquito doctor." For more than a decade Finlay conducted hundreds of experiments on the transmission of yellow fever, and the conclusion was always the same: The mosquitoes had to be the cause.

U.S. Army surgeon Dr. Walter Reed and his team went to Cuba in 1900 to study yellow fever. Finlay presented all of his research results to the group. The Americans didn't believe the documents and were convinced that the cause was unsanitary conditions. After all of their experiments failed, they finally used Finlay's data for more tests. This time the American doctors corroborated the Cuban scientist's findings. Mosquito-control programs were implemented throughout Cuba and in the Panama Canal Zone, where the illness was devastating. Dr. Reed returned to the United States with the results of his studies. He was bestowed with many honors, but he never mentioned Dr. Finlay. Finally, thirty-nine years after Finlay's death in Havana, his discovery was properly credited. In 1954 the International Congress of Medical History judged that Finlay's studies and conclusions were made first, and pronounced him the discoverer of how yellow fever is transmitted. In 1980 the United Nations established the biennial Dr. Carlos J. Finlay Prize for Microbiology. His birthday is celebrated as the Day of American Medicine in the Western Hemisphere.

Bibliography

Ada, Alma Flor, and Campoy, F. Isabel *Voces*. Miami: Santillana U.S.A. Publishing, 2000.

López Sánchez, José, transl. Carmen González Díaz de Villegas. *Carlos J. Finlay: His Life and His Work*. Havana: Editorial José Martí, 1999.

Pérez-Embid, Florentino, ed. *Forjadores del Mundo Contemporáneo*. Barcelona: Editorial Planeta, 1960.

Portell-Vilá, Herminio. *Finlay: vida de un sabio cubano*. Miami: La Moderna Poesía, 1990.

Varona, Frank de, ed. *Hispanic Presence in the United States*. Miami: Mnemosyne Publishing Company, 1993.

Juan José Flores

Ecuador's First President　　　Soldier and Statesman

- ❖ Born in Puerto Cabello, Venezuela.
- ❖ Birth date: July 19, 1800.
- ❖ Death date: October 1, 1864.

Career Highlights

- Joined revolution against Spain in 1814.
- Promoted to Brigadier General in 1827.
- Led Ecuador's secession from Greater Colombia in 1830.
- Appointed president in 1830.

Important Contributions

Juan José Flores was a distinguished soldier but failed miserably as a statesman. His most dubious achievement was that he led the movement that caused the collapse of *Gran Colombia* (Greater Colombia).

Career Path

Juan José Flores was born to a poor family. Lacking an education, he joined the Spanish colonial army in 1813; however, by the time he was fifteen years old, he had joined the revolutionaries fighting for independence. Flores showed his mettle and was promptly elevated to second lieutenant. He participated in more than twenty-three battles, and on October 1, 1822, Simón Bolívar himself promoted Flores to colonel. That same year, Antonio José de Sucre, the hero of Ayacucho, defeated the Spaniards in the Battle of Pichincha, consolidating the independence of the region that would become Ecuador. The newly independent territory promptly joined Greater Colombia. Four years later, at the battle of Tarquí, Flores distinguished himself again and Sucre promoted him to brigadier general.

By then, however, the seeds of partition had been planted. Bolívar had proven to be no democrat: The Peruvians and Ecuadorians resented the Venezuelans and Colombians that were in positions of power, and their economies were in shambles. General Flores became increasingly critical of the situation and began working to separate Ecuador from Greater Colombia. Ecuadorian leaders joined in, and on May 13, 1830, Ecuador seceded. Flores was appointed to the position of supreme commander, and on August 14, provisional president. He began his first administration on September 22.

His government was a disaster. Education received almost no funding, public works were nonexistent, and the nation's economy got even worse. Only Ecuador's landowners and upper classes were happy with Flores's rule. On September 10, 1834, his term was over, but the constitutional assembly appointed him to a second term beginning on February 1, 1839. Realizing that he was only a military man, Flores spent the five years between administrations educating himself, learning about law, economics, and civil works. During the first two years of his second administration, Flores reversed the policies of his first administration. He prioritized education, public works, industrialization, and farming, and the country prospered. Although he was still unpopular due to his desire to perpetuate himself in power and his involvement in Colombian politics, the constitutional assembly appointed him to a third term. But the middle classes revolted, leading to his resignation on March 6, 1845.

After his resignation, Flores traveled to Europe and assembled a fighting force of Spanish, English, and French soldiers to return to Ecuador. The British government, however, pulled its support from the expedition, which was subsequently cancelled. Eventually the Ecuadorian government took into account the services of Flores during the wars of independence and allowed his return. Flores was welcomed back with honors and parades. No sooner had he settled in, Flores raised an army and invaded Colombia, but was defeated. He retreated to his estate in the Puná Island in the Gulf of Guayaquil. There he lived for the rest of his life.

Bibliography

Aguado Cantero, Rodolfo. *Juan José Flores: Fundador de Ecuador*. Madrid: Anaya, 1988.

Andújar Persinal, Carlos, ed. *Historia y Geografía de América Latina y el Caribe*. Santo Domingo: Santillana, S.A., 1997.

Van Aken, Mark J. *King of the Night: Juan José Flores and Ecuador, 1824–1864*. Berkeley, CA: University of California Press, 1989.

Vasconez Hurtado, Gustavo. *El General Juan José Flores: La República, 1830–1845*. Quito: Banco Central del Ecuador, 1980.

Vasconez Hurtado, Gustavo. *El General Juan José Flores, primer presidente del Ecuador: 1800–1830*. Quito: Casa de la Cultura Ecuatoriana, 1981.

Vázquez, Germán y Martínez Díaz, Nelson. *Historia de América Latina*. Madrid: Sociedad General Española de Librería, 1990.

Bernardo de Gálvez

Hero of the American
Independence

Soldier,
Statesman

❖ Born in Macharaviaya, Spain.
❖ Birth date: July 23, 1746.
❖ Death date: November 30, 1786.

Career Highlights

- Arrived in Louisiana in 1776.
- Became governor of Louisiana in 1777.
- Took various southern British garrisons between 1779 and 1781.
- Appointed viceroy of México in 1785.

Important Contributions

Aside from being a personal friend of many leaders of the colonial independence movement, Bernardo de Gálvez made great military contributions to the American Revolution. As governor of Louisiana, he closed the Mississippi River to all British ships, while allowing the Americans to navigate freely. He also defeated the British in three southern garrisons, preventing those troops from moving north to fight the revolutionaries.

Career Path

The Maryland State Resolution on the Role Played by Hispanics in the Achievement of American Independence, recognizing Hispanic contributions to the birth of the nation, was passed on March 16, 1996.

Among the most prominent names in the document was that of Bernardo de Gálvez, for whom the city of Galvezton, now Galveston, Texas, was named. Even though his contributions to the American Revolution were great, the average American knows little of him.

De Gálvez was born in a mountain village near Málaga, a province of southern Spain. Following family tradition, he joined the army in 1762 at sixteen. The same year he was made a lieutenant, participated in a war with Portugal, and was elevated to captain. He first came to the New World in 1769 as part of an uncle's staff that had been ordered to inspect the viceroyalty of New Spain, today's México. Young de Gálvez distinguished himself in combat against the Apaches, being wounded many times, before returning to Spain in 1772. While there, he joined the Regiment of Cantabria, serving in France for three years. In 1775 he was part of a failed expedition to Algiers and was wounded again.

The following year de Gálvez was dispatched to Louisiana, promoted to colonel, and chosen as second in command of the armed forces in that Spanish colony. He replaced Luís de Unzaga as governor of Louisiana on January 1, 1777. By this time, de Gálvez had become sympathetic to the colonies' fight for independence. He exchanged letters with Thomas Jefferson and Patrick Henry, welcomed their agents, and, by fortifying New Orleans, ensured that no British ship could navigate the Mississippi. When Spain entered the war on June 21, 1779, the Spanish crown ordered de Gálvez to fight the British along the Mississippi and the Gulf Coast. The Louisiana governor took this command to heart. He raised an army of 7,000, a truly multinational force of Mexicans, Cubans, Spaniards, Puerto Ricans, Venezuelans, Italians, French, and even Native Americans. De Gálvez and his troops routed the British at Baton Rouge, Louisiana, on September 21, 1779. After a two-month siege, he captured Fort Charlotte, at Mobile in today's Alabama, on March 14, 1780. After another two-month siege, he defeated the British at Fort George in Pensacola, what was then the capital of Florida, entering the fort on May 10, 1781. When the American colonists won their independence, Congress cited de Gálvez for his contributions.

De Gálvez returned to Spain in 1783, only to be named captain-general and governor of Cuba, where he arrived on October of the following year. He then was appointed viceroy of México, succeeding his recently deceased father. While in México, he helped feed the population during trying periods, started the construction of the famous Castle of Chapultepec, and completed work on the Cathedral of México. Eventually, health problems forced his resignation on October 15, 1786, and he died the following month. De Gálvez was buried at the Church of San Fernando in México City, but his heart was placed in an urn and buried in that city's cathedral.

Bibliography

Boeta, José Rodulfo. *Bernardo de Gálvez.* Madrid: Publicaciones Españolas, 1977.

Caughey, John Walton. *Bernardo de Gálvez in Louisiana, 1776–1783.* Gretna, LA: Pelican, 1972.

Lafarelle, Lorenzo G. *Bernardo de Gálvez: Hero of the American Revolution.* Austin, TX: Eakin Press, 1992.

Lamar, Howard R., ed. *The Reader's Encyclopedia of the American West.* New York: Thomas Y. Crowell Company, 1977.

Varona, Frank de. *Bernardo de Gálvez.* Austin, TX: Raintree Steck-Vaughn, 1991.

Federico García Lorca

Gypsy Dreams

Playwright,
Poet

❖ Born in Fuente Vaqueros, Spain.
❖ Birth date: June 5, 1898.
❖ Death date: August 19, 1936.

Career Highlights

- Published his best-known book of poems, *El Romancero Gitano* (*Gypsy Ballads*) in 1928.
- Wrote *Poeta en Nueva York* (*Poet in New York*) circa 1929.
- Completed his greatest play, *La Casa de Bernarda Alba* (*The House of Bernarda Alba*), in 1936.

Important Contributions

García Lorca brought to the forefront of Spanish literature the color and passion of his Andalusian homeland. His works excel in the presentation of dramatic situations, and the language was quite raw for its time. After his death, he became a symbol of the subjugation of independent thinking by totalitarian states.

Career Path

Revered by devotees of poetry and the theater, Federico García Lorca is, without doubt, Spain's greatest twentieth-century playwright and one of its best poets. Even though García Lorca suffered from depression, was a social outcast, was disappointed in his lack of economic success, and had no love interests to speak of, his friends considered him a fun person. His gloomy character has always been known, as it came through in some of the tragedies he wrote for the theater, but had not been widely publicized until recent times.

García Lorca was born in Spain's Andalusian region, an area rich in Moorish history and Gypsy influence. Lorca spent a good part of his life unsuccessfully struggling against the Gypsy inspiration. As a child he showed great imagination and an inclination to music. He began writing poetry at an early age, and was so pleased with his youthful work that he performed his poems at his hometown cafés. When he entered the University of Granada, he majored in philosophy and law for a while, but art, theater, and literature were his true callings, and he changed his studies.

In 1918 he published his first book, essays stirred by an outing to Castile. The following year he transferred to the University of Madrid. While at Madrid he became part of the *Generación del 27* (Generation of 1927), a group of poets who brought new strength in imagery and metaphor to Spanish poetry. Filmmakers, essayists, and painters were also part of the group.

In 1920 one of his plays, *El maleficio de las mariposas* (The butterflies' evil spell), was performed for only one night, but still it made him somewhat of a luminary. The following year he published his first book of poems. However, García Lorca's fame was sealed in 1927 with the publication of *Canciones* (*Songs*), and again in 1928 with the publication of *El Romancero Gitano* (*Gypsy Ballads*). That same year he traveled to the United States to study English at Columbia University in New York. It is thought that García Lorca made the trip to get away from the label of Gypsy Poet, with which he had been branded in Spain. During this trip he wrote the verses for *Poeta en Neuva York* (*Poet in New York*), which would not be published until 1940, well after his death. In 1930 he wrote *La Zapatera Prodigiosa* (*The Prodigious Cobbler's Wife*). Back in Spain in 1931, he published *Poema del Cante Jondo* (*Poem of Gypsy Singing*), another compilation of related verses, and formed a theater troupe to tour the country. *Bodas de Sangre* (*Blood Wedding*), the first of his three illustrious tragedies, appeared in 1933. The following year he wrote *Llanto por Ignacio Sánchez Mejías* (*Lament for the Death of Ignacio Sanchez Mejias*), a eulogy to a famous bullfighter, and his second tragedy, *Yerma* (*Barren*). García Lorca finished the first draft of his third great tragedy, *La Casa de Bernarda Alba* (*The House of Bernarda Alba*), about a domineering mother and her five daughters, shortly before his death. By 1936 Spain was imbued in its civil war, and General Francisco Franco's Nationalists considered all intellectuals dangerous. García Lorca was no exception. He was arrested and summarily executed along with three other individuals. Their bodies were thrown into an unmarked grave.

The new Spanish government banned his works. For years he was studied and honored, but mostly outside of his native land. Not until the early 1970s, when the Franco regime began to crumble, were García Lorca's works sold at Spanish bookstores.

Bibliography

Cobo Borda, J.G. *Retratos de poetas*. Bucaramanga, Colombia: Editorial UNAB, 2004.

Gibson, Ian. *Federico García Lorca: Biografía Esencial*. Barcelona: Península, 1998.

Magariño, Arturo et al. *Caminos Abiertos por Federico García Lorca*. Madrid: Editorial Hernando, 1982.

Martínez Cutiño, Luís. *García Lorca para Principiantes*. Buenos Aires: Era Naciente, 1999.

Morales, Maria Luz. *Alguien a quien conocí: Maria Curie, Keyserling ....* Barcelona: Editorial Juventud, 1973.

Stainton, Leslie. *Lorca: A Dream of Life*. New York: Farrar, Straus, and Giroux, 1999.

Julius Peter Garesché

A Premonition of Death   Soldier

❖ Born in Havana, Cuba.
❖ Birth date: April 26, 1821.
❖ Death date: December 31, 1862.

Career Highlights

- Commissioned as a first lieutenant in 1846.
- Decorated by Pious IX as a Knight of St. Sylvester in 1851.
- Promoted to major in 1861.
- Became chief of staff of the Army of the Potomac in 1862.

Important Contributions

Garesché was a brilliant staff officer who rose quickly through the ranks to take his position in the Army of the Potomac. He was also a deeply religious man who was involved with the Society of Saint Vincent de Paul, a Catholic group that helps the needy. While in Washington D.C., he served as the society's president, assisting the city's poor.

Career Path

Julius Peter Garesché du Rocher is one of the few known high-ranking Hispanic officers to have served in the Union Army during the U.S. Civil War. A gifted strategist, he rose to the rank of lieutenant colonel and served as chief of staff in the Army of the Cumberland under General William Rosencrans.

Garesché was born to a prosperous Protestant family of French ancestry in Cuba. His mother, Mimika Louisa Bauduy of Wilmington, Delaware, was Catholic. Aided by the fact that her faith was the accepted one on the island, she had Julius baptized as a Catholic. When Garesché was about six, the family left Cuba for New York City, and in 1830 settled in his mother's hometown of Wilmington. With his brother, Alexander, Garesché attended a private school in the area. In 1833, at the age of twelve, Garesché enrolled in Georgetown College. However, financial problems forced him to leave Georgetown, and upon the recommendation of a friend, he was admitted to the U.S. Military Academy at West Point. At West Point Garesché was quite mischievous, getting demerits right and left, but he still managed to graduate in the middle of his class in 1841. It was at the military academy that he began a strong friendship with his future boss, Rosencrans. Shortly before graduating and accepting his first post, Garesché visited the family's newly acquired 2,000-acre estate. There he narrowly escaped death in an accident. Garesché and his family deduced that the mishap was a sign that he would meet a violent end. Commissioned a second lieutenant, Garesché was assigned to the 4th Infantry at Fort Brown, Texas, and was involved with the work of the Catholic Church. Over the next five years he served on western frontier garrisons, being promoted to first lieutenant in 1846. To while away the long hours of boredom, Garesché began to write. Under the pen name Catholicus he wrote articles on moral, political, and military matters for many Catholic publications, including the *Freeman's Journal* and *Brownson's Quarterly Review*. In one such article he went so far as to question the constitutional right of the president to be commander in chief of the armed forces. He married Mariquita de Laureal on February 17, 1849. He was promoted to the rank of brevet captain in 1855, then to assistant adjutant general, and finally to major in 1861. By then Garesché was serving in Washington, D.C. While in the nation's capital, he helped establish the local chapter of the Society of Saint Vincent de Paul. Just a few months after becoming a major, he was instrumental in facilitating the appointment of his old friend Rosencrans to general. Rosencrans appointed Garesché as his chief of staff in early November 1862. But the abrupt move to field action didn't last long for Garesché. The following month, while commanding a column trying to regain lost ground during the Battle of Stones River in Tennessee, Garesché was decapitated by a cannonball.

Initially buried on the battlefield in Tennessee, his body was later moved to Mount Olivet Cemetery in Washington, D.C. The Society of Saint Vincent de Paul and Georgetown College built a monument to his memory there. One of his sons, Louis, published his father's biography in 1880.

Bibliography

Matano, Lisette C. "Julius P. Garesché." Georgetown University. http://www.library.georgetown.edu/dept/speccoll/cl71.htm (March 24, 2004).

Meehan, Thomas F. "Julius Peter Garesché." *Catholic Encyclopedia,* http://www.newadvent.org/cathen/06384a.htm (March 24, 2004).

Pittard, Dr. Homer. "The Strange Death of Julius Peter Garesché." Latin American Studies. http://www.latinamericanstudies.org/civil-war-cubans/garesche-death.htm (November 24, 2004).

Roberto Goizueta

Company Man   Businessman

- ❖ Born in Havana, Cuba.
- ❖ Birth date: November 18, 1931.
- ❖ Death date: October 18, 1997.

Career Highlights

- Hired by the Coca-Cola Company in 1954.
- Appointed vice president of technical research and development in 1966.
- Named CEO of the Coca-Cola Company in 1981.
- Introduced a cluster of new Coca-Cola products.
- Under his leadership, Coca-Cola donated almost $100 million worldwide for educational programs.

Important Contributions

When Roberto Goizueta became Coca-Cola's CEO, the company was content with its market share and its products, but had lost its initiative. Under Goizueta's leadership, Coca-Cola completely revamped its product line, propelling its earnings and market share to unprecedented highs.

Career Path

Thanks to Roberto Goizueta, American icon Coca-Cola rebounded from the doldrums and became bigger and better than ever. The risk-taking, aristocratic, Cuban-born CEO was not just a clever executive; he was a humanitarian who donated his time and money to worthy causes and nudged his company into doing the same. He wanted to help others succeed.

Roberto Crispulo Goizueta was born into a family of industrialists and landowners. He attended a Jesuit school in his hometown, and later went to the Connecticut prep school, the Cheshire Academy, for one year. There he improved his English by watching movies. He was admitted to Yale University in 1948, and graduated with a bachelor's degree in chemical engineering. He returned to Cuba in 1953 to work in the family businesses. When Coca-Cola advertised in the Havana newspapers for a bilingual chemical engineer, he answered the ad and got the job.

When the revolutionary forces of Fidel Castro seized power on the island, Goizueta began thinking of leaving his homeland. In 1961 Goizueta and his wife, Olga, took a vacation to Miami, Florida. The couple's three children were already in the United States. Their entire fortune consisted of $40 and 100 shares of Coca-Cola stock. The company, however, rehired Goizueta and he went to work for Coca-Cola's Latin American venture. By 1964 he was assigned to Coca-Cola's headquarters in Atlanta, Georgia.

His hard work and business savvy were very impressive. In 1966, when he was just thirty-five, Goizueta became the company's youngest vice president of technical research and development. From there he rose rapidly, to vice chairman in 1979, to president in 1980, and to chief executive officer one year later.

Believing that the company was too conservative and stale, Goizueta went about reshaping it. He did away with the old "Have a Coke and a Smile" slogan and brought in "Coke Is It!" He also stopped using sugar in the soda recipe and began using high-fructose corn syrup, a manufacturing savings of 40 percent. In 1982 he introduced Diet Coke, the first new Coke brand since 1886. In 1985 he introduced New Coke, an infamous reformulation of the traditional Coca-Cola recipe. New Coke was widely derided by consumers. Goizueta was the first to admit that replacing the old formula with New Coke had been a disaster. Within ninety days of the fiasco, he brought the old formula back under the name of Coca-Cola Classic. He also changed the name of the new soda to Coke 2. Goizueta took the hullabaloo in stride. He believed in taking risks. Coca–Cola's market share in the United Sates increased, and thanks to Goizueta's cosmopolitan outlook, new bottling plants were opened overseas. Today nearly half of sodas sold the world over are bottled by the Coca-Cola Company.

Even though at times he was accused of being aristocratic, Goizueta made Coca-Cola one of the world's largest charity donors. He also established the Goizueta Foundation, which funds educational programs and provides scholarships to Hispanics and other minority students. During his sixteen years as Coca-Cola's CEO, he made many stockholders rich. Under his leadership, the company's stock appreciated 7,100 percent, an incredible business achievement that also made Goizueta a billionaire since he owned nearly sixteen million shares. He was the first executive in U.S. history to become a billionaire by holding stock in a business he neither started nor made public.

Goizueta, a heavy smoker, died in Atlanta of complications related to lung cancer at the age of sixty-five. As far as the Coca-Cola Company is concerned, "Goizueta was it."

Bibliography

"Coke CEO Roberto C. Goizueta dies at 65." CNN Interactive. http://www.cnn.com/US/9710/18/goizueta.obit.9am/ (November 24, 2004).

Greising, David. *I'd Like the World to Buy a Coke: The Life and Leadership of Roberto Goizueta.* New York: Wiley, 1998.

Hays, Constance L. *The Real Thing: Truth and Power at the Coca-Cola Company.* New York: Random House, 2004.

Huey, John. "In search of Roberto's secret formula. (Reflections on Coca-Cola Chief Executive Officer Roberto Goizueta)." *Fortune.* December 29, 1997, p. 230(4).

Morey, Janet Nomura, and Dunn, Wendy. *Famous Hispanic Americans.* New York: Dutton Juvenile, 1996.

Pendergrast, Mark. *For God, Country, and Coca-Cola: The Definitive History of the Great American Soft Drink and the Company That Makes It.* New York: Basic Books, 2000.

Francisco de Goya

The First Modernist   Artist

- ❖ Born in Fuendetodos, Spain.
- ❖ Birth date: March 30, 1746.
- ❖ Death date: April 16, 1828.

Career Highlights

- Appointed court painter in 1789.
- Director of painting at the Royal Academy of San Fernando from 1795 to 1797.
- Initiated his series of antiwar paintings in 1810 with *Los desastres de la guerra* (*The Disasters of War*).
- Created some of his most bizarre works in the five years prior to his death.

Important Contributions

Through his ability to portray drama, Goya influenced the romantics; through his treatment of light and color, the impressionists; and his fanciful, outlandish visions were a source of inspiration to the surrealists. The impact of his work was felt by artistic movements of the nineteenth and twentieth centuries.

Career Path

Francisco de Goya y Lucientes was ambitious, proud, and arrogant. He was a genius, but it took him time to develop his talents. One can learn of his growth as an artist by studying his paintings in chronological order. Not that there is a bad one among those that have survived. It is just that they kept on getting better, and at the same time, stranger.

117

Goya was born in the northern Spanish province of Saragossa. In his early teens he became the apprentice to José Luján, an artist in his hometown who taught him etching and painting. He studied under Luján for three years, and at about age seventeen, traveled to Madrid to expand his art education. In the Spanish capital he strove to win the important art contest of the Royal Academy of San Fernando. He tried twice, in 1763 and 1766, both times failing miserably. After a short trip to Italy, Goya went back to Saragossa in 1771. There he established something of a name for himself with the frescoes he painted for various churches in the province. In 1773 he married Josefa Bayeau, the sister of another artist. That same year he painted one of his self-portraits.

By 1775 Goya was back in Madrid doing designs for the Royal Tapestry Factory, where he drew his famous *cartones,* which are mis-shapen, fanciful scenes. He also impressed the Spanish upper classes as a portrait painter. He finally enrolled in the Royal Academy in 1780, thanks to the influence of his patron, Anton Raphael Mengs, a German who was court painter to King Charles III. Goya would replace Mengs in the position nine years later.

When Goya went deaf in 1792, his work began to change. Cut off from normal communications, he turned to the visions of his mind, visions filled with fantastic and sardonic images of the world around him. He depicted these visions in 1799 with *Los Caprichos (Caprices),* a sequence of bizarre etchings lampooning mankind's foolishness and vulnerability. The next year, however, painting in a more traditional style Goya turned out *La Familia de Carlos IV (The Family of Charles IV),* a portrait of Spain's royal family. Between 1803 and 1805 he produced his two *majas* (two portraits of the same woman in the same pose, but clothed in one painting and nude in the other): *La Maja Desnuda (The Naked Maja)* and *La Maja Vestida (The Dressed Maja).* The addition of *The Naked Maja* to his bizarre work, which was already banned by the Catholic Church, got him in trouble with the Inquisition.

When Napoleon invaded Spain in 1808, Goya became the French court painter. But even though he received no favor from the new king, he was pardoned when the Spanish monarchy was restored in 1814. That year he painted two of the most powerful artworks ever created depicting the horrors of war, *El dos de Mayo (May Second)* and *Los Fusilamientos en la Montaña del Príncipe Pío (The Executions in Prince Pio's Mountain).*

In 1819 he moved to a house just outside Madrid, and it became known as *La Quinta del Sordo (The Deaf One Villa).* For the next five years he would live in ever-increasing isolation from society. He painted *Las Pinturas Negras (Black Paintings)* on the walls of his house. This was a series of fourteen works that, critics agree, were meant for his eyes only. They are by far his most powerful expressions of his denunciation of the world. He also published a string of etchings known as *Disparates* (*Nonsense*) or *Proverbios* (*Proverbs*).

When an attempt to restore a liberal government to Spain failed in 1824, Goya moved to France. He would never return from this voluntary exile. Francisco de Goya died in Bordeaux, France, on April 16, 1828.

Bibliography

Blackburn, Julia. *Old Man Goya*. New York: Pantheon Books, 2002.

Connell, Evan S. *Francisco Goya*. New York: Counterpoint Press, 2004.

Herrera, Juan Ignacio. *Francisco de Goya*. Madrid: Ediciones Susaeta, 1979.

Hughes, Robert. *Goya*. New York: Alfred A. Knopf, 2003.

Litch, Fred. *Goya*. New York: Abbeville Press, 2001.

Symmons, Sarah. *Goya*. London: Phaidon Press, 1998.

Rita Hayworth

Don't Call Her Gilda   Actress

❖ Born in Brooklyn, New York.
❖ Birth date: October 17, 1918.
❖ Death date: May 14, 1987.

Career Highlights

- First appeared on film in 1926 at age eight.
- Made her official movie debut in 1934 at age sixteen.
- One of the most popular World War II pin-up girls.
- Her most famous movie, *Gilda*, appeared in 1946.

Important Contributions

At a time when few Hispanic actresses made it in Hollywood, Rita Hayworth did. She became one of the brightest stars in Tinseltown thanks to her talents, liveliness, and beauty. She could play a Spanish harpy opposite Tyrone Power or dance with Fred Astaire. At one time she was the most famous woman in the world.

Career Path

In *Entertainment Weekly's* "The 100 Greatest Stars of All Times," film critic Michael Sauter called Rita Hayworth's combination of looks and dancing ability "a rarity." Indeed she was. She was the only Hispanic to make that list, and she was the sole Hispanic female on the American Film Institute's list of the fifty greatest American screen legends (twenty-five women and twenty-five men). She was number nineteen.

Margarita Carmen Dolores Cansino was the daughter of a Spanish immigrant father and an Irish-English mother. Both of her parents were dancers, and from the time she could walk, her father, Eduardo, taught her the dances of his native Spain. Dancing became her passion.

Lured by the new film industry, the family moved to Hollywood when Hayworth was eight years old. At first things went well. Eduardo taught dance and choreographed a few movies, but then the Depression hit and things got tough. Eduardo danced at nightclubs, and eventually his daughter joined him in an act called "The Dancing Cansinos." Throughout the early 1930s they danced at various well-known nightclubs in Los Angeles and Tijuana, México. It was in one of these clubs that she was discovered by an executive from Fox Studios in 1935. After a screen test, Hayworth signed as a contract player.

From 1935 to 1937 Hayworth had an assortment of minor roles, mostly as a dancer, emphasizing her sultry Spanish looks. But Edward Charles Hudson, her husband and manager, got her a contract with Columbia Pictures for $200 a week, and her image began to evolve. Columbia changed her name to Rita Hayworth (her mother's maiden name was Haworth), subjected her to painful electrolysis to move up her hairline, and lightened her hair, all to make her more acceptable to the Anglo audiences of the day. Her career took off.

Most of her first acting jobs at Columbia were in B movies, but in 1938, thanks to her hard work and drive, she landed the part of Judy McPherson in Howard Hawk's *Only Angels Have Wings* opposite Cary Grant and Jean Arthur. From then on she made only A movies: *Music in my Heart*, *The Lady in Question*, and *Strawberry Blonde*. She was loaned to Fox Studios for *Blood and Sand*, in which she played the alluring and wicked Doña Sol. She returned to Columbia Pictures to film *You'll Never Get Rich*, showcasing her dancing talents opposite the great Fred Astaire. She became the studio's top female star. During World War II, Hayworth's pin-up pictures were second in popularity only to Betty Grable's.

In 1945 she began shooting the movie she is best remembered for, *Gilda*. It was released the following year, broke box-office records, and made her the most famous actress in the world. The movie forever changed her image, to the point that she was heard to complain: "Every man I have ever known has fallen in love with Gilda and awakened with me." In real life, Hayworth was the total opposite of Gilda; while her alter ego was sexy and alluring, she was shy and reclusive.

After three more movies, all of which were hits, Hayworth took a four-year hiatus. Then *Affair in Trinidad* was released in 1952. Its success rivaled that of *Gilda*. Hayworth had not lost one bit of her acting abilities or her appeal. "The Love Goddess," as *Time* magazine had dubbed her, was back. She continued working nonstop until 1972, when she more or less disappeared from the public eye. In the early 1980s it was revealed that she suffered from Alzheimer's disease. The one and only Rita Hayworth passed away quietly at the age of sixty-eight in New York City on May 14, 1987.

Bibliography

Dick, Bernard F, ed. *Columbia Pictures: Portrait of a Studio*. Lexington, KY: University Press of Kentucky, 1992.

Gwinn, Alison, ed. *The 100 Greatest Stars of All Time*. New York: Time, Inc., Home Entertainment, 1997.

Leaming, Barbara. *If This Was Happiness: A Biography of Rita Hayworth*. New York: Viking, 1989.

McLean, Adrienne L. *Being Rita Hayworth: Labor, Identity, and Hollywood Stardom*. New Brunswick, NJ: Rutgers University Press, 2004.

Reyes, Luís, and Rubie, Peter. *Los Hispanos en Hollywood*. New York: Random House Español, 2002.

Rodríguez, Clara E. *Heroes, Lovers, and Others: The Story of Latinos in Hollywood*. Washington, DC: Smithsonian Books, 2004.

Rafael Hernández

The Merry Maker   Composer

❖ Born in Aguadilla, Puerto Rico.
❖ Birth date: October 24, 1892.
❖ Death date: December 11, 1965.

Career Highlights

- Began taking music lessons at twelve.
- Appointed conductor and director of the Puerto Rican Symphony Orchestra and musical advisor to Puerto Rico's Public Broadcasting Corporation in 1947.
- Honorary president of the Association of Composers and Authors of Puerto Rico from 1956 to 1959.
- Wrote more than 3,000 songs.

Important Contributions

A versatile composer, Rafael Hernández's compositions run the gamut of popular Latin American music. From Puerto Rican *danzas* to Cuban rumbas, from love songs to witty ditties, just about anything he wrote became a hit. New versions of his songs are recorded and performed every year. Hernández had a knack for writing songs that touched Puerto Ricans' love for their homeland.

Career Path

Together with México's Agustín Lara and Cuba's Ernesto Lecuona, Puerto Rico's Rafael Hernández makes up the great triumvirate of Spanish American composers who filled the world with music during the early and middle twentieth century. Of the three, he was the most prolific, with more than 3,000 compositions. Hernández also cultivated more musical styles that either of his two illustrious colleagues.

As a child, Rafael Hernández Martín was very poor. His dream was to become a train engineer or a cigar maker; he became a great composer, not for the money but to make people dance. Through the coaxing of his grandmother, young Hernández turned to music. She owned an eatery in town that was inexpensive enough to be a favorite of struggling musicians. One of them agreed to teach the boy music. Hernández learned the trumpet, piano, guitar, trombone, banjo, and violin. In 1912 he wrote his first song, "María Victoria," named for a favorite Mexican actress. He then moved to San Juan, where he earned a living in the municipal band and playing during silent films at movie houses. Five years later he landed a recording contract and published his second composition, "Mi Provisa," a title derived from the names of three women he knew.

When the United States entered World War I, Hernández.enlisted in the Army and served in his regiment's band, which different sources identified as the 375th or 396th. He later saw front-line combat as a medic. Even so, he had enough time to compose "Oui Madame." Released from active duty, Hernández returned to Puerto Rico, where economic conditions forced him to migrate to New York. He soon went to Cuba, where he wrote many of his most popular songs, such as the love ballad "Capullito de Alelí" ("Little Flower Bud." or "Gilly Flower Little Blossom"), the witty "Buche y Pluma" ("Belly and Feathers"), and the world-famous rumba "El Cumbanchero" ("The Merry Maker"). To this day, many people swear that a Cuban composer penned these songs.

After four years in Cuba, Hernández returned to New York, where he formed the *Trío Borinquen* (Borinquen being the Indian name of Puerto Rico). During this time he wrote other well-known pieces, including "Mi Patria Tiembla" ("My Country Trembles"), and in 1929, the composition that would forever identify him, "Lamento Borincano" ("Borinqueneer's Lament"). The song tells of the struggles of a Puerto Rican *jíbaro* (peasant) to make ends meet.

In the late 1930s Hernández traveled to México for a three-month engagement, but ended up living there for sixteen years. He studied at the country's National Conservatory of Music and found he had a knack for writing songs that appealed to love of the homeland. Among his compositions that give rise to these patriotic feelings are "Preciosa" ("Beautiful"), about Puerto Rico, and "Linda Quisqueya" ("Pretty Quisqueya"), about the Dominican Republic. (*Quisqueya* is the Indian name for Hispaniola.) These are considered second national hymns. His song "Qué Chula es Puebla" ("How Beautiful is Puebla") is considered

Puebla's unofficial anthem. He returned to Puerto Rico for the last time in 1953, and succumbed to cancer in San Juan on December 11, 1965. The world continues to enjoy the songs of the man President John F. Kennedy once greeted as "Mr. Cumbanchero."

Bibliography

Cásares Rodicio, Emilio. *Diccionario de la Música Española e Hispano Americana.* Madrid: Sociedad General de Autores y Editores, 2000.

"Hernández Marín, Rafael-Bolero." Música de Puerto Rico. http://www.musicofpuertorico.com/es/rafael_hernandez.html (November 29, 2004).

"Rafael Hernández." Peermusic. http://latino.peermusic.com/artistpage2/Rafael_Hernandez.html (November 11, 2004).

Salazar, Jaime Rico. *Cien Años de Bolero.* Bogotá: Centro Editorial de Estudios Musicales, 1993.

Miguel Hidalgo

A Priest of the People 　　　Revolutionary,
Priest

- ❖ Born in Pénjamo, México.
- ❖ Birth date: May 8, 1753.
- ❖ Death date: July 31, 1811.

Career Highlights

- Ordained a priest in 1778.
- Proclaimed México's independence from Spain and the abolition of slavery in 1810.
- Established an independent Mexican government in 1811.

Important Contributions

With the *Grito de Dolores* (the Proclamation of Dolores), Miguel Hidalgo started the struggle for Mexican independence from Spanish colonial rule on September 16, 1810. His attempt was unsuccessful; within a year the Spaniards had defeated his forces and killed him. However, he had awakened the Mexican people to the fight, and ten years later, on September 21, 1821, México won its independence.

Career Path

If it had not been for a small, private vineyard, México might have never won its independence. Miguel Hidalgo y Costilla, *El Padre de la Independencia Mexicana* (Father of Mexican Independence), was cultivating the vineyard to relax while away from his priestly studies in the city of Valladolid (today's Morelia) when the Spanish colonial authorities ordered its destruction. It was the policy of Madrid's rules to allow no activities that might be detrimental to its commercial monopoly with the New World colonies. Even small personal vineyards were included. This minor but unjust act convinced Hidalgo, who was aware of the other abuses committed by the colonial authorities, that there would be no freedom in México until the Spaniards were overthrown. Eventually, he would begin the revolution that will do just that after his death.

Miguel Gregorio Antonio Hidalgo y Costilla Gallaga Mandarte y Villaseñor was born in the Hacienda de Corralejo, a farm near Pénjamo, in the Mexican state of Guanajuato. It was there that Miguel Hidalgo studied and was ordained a priest. As a student, Hidalgo became fluent in French and was attracted to the ideas of Jean-Jacques Rousseau and other French writers of the Enlightenment Period. His fascination with these progressive writers led officials of the Inquisition to launch a surreptitious investigation into his activities in 1800.

The poverty and social injustices perpetrated by the colonial Spanish government in New Spain (México's colonial name) moved Hidalgo ever closer to opposing Spanish domination of his homeland. Hidalgo felt that the people, not some distant monarch, should rule his country. His pro-democracy ideas caught the eye of the Inquisition authorities, who had close ties to the Spanish crown. After many years, nothing was found to suspect Hidalgo of any kind of anti-church activity, and the investigation was dropped.

After serving as professor of theology and as rector to the College of San Nicholas, Hidalgo became parish priest of Dolores, in his home state of Guanajuato.

The *buen cura de Dolores* (good priest of Dolores), was animated, diligent, and greatly concerned about the welfare of his parishioners. He set up tanning, pottery, carpentry, blacksmith, and looming shops. He also taught beekeeping to the Indians.

As in South America, the year 1810 was pivotal in México's push for self-rule. Napoleon's invasion of Spain had weakened the empire, and independence-minded individuals all over the Spanish-speaking Americas saw their chance at freedom. Mexicans, too, jumped at the opportunity. Hidalgo joined a pro-autonomy group that planned to start a revolution in October 1810. However, a fellow conspirator betrayed the group. Rather than abort the uprising, Hidalgo moved it forward. On September 16, he rang the church bells summoning the townfolk to a meeting. In a fiery speech Hidalgo condemned Spanish rule and called for independence. He carried a flag with a picture of the *Virgen de Guadalupe* (the Virgin of Guadalupe). Hidalgo ordered every single native-born Spaniard in town arrested. He took command of an army of disheveled, tattered Indians and *mestizos*. Hidalgo's forces won at Dolores and Celaya and took Guanajuato and Valladolid. The parish priest was soon excommunicated, but his followers ignored the edict and continued flocking to his side. His army grew to 82,000 and marched toward México City. Hidalgo routed the Spaniards just outside of the capital on October 30, 1810, but decided not to take it. The Spaniards then went on the offensive and defeated Hidalgo's forces at Aculco, the second battle of Guanajuato, and at *Puente Grande* (Large Bridge) near Guadalajara on January 17, 1811. After resigning command of the insurrection, he retired to Saltillo. But on March 21, 1811 his small retinue was ambushed near Acatita de Bajá. Hidalgo was judged by the Spanish authorities, defrocked, and executed by firing squad at Chihuahua on July 31.

Bibliography

Blanco Moheno, Roberto. *Historia de dos curas revolucionarios: Hidalgo y Morelos*. México: Editorial Diana, 1973.

Carrillo Díaz B, Roberto. *Presencia del Padre Hidalgo*. México: Secreataría de Obras y Servicios, 1973.

Crivelli, Camillus. "Miguel Hidalgo." *The Catholic Encyclopedia*. http://www.newadvent.org/cathen/16045a.htm (March 2, 2004).

De Varona, Frank. *Miguel Hidalgo y Costilla: Father of Mexican Independence*. Brookfield, CT: Millbrook Press, 1993.

Gleiter, Jan, and Thompson, Kathleen. *Miguel Hidalgo y Costilla*. Austin, TX: Raintree Steck-Vaughn, 1991.

Guzmán Pérez, Moisés. *Miguel Hidalgo y el gobierno insurgente en Valladolid*. Morelia, Michoacán, México: Universidad Michoacana de San Nicolás de Hidalgo, Centro de Estudios sobre la Cultura Nicolaita, 1996.

Ibarra Palafox, Francisco A. *Miguel Hidalgo: entre la libertad y la tradición*. México D.F.: Porrúa: Facultad de Derecho, U.N.A.M., 2003.

Johnson, Lyman L., ed. *Death, Dismemberment, and Memory: Body Politics in Latin America*. Albuquerque, NM: University of New Mexico Press, 2004.

Eugenio María de Hostos

The Great Educator

Patriot,
Educator

- ❖ Born in Mayaguez, Puerto Rico.
- ❖ Birth date: January 11, 1839.
- ❖ Death date: August 11, 1903.

Career Highlights

- Founded the newspaper *La Patria* (*The Motherland*) in Lima, Perú, in 1871.
- Established the Dominican Republic's first teacher's college in 1880.
- Appointed professor of constitutional law at the University of Chile in 1890.
- Wrote *Ensayo sobre la historia del la lengua castellana* (*Essay on the History of the Castilian Language*) in 1894.
- Appointed to the Cuban and Puerto Rican revolutionary parties of New York.

Important Contributions

Spanish-speaking America owes a debt of gratitude to Puerto Rican patriot Eugenio María de Hostos. Educator, sociologist, philosopher, essayist, and novelist, de Hostos spent more time away from his native land than in it. Throughout his life he struggled for the independence of not only Puerto Rico, but Cuba as well. He reformed the educational system of the Dominican Republic, promoted democracy in Spain, taught in Perú and Chile, and influenced the social fabric of almost every nation south of the Río Grande.

Career Path

De Hostos attended elementary school in Mayagüez and by 1852, following his father's wishes, went to Bilbao, Spain, to begin his secondary education at that city's *Instituto de Segunda Enseñanza* (Institute of Secondary Education). In 1858 he started to study law in Madrid, but his dissatisfaction with the teaching methods of the time and his refusal to receive a degree from a monarchic government prevented him from graduating. After his mother died four years later, he traveled to his native land, and then returned to Spain the same year. There he wrote *La Peregrinación de Bayoán* (*Bayoan's Pilgrimage*) and joined *La Sociedad Abolicionista de la Esclavitud* (the Society for the Abolition of Slavery). In 1869 de Hostos went to New York, where he promoted the independence of Puerto Rico and Cuba from Spain. For four years he traveled throughout South America seeking support for the Cuban cause and promoting his ideas: In Perú he advocated for better treatment for Chinese immigrants; in Chile he encouraged scientific education for women; and in Argentina he taught at the University of Buenos Aires and pushed for the construction of the first railroad across the Andes. He also traveled to Colombia and Brazil where he promoted Puerto Rico's and Cuba's independence.

Once he was back in the United States, de Hostos set out from Boston on an ill-fated armed expedition to Cuba in 1875. The mission failed because the ship was so old and shattered that it almost sank two days into the trip and had to return to American soil. De Hostos began traveling again. While living in Venezuela, he married Belinda Otilia de Ayala, a Cuban natural, and was appointed principal of two schools in 1877. The rest of his life was dedicated to writing educational treatises, establishing schools in South American and Caribbean countries, and continuing his work for the independence of Cuba and Puerto Rico.

In 1900 de Hostos was appointed to the position of inspector general for public education in the Dominican Republic, where he spent the next few years revamping the educational system.

Eugenio María de Hostos died at Las Marías, Santo Domingo, Dominican Republic, and was buried with honors in the National Pantheon. His work as a writer, educator, and revolutionary ranks him among the great men of the Western Hemisphere.

Bibliography

Balseiro, José Agustín. Eugenio María de Hostos; Hispanic America's Public Servant. Coral Gables, FL: University of Miami, 1949.

Cassá, Roberto. *Eugenio María de Hostos: El Maestro*. Santo Domingo: Tobogán, 2000.

Castro Ventura, Santiago. *Hostos en el perímetro dominicano*. Santo Domingo: Editorial Manatí, 2003.

Henríquez Ureña, Camila. *La ideas pedagógicas de Hostos y otros escritos*. Santo Domingo: Secretaría de Estado de Educación, Bellas Artes y Cultos, 1994.

Méndez, José Luis. *Hostos y las ciencias socials*. San Juan, PR: Editorial de la Universidad de Puerto Rico, 2003.

Palmer, Joy A., ed. *Fifty Major Thinkers on Education: From Confucius to Dewey*. London: Routledge, 2001.

Ignatius of Loyola

Soldier of God   Priest

❖ Born in Azpeitía, Spain.
❖ Birth date: December 24, 1491.
❖ Death date: July 31, 1556.

Career Highlights

- Began conversion in 1522.
- Wrote *Spiritual Exercises* in about 1523.
- Jailed for forty-two days by the Inquisition in 1526.
- Founder of the Society of Jesus (the Jesuits); recognized by the Vatican in 1540.
- A key leader of the Counter-Reformation.

Important Contributions

Ignatius of Loyola was not only a religious leader but also a revolutionary. At a time when only the very wealthy were educated, the Jesuit charter called for the order's members to educate the masses. They began with six schools, including one in India for future Jesuits. The first Jesuit school for lay students and seminarians was established at Messina, Sicily, in 1548.

Career Path

Ignatius of Loyola was one of the most controversial figures to emerge from the Reformation and Counter-Reformation. A former military man, Loyola brought a never-before-seen stern discipline to religious life that served the Catholic Church well during the Reformation.

Loyola was born at the family castle in the Spanish province of Guipozcoa. He was one of thirteen children and his baptismal name was Iñigo. Growing up in the service of the treasurer of Castile, Juan Velázquez, he developed a taste for life at court, ladies, gambling, and swordplay. He later joined the Duke of Nágara's military forces, fighting the French at Pamplona, who claimed the territory. During the March 10, 1521, Battle of Pamplona, a cannonball shattered both of his legs

Out of respect for his courage, the French took Loyola back to the family castle; one leg healed, but the other did not. Doctors had to break it and reset it. He nearly died, but eventually recovered, although one of his legs was left shorter than the other. To pass the months of recovery, Loyola took to reading. He was interested in tales of chivalry, but the only books available in the castle were one about the life of Christ and another on the saints. So began his conversion.

After healing, he set out on a pilgrimage to Montserrat, where he hung his sword and dagger at the altar of the Virgin Mary. From there Loyola went to Manresa on the way to Barcelona, his planned destination. In Manresa he lodged at a cavern outside the village. He intended to stay just a short time, but wound up living there for ten months. He had a vision of God that enabled Loyola to see Him in all things. It was also at this cavern that he wrote most of the *Spiritual Exercises*, a guidebook for prayer and self-control.

At the age of thirty-three, he lacked the education to be a priest, so he studied at Barcelona, Alcalá, and Salamanca from 1524 to 1528. While at Salamanca he was accused of preaching heresy, but was cleared. He went to Paris in 1528 to study philosophy, theology, and Latin, and received his master's degree in art in 1534. With six other students, founded the Society of Jesus—the Jesuits. During this time, Loyola survived by begging and working among the poor.

Intending to travel to the Holy Land, he left Paris in 1535 and went to Italy, but was not able to leave for Palestine due to the war between Christians and Moslems. While waiting, Loyola and his companions worked in hospitals and with the poor. Once ordained in 1537, he and the other Jesuits went to Rome to get the Pope's sanction for their order. Loyola claims that God told him it would happen in a vision. Three years later Pope Paul III did so. That same year, Loyola was elected the superior general of the order and wrote its charter. The document called upon Jesuits to educate children of all classes, instruct the ignorant and the poor, and minister to the sick, prisoners, and other downtrodden people.

The Jesuits became a kind of shock troops of the Papacy during the Counter-Reformation. Their profound knowledge of Scriptures, science, and philosophy made them the ideal defenders of the faith as articulated by the Vatican.

Ignatius of Loyola died in Rome at the age of sixty-four. By then, the Jesuits had about 13,000 members and had missions in Europe, Asia, and the New World. The Catholic Church canonized Loyola in 1622. However he is not the only Jesuit so honored by his church. The order counts more than thirty-five saints and many blessed among its members.

Bibliography

Boehmer, Heinrich. *The Jesuits: An Historical Study*. New York: Gordon Press, 1975.

Brodrick, James. *The Origin of the Jesuits*. Garden City, NY: Doubleday, 1960.

Butler, Alban. *Vidas de los Santos*. Madrid: Editorial LIBSA, 1998.

Donnelly, John Patrick. *Ignatius of Loyola: Founder of the Jesuits*. New York: Pearson/Longman, 2004.

Luebke, David M., ed. *The Counter-Reformation: The Essential Readings*. Malden, MA: Blackwell, 1999.

Tellechea Idígora, José Ignacio, trans. Cornelius Michael Buckley. *Ignatius of Loyola: The Pilgrim Saint*. Chicago: Loyola University Press, 1994.

Wright, Jonathan. *God's Soldiers: Adventure, Politics, Intrigue, and Power: A History of the Jesuits*. New York: Doubleday, 2004.

Isabella of Castile

Ahead of Her Time

Monarch

- ❖ Born in Madrigal de las Altas Torres, Spain.
- ❖ Birth date: April 22, 1451.
- ❖ Death date: November 26, 1504.

Career Highlights

- Became Queen of Castile in 1474.
- Married Ferdinand of Aragon in 1469.
- Together with Ferdinand established the Spanish Inquisition in 1478.
- Sponsored Christopher Columbus's first exploration voyage in 1492.
- Expelled Jews from Spanish territories in 1492 and Moors in 1502.

Important Contributions

It can be said that *Isabel I, la Católica* (Isabella I, the Catholic) was one of the first liberated women in the modern sense. At a time when all power and wealth were in the hands of male rulers, Isabella challenged the odds, convention, and male authority, and became the most powerful woman in the world. When she funded Columbus's voyage of discovery, she set Spain on a course to become the world's most powerful nation, and changed the course of human history.

Career Path

Isabella of Castile's ancestors included Spanish, Portuguese, French, and English nobility. She was the daughter of Juan II of Castile and his Portuguese wife Doña Isabel, and a descendant of William the Conqueror, Henry II of England, Eleanor of Aquitaine, and Phillip the

Bold of France. She was also a pious, religious woman and remarkably politically astute. When she was only three years old, King Juan II died, and her half-brother, Henry IV, inherited the crown of Castile. Henry's rule, however, was unstable due to the power the Spanish nobility had acquired under the reigns of his grandfather and father. Another problem Henry had was that the nobles considered Isabella's younger brother Alfonso the true heir to the throne. Henry IV managed to hold the crown by taking Isabella and Alfonso to his court as hostages under the facade of completing their educations. But on July 5, 1468, Alfonso died under mysterious circumstances, and the nobles rallied behind Isabella. Yet the future queen rejected their offers and would not take the crown until Henry died. To mollify the nobles, Henry named Isabella as his heir, took it back, and then chose her again as successor. Political and military conflicts over the matter, but Isabella would not ensued take power in Castile until 1474, when Henry died.

By then, she had married Ferdinand of Aragón, even though she had been promised at different times to Ferdinand's oldest brother and, after his death, to Alfonso V of Portugal, as well as to various other powerful Spanish nobles. However, the young princess was truly in love with Ferdinand, and married him over her brother's opposition.

The stories about the war with the Moors, the expulsion of the Jews and Moors, the Inquisition, all moves designed to unite Spain, and the sponsorship of Columbus's voyages of exploration are thoroughly documented, although they are shrouded in fable and anti-Spanish bias. Less well-known is that Isabella was a protector of Native Americans. When Columbus brought some New World inhabitants to Spain, Isabella ordered their freedom and sent them back to their homeland. She was always concerned about the natives' well-being and prevented many abuses by the colonists.

Isabella also stimulated the manufacture of steel weapons, silk, glass, leather, cloth, and silverware. In addition, she sponsored many artists and scholars. She was able to develop industry and arts by using the riches that came from Spain's new colonies. Isabella also obtained large funds from the production of wool, an enterprise she promoted through special grazing rights to sheep ranchers, a measure that helped make Spain one of the largest exporters of wool at the time. All these efforts brought about a true Golden Age of Spain.

Isabella died on November 26, 1504, at Medina del Campo. As Queen of Castile, she had shaped the future not only of Spain, but also of the world.

❖   ❖   ❖

Bibliography

Ashby, Ruth, and Ohrn, Deborah. *Herstory: Women Who Changed the World*. New York: Viking, 1995.

Fernández Alvarez, Manuel. *Isabel La Católica*. Pozuelo de Alarcón, Madrid: Espasa, 2003.

Kamen, Henry. *Empire: How Spain Became a World Power*. New York: HarperCollins Publishers, 2003.

Liss, Peggy K. *Isabel the Queen: Life and Times*. New York: Oxford University Press, 1992.

Rubin Stuart, Nancy. *Isabella of Castile: The First Renaissance Queen*. New York: St. Martin's Press, 1991.

Walsh, William Thomas. *The Last Crusader, Isabella of Spain*. Rockford, IL: Tan Books and Publishers, 1987.

Juan Ramón Jiménez

Thank the Donkey!   Writer

❖ Born in Moguer, Spain.
❖ Birth date: December 23, 1881.
❖ Death date: May 29, 1958.

Career Highlights

- Founded *Helios*, a historically significant literary review magazine in 1902.
- Published the classic *Platero y yo* (*Platero and I*) in 1914.
- Translated Shakespeare's works into Spanish.
- Awarded the Nobel Prize in Literature in 1956.

Important Contributions

Juan Ramón Jiménez's poetry evolved from early symbolism to a simple style that has been described as "naked" poetry. His early romantic expressions later gave way to a pantheistic religious belief. He had a definite influence on Spanish poetry of the 1920s and 1930s. *Platero y yo* is usually required reading in college Spanish-language programs.

Career Path

Juan Ramón Jiménez owes most of his fame to a donkey. Indeed, his best-known work is *Platero and I*, about the relationship between a young poet and his donkey. *Platero and I* rivals Miguel de Cervantes's *Don Quixote* as the most-translated Spanish language book.

As his father was a lawyer, Jiménez was able to attend Cadiz's Jesuit Academy and then, in 1896, to study law at the University of Seville. His interest in jurisprudence didn't last long. Jiménez was more interested in painting, but this endeavor was also unsatisfactory, so he turned to poetry. By 1900, when he moved to Madrid, Jiménez had already published some poems in the literary review *Vida nueva* (*New Life*). That year he published two of his early anthologies, *Alma de Violeta* (*Violet Soul*) and *Ninfas* (*Nymphs*). His stay in the Spanish capital didn't last long. Just two months after arriving, his father died, so Jiménez returned home. The tragedy sent him into a deep depression, and his family took him to a sanatorium in France. His fixation with death emerged as a theme that would appear again and again in his poems. By late 1901 Jiménez was back in Madrid working feverishly. Over the next four years he would publish a number of new collections, 1904's *Jardines lejanos* (*Far Away Gardens*) among them.

He moved back to Moguer in 1905. There he wrote and tried out assorted verse forms. In 1912 Jiménez returned to Madrid, where he created a series of what he called prose poems about a donkey that became *Platero and I*. In this beautiful fable, Jiménez talks to the donkey Platero, who tags along on the writer's excursions, listening to his thoughts and ideas, but who never answers. The book was published two years later.

Jiménez met Zenobia Camprubí Aymar and courted her for three years. The romance took Jiménez to New York, where he married her at Saint Stephen's Church in 1916. Zenobia was a good choice for Jiménez. She became his collaborator and his secretary. He published *Diario de un poeta reciencasado* (*Diary of a Newlywed Poet*) two years later. In this book he continued writing poetry that was almost like prose, as in *Platero and I*.

During the 1930s Zenobia was diagnosed with cancer. In 1935, for reasons unknown, he refused a seat in the prestigious Spanish Academy. The next year the Republican government appointed him cultural attaché to the United States, but he didn't last long in the position. In 1937 he moved to Havana, Cuba, where he was wined and dined by important people. After a short stay in New York, the poet and his wife settled in Coral Gables, Florida, where Jiménez wrote *Voces de mi copla* (*Voices of my Verse*) and *Animal de dondo* (*Animal Disposition*), among others. During this time he had another bout with depression that kept him hospitalized for eight months. Later he traveled through Argentina and Uruguay and, in 1950, settled in Puerto Rico.

Six years later, on October 25, he won the Nobel Prize for Literature, and just three days later, Zenobia died. Jiménez remained a recluse until his death on May 29, 1958. Less than a month after his death, his remains and those of Zenobia were transported to Spain. The country received them in mourning.

Bibliography

Alarcón Sierra, Rafael. *Juan Ramón Jiménez: pasión perfecta*. Madrid: Espasa Calpe, 2003.

Baquero, Gastón. *Eternidad de Juan Ramón Jiménez*. Madrid: Huelga y Fierro Editores, 2003.

Haro, Pedro Aullón, et al. *Como Dominar la Historia de la Literatura Española*. Madrid: Editorial Playor, 1991.

López Martínez, and Maria Isabel. *La poesía popular en la obra de Juan Ramón Jiménez*. Sevilla: Diputación Provincial de Sevilla, 1997.

Pérez-Embid, Florentino, ed. *Forjadores del Mundo Contemporáneo*. Barcelona: Editorial Planeta, 1960.

Porto-Bompiani, González. *Diccionario de Autores*. Barcelona: Montaner y Simón, 1963.

Benito Juárez

The Only One   Statesman

❖ Born in San Pablo Guelatao, México.
❖ Birth date: March 21, 1806.
❖ Death date: July 18, 1872.

Career Highlights

- Wrote the moderate liberal Mexican Constitution of 1857.
- Elected to first term as president in 1861.
- Led resistance to the French occupation.
- Elected to second term in 1867.

Important Contributions

México's most revered and beloved national hero, Benito Juárez is the first of two known Native Americans to have served as president of a New World country. In the Constitution of 1857, which he wrote, freedom of the press was guaranteed and civil marriage established, both concepts unthinkable in México prior to that time.

Career Path

Benito Juárez once said, "Respect for other people's rights is peace." He spent most of his life fighting to make others respect the rights of Native Americans, the poor, and the Republic of México. He was an intelligent, honest, tough individual who would stand his ground against enormous odds and win.

Benito Pablo Juárez García was born to full-blooded Zapotec Indian parents in the state of Oaxaca. His parents died when he was three years old. He and one of his sisters, Rosa, went to live with their grandparents, but they soon died, too. An uncle raised them.

For the first years of his life, Juárez was illiterate and spoke only Zapotec. As a boy, he worked as a shepherd while his uncle taught him to read and write Spanish. Unhappy with the slow pace of his learning, Juárez packed up and walked to the city of Oaxaca on December 17, 1918, to further his education. Once there, Juárez found that his studies were not moving along any faster. He changed schools and teachers at various times, studied at a seminary, and at graduation in 1827, decided to take up law.

After getting his law degree in 1831, he dabbled in politics as an antiestablishment liberal. Eleven years later Juárez was appointed to a judgeship and married Margarita Mazza, the daughter of one of the region's wealthiest families of Spanish descent. Since Juárez cared little for money, the marriage was surely for love, although it provided him with the backing he needed to obtain his ultimate goal of political power. Eventually he was appointed and later elected governor of Oaxaca, but by 1852, he had to go into exile due to his opposition to the corrupt government of Antonio López de Santa Anna. Juárez first went to Havana and then to New Orleans, where he led a revolutionary group for the next two years. In 1855 he returned to México as part of the liberal uprising. Santa Anna was overthrown and fled to Cuba, and Ignacio Comonfort became president. With this victory, Juárez became the first chief justice and then vice president. He was also selected leader of the Liberal Party.

The Conservative Party rebelled against the Liberal Party triumph and a civil war ensued. Comonfort crumbled and Juárez was appointed provisional president. For three years, the liberals, whose headquarters were in Veracruz, fought the conservatives, who controlled México City. Finally, on January 11, 1861, Juárez entered México City. Three months later he was elected to his first term as president. Juárez immediately began instituting the reforms he considered necessary. He authorized land reform and instituted the Mexican Constitution of 1857, which guaranteed free speech and free press among other rights. He championed the rights of the Indians and curtailed the power of the Catholic Church. The country was bankrupt due to the civil war, so Juárez suspended all payments of the foreign debt. This move displeased England, France, and Spain and gave them an excuse to interfere in México. British, Spanish, and French troops occupied Veracruz. Juárez was able to negotiate the withdrawal of the British and Spanish troops, but not the French.

With the collaboration of the conservatives, the French invaded the rest of the country in 1862. The following year the French took México City, and Juárez fled to northern México. Maximilian I, an Austrian noble, was crowned emperor. Maximilian wanted Juárez to be his prime minister, but the Mexican leader refused to collaborate, choosing instead to lead the resistance from El Paso del Norte, today's Ciudad Juárez. Pressure from the United States and other nations forced the French to leave in 1866. With only the conservative support, Maximilian was defeated within a year. Juárez returned to the presidency and sentenced the former emperor to death. He demonstrated his strength by not succumbing to the international pleas and pressures for him to spare Maximilian's life. Juárez was then elected for a second term as president.

Four years later, Porfirio Díaz, a conservative *caudillo* (military leader), embarked on a revolution against Juárez. In the long run the revolt would be suppressed, but Juárez would not live to see it. He died of a heart attack while working at his desk at the National Palace in the Mexican capital.

Today, his birthday is a national holiday in México, five towns are named for him, El Paso del Norte was renamed Ciudad Juárez, and México City's international airport bears his name.

Bibliography

Ada, Alma Flor, and Campoy, F. Isabel. *Sonrisas*. Miami: Santillana U.S.A. Publishing, 2000.

Fuentes Mares, José. *Juárez: El Imperio y la República*. México City: Editorial Grijalbo S.A., 1983.

Galeana de Valadés, Patricia. *Benito Juárez: el indio zapoteca que reformó México*. Madrid: Anaya, 1988.

Hammett, Brian R. *Juárez*. London, New York: Longman, 1994.

Pérez-Embid, Florentino, ed. *Forjadores del Mundo Contemporáneo*. Barcelona: Editorial Planeta, 1960.

Ridley, Jasper Godwin. *Maximilian and Juárez*. New York: Ticknor & Fields, 1992.

Frida Kahlo

A Painful Life   Painter

- ❖ Born in México City, México.
- ❖ Birth date: July 6, 1907.
- ❖ Death date: On July 13, 1954.

Career Highlights

- Painted 143 canvases of which 55 are self-portraits.
- *Mi nacimiento* (*My Birth*), one of her most outrageous works, appeared in 1932.
- Painted *Las dos Fridas* (*The Two Fridas*) in 1939.

Important Contributions

Kahlo was part of the movement toward indigenous themes that spread through Mexican art in the late 1920s and 1930s. She also incorporated expressionist and surrealist elements into her highly personal style. She liked to shock her audience and integrated detailed elements of her anatomy in her work. In the late twentieth century, she became a kind of feminist symbol, and her fame grew as she became the subject of various documentaries and feature films.

Career Path

Unconventional is just about the kindest word one can use when describing Mexican painter Frida Kahlo. Her work was exceptional, but it might be her lifestyle, politics, and personal suffering that most set her apart. Even though her birth certificate says she was born the day before, Kahlo told everybody she was born on July 7, 1910. It is widely believed that she found pleasure in lying.

When Kahlo was six years old she was stricken by polio in her right leg. Then in 1925 she was in a tragic bus accident. She suffered fractures in her ribs, collarbone, and right leg, her right foot was crushed, and her spine broken. This accident forced her to undergo some thirty-five surgeries over her lifetime. To fight boredom during her long and painful recoveries, she began to paint. It became her lifelong career.

She was a brilliant student, so much so that she was one of the few females at the National Preparatory School. But the honor did not prevent her from getting into all sorts of trouble and being expelled once. Her fellow students disrespected her because of her physical problems.

Around 1928 Kahlo started attending gatherings of Communist sympathizers and met Diego Rivera, already a famous painter. Rivera encouraged her painting, and perhaps a little put off with the dark, shapeless clothes she wore as a good Communist, recommended that she dress in traditional Mexican outfits, which she would do for the rest of her life. Kahlo and Rivera were married on August 21, 1929, and traveled to San Francisco, where Rivera was doing a mural. There Kahlo became friends with Dr. Leo Eloesser and painted his portrait, the *Retrato del Doctor Leo Eloesser* (*Portrait of Dr. Eloesser*), in 1931. The following year, Kahlo painted *Autorretrato de pie en la frontera México-Estados Unidos* (*Self-Portrait Between the Borderline of México and the United States*).

From the West Coast, Rivera and Kahlo went to New York, where she painted *Mi vestido cuelga aquí* (*Here Hangs My Dress*) in 1933. Then she left alone for Paris. Kahlo's talent and exotic appearance captivated the French.

Back in México, her marriage with Rivera was on the rocks. Both of them were notorious for their many illicit relationships. They divorced in 1939, the same year she painted *The Two Fridas*, one of her masterpieces. Nonetheless, they continued to be comrades, participating in Communist demonstrations and in the Revolutionary Artist Union, an organization of left-wing artists.

When Russian Communist leader Leon Trotsky arrived in México as an exile, he stayed at Kahlo's house. By then Rivera and Kahlo had remarried, and when Trotsky was murdered on August 21, 1940, they were suspects. Eventually, they were cleared and divorced again that same year. Afterward, Kahlo became an art teacher and continued her radical politics, rejecting Stalinism but embracing the ideas of China's Mao Zedong.

Neither the alcohol she drank in large quantities, nor the cigarettes she smoked continuously, nor even the illegal drugs she used could alleviate her physical and spiritual pain. Kahlo tried to kill herself at least twice, and in all probability finally succeeded, for she died under mysterious circumstances. No autopsy was performed.

Bibliography

Ada, Alma Flor, and Campoy, F. Isabel. *Caminos*. Miami: Santillana U.S.A. Publishing, 2000.

Ankori, Gannit. *Imaging Her Selves: Frida Kahlo's Poetics of Identity and Fragmentation*. Westport, CT: Greenwood Press, 2002.

Kahlo, Frida. *The Diary of Frida Kahlo: An Intimate Self-Portrait*. New York: Harry N. Abrams, 1995.

Krull, Kathleen. *Lives of the Artists*. New York: Harcourt Brace, 1995.

Lozano, Luis Martin, et al. *Frida Kahlo*. Boston: Bullfinch Press, 2001.

Rummel, Jack. *Frida Kahlo: A Spiritual Biography*. New York: Crossroad Publishing Company, 2000.

Agustín Lara

A Poet's Soul

Composer

- ❖ Born in México City, México.
- ❖ Birth date: October 30, 1896.
- ❖ Death date: November 6, 1970.

Career Highlights

- Wrote more than 500 popular songs.

- Created scores for movies during the golden age of Mexican cinema, 1925–1950.

- Composed "Granada," one of the most popular songs of all time, in 1936.

- Composed his renowned waltz "María Bonita" ("Pretty Maria") in 1945.

Important Contributions

Few composers have done as much as Agustín Lara to improve the attractiveness of romantic Spanish popular music. His highly personal style fused bolero, jazz, tango, and waltz. Tropical rhythms such sambas and rumbas were also part of his blend. Since the revival of the bolero in the 1990s Lara's music has enjoyed renewed popularity.

Career Path

Agustín Lara was always romantic, unabashed, brash, and without fear. Angel Agustín María Carlos Fausto Mariano Alfonso del Sagrado Corazón Lara y Aguirre del Pino claimed the picturesque, sultry town of Tlacotalpan, in the state of Veracruz, as his hometown. However, it was partly his romanticism that led him to make this claim, as all records point to México City as the birthplace of one of México's best-known composers. Soon after his birth his family moved to Tlacotalpan, where he spent the first five years of his life. The irresistible tropical beauty and rhythms of Tlacotalpan had an impact on Lara's life and music. Three types of tropical music genres had the most influence: the *son jarocho*, the *bolero*, and the *danzón*, the latter two of Cuban origin. While others excelled at composing and interpreting *bolero* and *danzón* music, Lara was the best.

His father, a doctor, enjoyed playing the piano, and introduced Lara to the instrument. Although the young man had talent and showed an inclination to become a professional musician, his father opposed a career in music. The elder Lara thought music was not an honest profession. Due to family financial problems, Agustín went to work playing the piano at a bordello. This stage of his life would have lasting emotional and physical consequences. Observing the prostitutes firsthand inspired him to write many sorrowful ballads about their rough lives. Also, during a fight in the bordello, he was hit in the face with a broken bottle. The large scar it left deformed his face.

Lara's father interrupted his son's musical career by sending him to military school, but the young man ran away and went back to work as a musician. Early in his career he married his first wife, Angelina Brusquetta, whose father owned a famous nightclub in México City. At the club he met a popular tenor, Juan Arvizu, who hired Lara to write songs for him. In 1928 his first recorded songs, "Imposible" ("Impossible") and "Clavelito" ("Small Carnation"), both sweet, soulful ballads, were published. He then began a radio show that put his career in high gear. RCA offered him a recording contract as a result.

From 1930 to 1950, the golden age of Mexican movies, Lara wrote some of his most famous songs for the movies: "Farolito" ("Small Street Light"), "Santa" ("Saint"), and "Noche de Ronda" ("Serenade Night"), among others. His most famous works are also from this period: "Granada," written before he visited that Spanish City, and "Pretty Maria," composed for his second wife, Mexican actress María Félix. Lara also tried his hand at acting, but his movies were far less memorable than his songs.

With the arrival of the 1960s, shifting musical tastes and failing health diminished his work and prominence. However, with the resurgence of interest in the bolero, his popularity rose again in the 1990s. Lara died of a heart attack in México City at the age of seventy-three. Many great Spanish-language singers have recorded his music.

❖ ❖ ❖

Bibliography

"Agustín Lara." Servicioweb. http://www.servicioweb.cl/bolero.agustinlara.htm (March 16, 2004).

Aura, Alejandro. *La Hora Intima de Agustín Lara*. México City: Cal y Arena, 1993.

Cásares Rodicio, Emilio. *Diccionario de la Música Española e Hispano Americana*. Madrid: Sociedad General de Autores y Editores, 2000.

Martínez, Gabriel Abaroa. *El Flaco de Oro*. México City: Grupo Editorial Planeta, 1993.

Rodríguez, David, et al. *Todo lo que Usted Quería Saber sobre Agustín Lara*. Col. Azures, México: Editorial Contenido, 1993.

Octaviano Larrazolo

First in the Senate   Statesman

❖ Born in El Valle de San Bartolo, today's Allende, México.
❖ Birth date: December 7, 1859.
❖ Death date: April 7, 1930.

Career Highlights

- First elected to office in Texas in 1886.
- Admitted to the bar in 1888.
- Elected governor of New Mexico in 1918.
- Elected to the U.S. Senate in 1928.

Important Contributions

The first Hispanic to serve in the U.S. Senate, Larrazolo was deeply committed to equality among all Americans. He abandoned the Democratic Party over equal opportunities for the Hispanic majority in New Mexico, and, as governor of the state, went against the Republican Party's position on taxes and universal suffrage.

Career Path

Octaviano Larrazolo was a man who did not give up easily. Even though he was well-connected in New Mexico's political circles, and the public thought him a great orator, he managed to lose more elections than he won. But he was persistent: Some might say he kept banging his head against the wall until the wall broke enough to make him part of history.

Larrazolo was a Mexican immigrant. As a protégée of Arizona Bishop J.B. Salpointe, Larrazolo moved from México to Tucson, Arizona, when he was ten years old, and began to study theology. In 1865 Salpointe moved to Santa Fe, New Mexico, and Larrazolo went with him. He finished his studies at Santa Fe's Saint Michael's College. After earning his degree, Larrazolo taught in Tucson and in the El Paso County public schools. While in Texas, he became interested in politics and joined the Democratic Party. He was first appointed to public office as Clerk of the U.S District Court and the Circuit Court of El Paso County in 1885. The following year he was elected Clerk of the 34th District Court at El Paso. He went on to serve two terms as district attorney for the western district of Texas. Nevertheless, he found time to study law.

In 1895 Larrazolo relocated to Las Vegas, New Mexico, where he practiced law and ran for political office. He was the Democratic candidate for Territorial Delegate to Congress three times and he lost each race. When the leaders of New Mexico began the drive for statehood, Larrazolo began having problems with the Democratic Party. While he was deeply committed to a constitution that assured equal rights to people of Spanish heritage in New Mexico, the Democratic Party opposed such provisions. His fellow Democrats accused him of racism. Undaunted, Larrazolo became one of the most outspoken leaders for approving the state constitution as it was written.

While not physically present at the New Mexico Constitutional Convention of 1911, Larrazolo nevertheless exerted a powerful influence. Clauses were inserted that protected the vast Hispanic majority in the state, 60 percent of the population at that time, from discrimination and disfranchisement due to race or language. That same year, he finally broke away from the Democratic Party over his request that half of New Mexico's Democratic candidates be Hispanics. The Democrats' loss was the Republicans' gain.

It was seven years before Larrazolo held another elected political office in New Mexico, but on November 5, 1918, he was elected as the state's first Republican governor. Although he only lasted four years in office, his work for welfare homes for children and a state health board, as well as his support for women's suffrage, were popular. But his support for stronger income tax laws and women's rights put him at odds with the Republican Party. He was not re-nominated to run for governor.

By 1924 the Republicans were somewhat mollified and nominated Larrazolo to the New Mexico Supreme Court. He was defeated yet again. Larrazolo managed to get himself nominated and elected to the state legislature in 1927. Andieus Jones, then New Mexico's Democratic senator, died in office the following year, and Larrazolo was elected to complete the term. Larrazolo served in the Seventieth Congress, from December 7, 1928, to March 3, 1929.

Illness overtook Larrazolo while in Washington, D.C., and he decided not to run for a full term. He moved back to New Mexico, this time to Albuquerque, and practiced law there until his death.

Bibliography

"Larrazolo, Octaviano Ambrosio, (1859–1930)." Biographical Directory of the United States Congress. http://bioguide.congress.gov/scripts/biodisplay.pl?index = L000101 (November 11, 2004).

"Octaviano Larrazolo." Hispanic Americans in Congress, 1822–1995. http://www.loc.gov/rr/hispanic/congress/larrazolo.html (November 11, 2004).

Larrazolo, Paul, E. *Octaviano Larrazolo: A Moment in New Mexico History.* New York: Carlton Press, 1986.

Stein, R. Conrad. *New Mexico.* Chicago: Children's Press, 1998.

Zannos, Susan. *Octaviano Larrazolo.* Hockessin, DE: Mitchell Lane Publishers, 2004.

Ernesto Lecuona

Cuba's Songwriter   Composer

- ❖ Born in Guanabacoa, Cuba.
- ❖ Birth date: August 7, 1896.
- ❖ Death date: November 29, 1963.

Career Highlights

- Published his first composition in 1908.
- Composed more than 400 songs.
- Wrote eleven scores for American, Mexican, and Argentinian movies.
- Composed five ballets, thirty-one orchestral scores, and fifty-three operettas and *zarzuelas* (a Spanish type of operetta).
- Inducted into the Songwriters Hall of Fame in 1997.

Important Contributions

Lecuona fused the African and Spanish influences of popular Cuban music into a classical and semi-classical style that won him the admiration, not only from audiences worldwide, but also from other great composers such as George Gershwin and Maurice Ravel.

Career Path

Considered by countless music lovers around the world the greatest Cuban composer of all time, Ernesto was born in a working-class suburb of Havana. A precocious talent, he was playing the piano at age five, and benefited from the tutelage of his sister, Ernestina, fourteen years his senior. She also became well known as a concert pianist and composer. Following his sister's guidance, Lecuona studied under various important music teachers in Havana. At age twelve he published his first song, appropriately named "Cuba." At the time he was also working as a piano player in movie houses. Lecuona graduated with honors at seventeen from the National Conservatory in Havana.

In 1916, he moved to New York City in search of a career as a concert pianist. He found that and more. For the next forty-six years Lecuona produced a massive amount of work. Warner Brothers, MGM Studios, and Twentieth Century Fox, as well as Mexican and Argentinian productions, vied for his services. It was his score for the 1942 Warner Brothers' film *Always in My Heart* that earned him an Academy-Award nomination. The movie's theme song, *Siempre en mi Corazón* ("Always in My Heart") is closely identified with him and is a kind of unofficial anthem for exiled Cubans.

Another song that is simply Lecuona is *Andalucía,* which is part of his *Spanish Suite*. It became a number-one hit in 1940 for big-band singer Bob Eberly and the Jimmy Dorsey Orchestra when American lyricist Al Stillman added English lyrics and renamed it "The Breeze and I." A more traditional version of "Andalucía" was on the soundtrack of the 2004 Richard Gere and Jennifer Lopez movie *Shall We Dance?* Other songs by Lecuona that have enjoyed multiple recordings are *Malagueña, Siboney,* and *Canto Carabalí.*

Having become quite wealthy by 1945, Lecuona practically disappeared from the public eye, preferring to spend time in his country house raising tropical birds and farming.

Lecuona was a co-founder of the Havana Symphony Orchestra, and directed two bands, Lecuona Cuban Boys and *La Orquesta de la Habana* (Havana's Orchestra). He toured the United States, Latin America, and Europe with the two groups. This was no small feat, since he was terrified of flying and would go to any length to avoid getting on an airplane, including taking long train or bus rides. In 1960, after Fidel Castro overthrew the Cuban government, Lecuona moved permanently to the United States, residing in Tampa, Florida. He died of a heart attack during a trip to Santa Cruz de Tenerife in the Canary Islands. His grave, at the Gate of Heaven Cemetery in Hawthorne, New York, has become a pilgrimage site for music lovers.

❖ ❖ ❖

Bibliography

Cásares Rodicio, Emilio. *Diccionario de la Música Española e Hispano Americana*. Madrid: Sociedad General de Autores y Editores, 2000.

León, Carmela de. *Ernesto Lecuona*. Havana: Editorial Letras Cubanas, 2000.

León, Carmela de. *Ernesto Lecuona: el Maestro*. Havana: Música Mundana, 1995.

Martínez, Orlando. *Ernesto Lecuona*. Havana: Unión de Escritores y Artistas Cubanos, 1989.

Rozada Bestard, Hamilé. *Catálogo de obras de Ernesto Lecuona*. Madrid: Sociedad General de Autores y Editores, 1995.

Vian, Enid, ed. *Ernesto Lecuona, 1895–1963*. Havana: Instituto Cubano del Libro, Editorial Ciencias Sociales, 1992.

Luís Federico Leloir

Another Overnight Success 　　Biochemist

- ❖ Born in Paris, France.
- ❖ Birth date: September 6, 1906.
- ❖ Death date: December 2, 1987.

Career Highlights

- Began research career in 1932.
- Established his research laboratory in 1947.
- Awarded the Nobel Prize in Chemistry in 1970.
- Awarded honorary degrees from the universities of Granada, Spain; Paris, France; and Tucumán and La Plata, Argentina.
- Received awards from the Argentine Scientific Society and the Helen Hay Whitney Foundation, among others.

Important Contributions

Luís Leloir's lifetime work provided an understanding of how mammals, including humans, manufacture the fuel necessary for the body to function. His research also discovered the cause of a serious illness related to milk intolerance.

Career Path

Most scientists labor in obscurity. They might be studying something of great importance, but nobody would know them if they walked by. Recognition usually goes to movie stars and athletes. For most of

156

his life, Luís Federico Leloir was one of those anonymous scientists, unknown even to his countrymen. but Leloir catapulted to international fame when he became the first Argentinian to win the Nobel Prize in Chemistry.

Leloir was born in Paris while his well-to-do Argentinian parents were traveling through Europe. The family returned to Buenos Aires two years later. The young Leloir showed an early inclination to observe nature, something he could enjoy as his family had large land holdings. He attended elementary and secondary school in Buenos Aires and later attended that city's university. Leloir received his medical degree in 1932, and immediately took a research job with the team of Dr. Bernardo Houssay, the winner of the Nobel Prize in Medicine in 1947.

In 1936 Leloir took a position with the biochemical laboratory at Cambridge University in Great Britain. Returning to Argentina a year later, Leloir went back to work with Houssay. The research funds were meager and work proceeded slowly; however, Leloir was able to make some inroads into how humans metabolize alcohol.

In 1941 Leloir became a professor of physiology at his old alma mater, the University of Buenos Aires. Two years later, following Juán Domingo Perón's coup of June 4, Houssay and many other college professors signed a document demanding the return to a democratic government. Houssay and the others were removed from their positions. Leloir resigned in protest and moved to the United States. There Leloir joined the Carl and Getty Cori research team at Washington University in Saint Louis, Missouri, and later worked at Columbia University in New York City.

Leloir returned to Argentina in 1946 and rejoined his old mentor Houssay at a private research facility. Wealthy textile merchant Jaime Campoamor granted Houssay the necessary funds the following year to establish what would become the *Instituto de Biología y Medicina Experimental* (Institute of Experimental Biology and Medicine), a facility that Leloir would head for the next forty years. By 1948 his team was already making inroads in the breakdown of lactose (milk sugar) in the human body. Twelve years later Leloir described the metabolism of carbohydrates and their storage in the body of mammals, which means in lay terms how food becomes sugar and is stored in the body to fuel human activity. That discovery won him the Nobel Prize in Chemistry.

Afterward Leloir continued his investigations on the use of glycogens, but now he had recognition and funding. He was appointed to the national academies of science in the United States, Chile, France, and Argentina. London's Royal Society and Paris' Societé de Biologie also made him a member. But more important, his country's

Antonio Machado

Castile in the Soul

Poet,
Playwright

❖ Born in Seville, Spain.
❖ Birth date: July 26, 1875.
❖ Death date: February 22, 1939.

Career Highlights

- Published first essays in 1893.
- Published first poems in 1901.
- Published his first book, *Soledades* (*Solitude*), in 1903.
- *Nuevas Canciones* (*New Songs*) appeared in 1924.

Important Contributions

Perhaps because his writings interlaced such universal themes as loneliness, love for the motherland, fondness for the common man, and good doses of existentialism, Antonio Machado is still exceptionally popular in the Spanish-speaking world. His popularity surged towards the second half of the twentieth century, and was greatly advanced by songwriter Joan Manuel Serrat, who put music to many of Machado's verses in an album entitled *A Antonio Machado, Poeta* (*To Antonio Machado, Poet*). It was a huge hit.

Career Path

Even though Antonio Machado was born in the Spanish province of Andalusia, he was Castilian. At the turn of the century Machado moved to the desolate, gloomy countryside imbued in local folklore and found an environment that mirrored his soul. The outcome was stunning; Machado became the poetic voice of Spain.

Antonio Machado y Ruíz was born one year after his brother Manuel, also a writer and his occasional collaborator. Soon after his birth, the family moved to Madrid, where Antonio Machado attended the city's Institute of Free Learning, a liberal, humanist school. Machado's early works, published toward the end of the nineteenth century earned him little renown or money. He visited Paris in 1899 and 1902. On his second trip, he met the great English author Oscar Wilde and the prolific Nicaraguan poet Rubén Darío. He also met Leonor Izquierdo, who would become his wife. After returning to Spain he established himself in Castile. Shortly thereafter the poetry collection *Solitude* was published. The poems, emotional and full of wonder, captured the angst of the nation, which at that point was no longer a world power. The title might also refer to traditional Andalusian songs.

About this time he met Miguel de Unamuno, Juan Ramón Jimenez, Pío Baroja, and other members of the *Generación del 98* (Generation of '98), and under their influence, became part of that important literary and philosophical movement. In 1907 he became a professor of French at the Soria Institute.

In 1909 he married Leonor and his life seemed to be tranquil. But Leonor died of tuberculosis three years later. Profoundly saddened by his loss, his philosophical outlook was reflected in the melancholic and sorrowful *Campos de Castilla* (*Fields of Castile*), a book published the same year. He took a new teaching position in the city of Baeza, Andulusia.

Seven years later Machado moved to Segovia where he met a woman known only as Guiomar, the subject of many of his subsequent poems. This relationship inspired him to write poems of a candidly erotic and romantic nature that were compiled and published in a book entitled *New Songs*.

From 1926 to 1932, in a fruitful collaboration with his brother Miguel, Machado wrote six plays that were extremely successful. The most famous was 1929's *La Lola se va a los Perros* (*Lola Went to the Dogs*). In 1927 Machado became a member of the Academia Española (Spanish Academy), and took a position in 1931 at the Instituto Calderón (Calderon Institute) in Madrid.

That was the same year the second Spanish Republic was proclaimed. Before moving to Madrid, Machado, then teaching in Segovia, north of Madrid, was one of three men who took over the city hall in the name of the republic. After three days in the city's interim government, Machado and the others turned it over to proper Republican authorities. Then he let it be known that he planned to stay as far away from the new regime as he had been from the old one. He wrote to friend, "I think I would form a party that can stay as far as possible from power."

It was not to be. When the Spanish civil war broke out in 1936, Machado, like most intellectuals, sided with the Republicans. His brother Antonio, however, sided with the Nationalists, creating a serious family rift. Machado, who had just published his most famous book of prose, *Juan de Mairena*, became something of a fugitive. He had to quickly move to Valencia and later to Barcelona, in the process becoming heavily involved with the publication of *Hora de España* (*The Hour of Spain*), a pro-democracy magazine. When the victory of Francisco Franco's Nationalists became apparent in late 1938 and early 1939, he departed for France in a self-imposed exile. Machado went to live at Collioure, a small town near the Spanish border, where he died and is buried.

Bibliography

Alonso Seoane, and María José. *Antonio Machado, Verso a Verso:Comentarios a la Poesía de Antonio Machado*. Seville: Publicaciones de la Universidad de Sevilla, Departamento de Literatura Española, 1975.

"Biografía de Antonio Machado." Biografías y Vidas. http://biografíasyvidas. com/biografía/m/machado.htm (January 2, 2005).

Caro, José Luis. *Antonio Machado*. Barcelona: Salvat, 1985.

Cobb, Carl W. *Antonio Machado*. New York: Twayne Publishers, 1971.

Gutiérrez Girardot, Rafael. *Machado, Reflexión y Poesía*. Bogotá: Tercer Mundo Editores, 1989.

López, Francisco, ed. *En Torno a Antonio Machado*. Madrid: Ediciones Júcar, 1989.

José Martí

For Love of the Motherland   Writer, Statesman

- ❖ Born in Havana, Cuba.
- ❖ Birth date: January 28, 1853.
- ❖ Death date: May 19, 1895.

Career Highlights

- Published his first political writings in 1869.

- Arrested by Spanish colonial troops for the first time in 1870.

- Published *Los Versos Sencillos* (*The Simple Verses*) in 1891.

- Wrote the *Manifest of Montecristi* explaining the reasons for Cuban self-rule.

- Became a major general in the Cuban Revolutionary Army in 1895.

Important Contributions

Martí was a poet, journalist, playwright, lawyer, orator, teacher, diplomat, and revolutionary. Like no other before or after, Martí was able to rally Cubans in favor of their independence. As a poet, his style greatly influenced the modernists.

Career Path

Cuba in the mid-nineteenth century was politically and socially speaking similar to the thirteen colonies of the mid-eighteenth century. It was a land governed by a European power determined to control the territory forever. It was also a place where the descendants of the European colonists were treated as second-class citizens in their own land. That was where José Julián Martí y Pérez, the *Apóstol de la Independecia de Cuba* (Apostle of Cuban Independence), was born. Martí was the son of Spanish parents, but he felt Cuban. From an early age he saw how the *peninsulares* (those born in the Iberian peninsula, that is, Spaniards) had greater opportunities and were treated better by the authorities than the *criollo* (those of Spanish ancestry but born in the New World, in this case Cuba). By the time he reached his early teens he embraced the concept of a Cuba governed by Cubans. In his opinion, the important element in being Cuban was being Cuban, without regard to race or wealth.

A bright young man, Martí took to writing at an early age and was a published journalist and author by the time he was sixteen years old. A letter reproaching a friend for joining the Spanish army earned Martí a jail sentence in Cuba, and in January 1871 he was deported in shackles to Spain. However, once in the city of Saragossa he was allowed to move freely. There he continued writing and studying. His work *La República Española ante la revolución cubana* (*The Spanish Republic in View of the Cuban Revolution*) was completed in 1873, and he received his law degree in 1874.

The next few years Martí traveled through France, England, México, Cuba (under an assumed name), and Guatemala, where in 1877 he was appointed to a chair at the national teacher's college. That same year he went back to México to marry Carmen Zayas Bazán, like him a Cuban. In 1878 he resigned his chair at the Guatemalan college, went back to Cuba, worked as a lawyer, celebrated the birth of his son José, and dedicated to him a book of poems, *Ismaelillo* (*Little Ishmael*).

Deported to Spain once again in 1879 for anti-Spanish activities, Martí escaped to France, and then to New York, where by 1880 he was working for the English-language daily *The Sun*. He also wrote in Spanish for many Latin American newspapers. His essays about life in the United States made him one of the most popular columnists of his time in the Spanish-speaking world.

He moved again, and in 1881 in Caracas, Venezuela, taught French and literature. But his writings made him unpopular with Venezuela's president, and Martí was forced to return to New York. By then a well-known poet and revolutionary, Martí was appointed consul of Uruguay in New York in 1887. In 1889 he published his children's magazine *La Edad de Oro* (*The Golden Years*). Two years later, Argentina and Paraguay also appointed him their consul in New York.

His most famous collection, *The Simple Verses*, was published in 1891, and Martí resigned his consular posts due to complaints from the Spanish consul. He had given a scorching anti-Spanish speech, and

Madrid's representative felt that Martí's diplomatic posts were incompatible with his political activism.

On March 14, 1892, he published the first issue of *Patria* (*Motherland*), the official periodical of the Cuban Revolutionary Party. The following month Martí was appointed party leader. In the spirit of other reformers who would follow him, Martí did not preach hate. He always felt that it was unfortunate that Cubans would have to fight Spaniards for independence. While repudiating the activities of the government in Madrid, he always proclaimed his love and admiration for the Spanish people and nation.

Martí was busy with a flurry of revolutionary activities over the next few years. He met with other Cuban autonomist leaders, including Máximo Gómez, a Dominican who would become military chief of the Cuban insurgents. Martí publicized the struggle for the island's independence, and, after meeting with Gómez in Montecristi, Dominican Republic, he wrote the *Manifest of Montecristi*.

On February 24, 1895, the Cuban War of Independence began. Martí wanted to join the fighting, and was goaded by criticism that he sent others to die for Cuba's independence but would not fight himself. Gómez and other leaders tried to talk him out of it, but on April 11, Martí landed in what was then Oriente, the eastern-most province of Cuba. Gómez appointed the poet and orator a mayor general. A little over a month later, he was mortally wounded in the Battle of *Dos Rios* (Two Rivers).

Martí is universally recognized and revered as a writer and a patriot. To Cubans of all races and political viewpoints, he is a symbol of independence, sacrifice, and love of country.

Bibliography

Ada, Alma Flor, and Campoy, F. Isabel. *Caminos*. Miami: Santillana USA Publishing, 2000.

Báez, Vicente, ed. *La Enciclopedia de Cuba*. San Juan and Madrid: Enciclopedia y Clásicos Cubanos, Inc., 1973.

Guerra, Lillian. *The Myth of José Martí: Conflicting Nationalisms in Early Twentieth-Century Cuba*. Chapel Hill, NC: University of North Carolina Press, 2005.

Mañach, Jorge. *Martí: El Apóstol*. Madrid: Espasa-Calpe SA, 1975.

Montero, Oscar. *José Martí: An Introduction*. New York: Palgrave Macmillan, 2004.

Ripoll, Carlos. *Cuba en la Poesía de Martí*. New York: Editorial Dos Rios, 2005.

Varona, Frank de, ed. *Hispanic Presence in the United States*. Miami: Mnemosyne Publishing Company, 1993.

José Martínez Ruíz (Azorín)

The Unimportant Philosopher   Writer

- ❖ Born in Monóvar, Spain.
- ❖ Birth date: July 8, 1873.
- ❖ Death date: March 2, 1967.

Career Highlights

- Elected to Spain's House of Deputies in 1906 and 1919.
- Appointed to the Royal Academy of the Spanish Language in 1924.
- Awarded the *Gran Cruz de Isabel la Católica* (Great Cross of Isabella the Catholic) in 1946.
- Honored with the *Gran Cruz de Alfonso X, el Sabio* (Great Cross of Alfonse X, the Wise) in 1956.

Important Contributions

Azorín is one of the most controversial figures to come out of what is called the *Generación del 98* (Generation of '98, a group of Spanish intellectuals who struggled against the angst and corruption the lost empire left in Spain). His political views were, and in many cases still are, hotly debated. His precise, serious, terse style is also a matter of continued disagreement. Admirers defend him for presenting his thoughts in a straight, clear manner, but his opponents believe it was just lack of creativity. The deliberations continue to this day.

Career Path

Azorín gave the Generation of 98 its name. José Martínez Ruíz, who wrote under the pseudonym Azorín, was also the leading Spanish literary critic of his day. Azorín led a calm, methodic life, and except for some minor incursions into politics, was first and foremost a writer.

165

José Augusto Trinidad Martínez Ruíz was born in a town of Alicante province, in southeastern Spain. He attended primary school in his hometown and secondary school at Yecla, in Murcia, a territory near Alicante. In 1888 Azorín enrolled at the University of Valencia to study law. He transferred to the University of Madrid but never finished his studies. During his university years he frequented literary hangouts and was saturated with all the latest liberal ideas circulating around Spain at the time. He also wrote a series of political documents under various pen names, and by 1896 was on the staff of *El País* (*The Nation*). At the newspaper his independent thinking and anarchist outlook got him in trouble, and he was asked to resign.

A quiet, soft-spoken man, Azorín did not reach his literary maturity until the publication of his first great trilogy in which, through the main character, he analyzes his own disappointment with Spanish society. The title of his second novel, published in 1903, was *Antonio Azorín*. As a writer, he took the name of the main character and from then on would never use his own or any other pen name. The third part of the trilogy, 1904's *Confesiones de un Pequeño Filósofo* (*Confessions of an Unimportant Philosopher*), is one of his most popular works and is still widely read. The work is highly autobiographical.

Over time, Azorín, who began as an anarchist, moderated his views and was elected to the House of Deputies on two occasions. He even served as undersecretary of public education in 1917 and 1919.

Never one to travel much outside his homeland, Azorín did visit France during World War I and actually lived in Paris, probably to escape the violence of the Spanish civil war. During the late 1920s Azorín dedicated most of his writing efforts to drama, and in 1927 published two of his best works, *Lo Invisible* (*That Which is Invisible*) and *Brandy, Mucho Brandy* (*Brandy, Lots of Brandy*). However, an important part of Azorín's body of work is found in the many articles and critical essays he wrote for newspapers, magazines, and other publications all over the Spanish-speaking world. In his later years he wrote for such stalwart Spanish dailies as *El Imparcial* (*Impartial*) and *ABC*. He also wrote for Latin American newspapers such as Argentina's *La Prensa* (*Printing Press*) and Cuba's *Diario de la Marina* (*Navy Daily*).

Among his later works, which include novels, literary essays, and his memoirs, his 1942 novel *El Escritor* (*The Author*) and 1943's *Obras selectas y biblbiografía* (*Selected Works and Bibliography*) are of particular importance.

Azorín died in his Madrid home on March 2, 1967.

❖   ❖   ❖

Bibliography

Aguirre Bellver. *Azorín, Cronista de Cortés*. Alicante: Instituto de Cultura Juan Gil-Alberti, 1998.

Diez Mediavilla, Antonio. *Azorín: Fines de Siglos (1898–1998)*. Alicante: Instituto de Cultura Juan Gil-Alberti, Editorial Aguaclara, 1998.

Fernández Pombo, Alejandro. *Maestro Azorín*. Madrid: Doncel, 1973.

García Mercadal. *Azorín: Biografía Ilustrada*. Barcelona: Ediciones Destino, 1967.

Livingstone, Leon. *Tema y Forma en la Novela de Azorín*. Madrid: Editorial Gredos, 1970.

Piñera, Humberto. *Novela y Ensayo de Azorín*. Madrid: Agesa, 1971.

César Milstein

Biochemist

- ❖ Born in Bahía Blanca, Argentina.
- ❖ Birth date: October 8, 1927.
- ❖ Death date: March 24, 2002.

Career Highlights

- Obtained PhD in chemistry from the University of Buenos Aires in 1957.

- Appointed to biochemistry research staff at Cambridge University in 1960.

- Received the 1980 Adolph Rosenberg Award from the University of Miami.

- Awarded the Nobel Prize in Physiology or Medicine in 1984.

- Received 1984 John Scott Award from the Board of Directors of City Trusts in Philadelphia.

Important Contributions

The discovery of monoclonal antibodies that Milstein shares with the German Georges Köhler has remarkable applications for the diagnosis of illnesses, oncological treatments, and the production of vaccines.

Career Path

César Milstein's research on the human immune system propelled him to international fame and a share of the Nobel Prize in Physiology or Medicine in 1984.

Milstein was born to a modest Jewish immigrant family who worked hard and made sacrifices to ensure that César and his two brothers would get college educations. After attending local schools in his hometown, Cesar studied at the University of Buenos Aires. He graduated in 1949 and married Celia Prilleltensky, a fellow student. They spent their year-long honeymoon hitchhiking through Europe and even working in an Israeli kibbutz for two months.

Back in Buenos Aires, Milstein began his studies for a doctorate in chemistry and received his degree four years later. These were lean years, with he and Celia working and attending classes. Shortly after obtaining his PhD, he went to work for one of the best microbiological research laboratories in Argentina. Milstein had just begun his work when he received a fellowship offer from Great Britain's world-famous Cambridge University. After four years in Britain, he returned to Argentina and became director of the Department of Molecular Biology at the Malbran Institute, one of the most important research laboratories in his country. In 1962 the military took over the government and for political and economic reasons, the research was stopped. This was fortuitous, however. He left for Cambridge again in 1963, and with his colleague, Georges Köhler, obtained the first encouraging results in their investigations into human immunology.

By the early 1970s, Milstein and Köhler had a working hypothesis on how to produce antibodies. They worked hard from 1973 to 1976, when they succeeded in developing procedures to produce monoclonal antibodies. These are antibodies with a particular attraction to specific body areas; they can effectively treat diseases by attacking sick cells and leaving healthy ones alone. The findings caused a revolution in the treatment of many illnesses and in procedures governing organ transplants. Both men were honored the world over.

In 1983, Milstein, who by then had become a British subject, was appointed head of the Protein and Nucleic Acid Chemistry Division at Cambridge University. The next year he and Köhler shared the Nobel Prize for Physiology and Medicine. Milstein spent most of the next decade and a half doing research, what he did best. He traveled frequently to his home country but continued to reside in Britain. He died in Cambridge on March 24, 2002.

Francisco de Miranda

Three Revolutions Hero

Soldier,
Statesman

❖ Born in Caracas, Venezuela.
❖ Birth date: March 28, 1750.
❖ Death date: July 14, 1816.

Career Highlights

- Appointed as Spanish liaison to Continental army staff in 1781.
- Joined the French Revolution in 1792.
- Escaped the guillotine in 1795.
- Attempted to free Venezuela in 1806.

Important Contributions

Francisco de Miranda is the predecessor of the celebrated patriots who liberated South America from Spanish rule. He started the struggle for independence, and the rest followed. Miranda also helped the American colonies gain their independence from England and took part in the French Revolution.

Career Path

Francisco de Miranda might be the only man who was a hero of the American Revolution, the French Revolution, and the independence of his own country, Venezuela.

Born to a wealthy Spanish father and a Venezuelan mother, Miranda attended schools that were part of the city's university system.

By 1764 discord between Spaniards and *criollos* (those of Spanish heritage born in the New World) was obvious, but Miranda remained a loyal Spanish subject. On January 21, 1771, Miranda sailed to Spain, and less than a year later was an infantry captain in the Spanish army fighting in North Africa against the forces of the Sultan of Morocco. When Juan Manuel de Cagigal, captain general (governor) of Cuba and Venezuela, prepared his 1781 expedition to attack the British stronghold of Pensacola, Florida, Miranda joined as a regimental captain. Miranda distinguished himself in the capture of the city and Cagigal attached him to George Washington's staff. It was about this time that Miranda first thought of the emancipation of the South American territories.

His main contribution to American independence came during the Battle of Yorktown, Virginia, in late September 1781. The American revolutionaries and the French troops attacking the city were running out of money for supplies and were close to withdrawal. Miranda made a passionate plea to the Spanish colonial government and the people of Cuba. Such was his eloquence that, not only did he receive funds from the island's governor, the *criollo* ladies pawned their jewelry and fancy silk dresses to buy supplies for the troops.

During the next few years, Miranda continued fighting for the Spanish crown and also traveled. He met Russian empress Catherine the Great at Kiev in 1787 and quickly became one of her favorites. Court intrigues forced him to leave for England, where he unsuccessfully tried to convince Prime Minister William Pitt to help liberate the New World's Spanish colonies. Frustrated, Miranda went to Paris right in the middle of the French Revolution. He was soon caught up in the action and within four months was appointed a field marshal of the revolutionary forces. At first he won several battles, but later suffered a few losses. Political enemies, mostly the Jacobins (one of the most radical groups during the French Revolution), accused him of treason. Miranda was tried, but his own masterful defense at court spared him the guillotine and secured his freedom.

Failing again to get assistance from England, Miranda, with the probable support of Thomas Jefferson, decided to liberate his homeland on his own. On August 3, 1806, he landed in Venezuela, and after taking the small fort of La Vela de Coro, went to the nearby city of Coro, but lack of local support forced him to flee. Not ready to give up, and after gaining support from other independent-minded leaders, Miranda landed at La Guaira with a larger force, on December 10, 1810. Three weeks later he was appointed lieutenant general of the Venezuelan army and beat the Spaniards on the field. On July 5, 1811, he declared Venezuela's independence from Spain. But a devastating earthquake, Miranda's iron-fisted rule, and Simón Bolívar's defeat at Puerto Cabello were too much for the young republic. Miranda negotiated with the Spaniards and on July 25, 1812, Venezuela became a colony once again. As Miranda tried to leave on July 31, he was arrested and charged with treason by a faction of loyalists, Bolívar among them. He was turned over to the royalists and dispatched to Spain. After three years of captivity, Miranda died in prison in San Fernando, Spain on July 14, 1816.

Bibliography

Díaz-Trechuelo Sínola, María Lourdes. *Bolívar, Miranda, O'Higgins, San Martín: cuatro vidas cruzadas.* Madrid: Ediciones Encuentro, 1999.

Egea López, Antonio. *El Pensamiento Filosófico y Político de Francisco de Miranda.* Caracas: Academia Nacional de la Historia, 1983.

Henríquez Uzcátegui, Gloria. *Los Papeles de Francisco de Miranda.* Caracas: Academia Nacional de la Historia, 1984.

León Berruezo, María Teresa. *La Lucha de Hispanoamérica por su Independencia en Inglaterra.* Madrid: Ediciones de Cultura Hispánica, 1989.

Lucena Giraldo, Manuel. *Francisco de Miranda el Precursor de la Independencia de Venezuela.* Madrid: Anaya, 1988.

Rodríguez de Alonso, Josefina. *Miranda y sus Circunstancias.* Caracas: Academia Nacional de la Historia, 1982.

Gabriela Mistral

Sorrowful Poet   Poet

❖ Born in Vicuña, Chile.
❖ Birth date: April 7, 1889.
❖ Death date: January 10, 1957.

Career Highlights

- Received the Nobel Prize in Literature in 1945.

- Awarded honorary degrees from the University of Guatemala and the University of Florence, Italy.

- Appointed to the United Nations Subcommittee on the Status of Women in 1946.

- Awarded Chile's National Prize for Literature in 1951.

Important Contributions

The hardships Mistral faced throughout her life—poverty, the suicides of a lover and a nephew, the death of various friends, as well as her own health problems—enabled her to produce a body of work full of kindness, tenderness, and compassion for others, especially children. As an educator she helped shape the educational systems of her native Chile and México.

Career Path

Lucila Godoy Alcayaga was the first Hispanic American to receive the Nobel Prize in Literature. She was known the world over by her pen name Gabriela Mistral. The poignant tone of her poetry was the result of the many sorrows—poverty, lost love, lack of children—she suffered throughout her life. Poverty kept her out of school until she was nine years old. Even at that early age, she had to work odd jobs to afford school supplies. Mistral was a good student, eventually becoming a teacher. She was also involved in many social causes.

When she was eighteen and teaching at the small town of La Cantera, Mistral had a passionate romance with a railroad worker. He committed suicide after his involvement in a fraud was discovered. Her pain at the loss fired her creativity.

Mistral was something of a paradox. She was a devoted Roman Catholic but condemned the Catholic Church's lack of concern for the political repression in Latin America. She was an admirer of the United States, but she vocally criticized Washington's policies toward its neighbors to the south.

In 1914 she published *Sonetos de la Muerte* (*Death Sonnets*), which won her a prize in the national literary contest *Juegos Florales* (Flower Games). Her pen name, which she made up from two of her favorite poets, Italian author Gabriele D'Annunzio and French Nobel laureate Frédéric Mistral, became well known throughout the Spanish-speaking world. *Death Sonnets*, like most of her work, is about loneliness, emptiness, and the memory of the dead.

She continued to teach while her writing career flourished. Her celebrated collection of poems *Desolación* (*Despair*) was published in 1922, and in 1924 *Ternura* (*Tenderness*), poems about nurturing children, compassion, and a longing for motherhood, appeared. *Tara*, another collection of poems about frustrated maternity and the love of children, was published in 1938. She received the Nobel Prize in Literature in 1945. The poor, sad Chilean schoolteacher had made a name for herself all over the world. When she returned home, more than 45,000 children packed a stadium in Chile to welcome her.

Mistral died of cancer in Hempstead, New York, on January 10, 1957. She had been influential in the educational systems of her native Chile and México, taught Spanish at Columbia University and Vassar College, and served as Chilean consul in Madrid, Lisbon, and Naples. She has been honored in Panama, Cuba, Spain, the United States, and many other nations. She is still beloved by all who read her work.

❖　❖　❖

Bibliography

Ada, Alma Flor, and Campoy, F. Isabel *Sonrisas*. Miami: Santillana USA Publishing, 2000.

Agosín, Marjorie, ed. *Gabriela Mistral: The Audacious Traveler*. Athens, OH: Ohio University Press, 2003.

Arrigoitia, Luis de. *Pensamiento y Forma en la Prosa de Gabriela Mistral*. Rio Piedras, PR: Editorial de la Universidad de Puerto Rico, 1989.

Concha, Jaime. *Gabriela Mistral*. Madrid: Júcar, 1987.

Flores, Angel. *Spanish American Authors: The Twentieth Century*. New York: H.W. Wilson, 1992.

Zemboraín, Lila. *Gabriela Mistral: Una Mujer sin Rostro*. Rosario, Argentina: B. Viterbo Editora, 2002.

Bartolomé Mitre

Doing it All for Argentina

Statesman,
Soldier,
Journalist

- ❖ Born in Buenos Aires, Argentina.
- ❖ Birth date: June 26, 1821.
- ❖ Death date: January 19, 1906.

Career Highlights

- Established the *Instituto Histórico y Geográfico del Uruguay* (Uruguay's Historic and Geographic Institute) in 1844.

- Fought against dictator Juan Manuel Rosas in 1852.

- Appointed commander of the Buenos Aires National Guard in 1852.

- Elected first president of a united Argentina in 1862.

- Founded the daily *La Nación* (*The Nation*) in 1870.

Important Contributions

Mitre influenced the cultural and political development of Argentina. He was the driving force behind the creation of an Argentinian national identity out of the warring provinces surrounding the La Plata River estuary.

Career Path

As a journalist, Bartolomé Mitre founded a newspaper. As a soldier and statesman, he helped create a nation. Both have survived for more than a century.

When Mitre was born, Buenos Aires was just one of the quarreling provinces left after Argentina won its independence from Spain five years earlier. His father, Ambrosio, was Mitre's main educator during his early life. When Mitre was four years old, the family moved to Montevideo, Uruguay, where he would eventually enroll in business school. He returned to Buenos Aires in 1836 as an employee of the family estate of Juan Manuel de Rosas, the famous *caudillo* (military leader) and future dictator. They did not get along. Later the same year Mitre returned to Montevideo to attend a military academy. In less than a year, he left with the rank of second lieutenant. In 1937 he enrolled in journalism school and published his first anthology of poems, *Décimas, Glosa, y Epigrama* (*Stanzas, Gloss, and Epigram*).

From 1837 to 1839, Mitre wrote for various newspapers and polished his knowledge of English, French, and German, languages he would find useful in his political career. Between 1840 and 1843 he participated in many domestic battles between the interior provinces and Buenos Aires, and rapidly rose to the rank of lieutenant colonel. Discontented with the fratricidal war, Mitre moved back to Montevideo where he founded Uruguay's Historic and Geographic Institute and published *La Montonera y la Guerra Regular* (*The Guerilla and Regular War*).

From 1848 to 1851 Mitre traveled to Brazil, Chile, and Bolivia, where he founded a military school. While in Chile, he bought the famous daily *El Comercio* (*Commerce*) and was its publisher until political unrest forced him to move to Perú.

Back in his country, he joined other Argentinian leaders in the fight against Rosas and participated in many battles. More internal struggles forced him to leave the country again, but later the same year, Buenos Aires broke away from the other provinces and he returned home as commander of the city's national guard. A fierce defender of provinces' rights, like states' rights in the United States, Mitre was opposed to a loose confederation. As a political pragmatist, he recognized that bringing all the territories in the region under one government was the only way to mold a nation.

Now an important military and political figure, he was rapidly promoted to foreign and government minister. He became commander in chief of the forces of Buenos Aires and was wounded defending the city in June 1853. Even though he suffered some military defeats, Mitre was elected governor of Buenos Aires in 1860. He then acted as head of the national government, and two years later was elected president of Argentina. Mitre served as president for six years. During his term he improved finances and public administration, created the Supreme Court, established commercial and penal codes, and led the Triple Alliance, with Brazil and Uruguay, against Paraguayan dictator Francisco Solano López.

After leaving office, Mitre established *The Nation* and served as ambassador to Brazil and Paraguay. Because of political turmoil he was imprisoned and then went into exile. Between 1887 and 1890 he wrote one of his seminal works, *La Historia de San Martín y de la Emancipación Sudamericana* (*The History of San Martin and South American Emancipation*). There was an attempt to elect him president again when he returned home from Europe in 1891, but Mitre refused to participate.

After a long illness, Mitre died in his Buenos Aires home on January 19, 1906. So many mourners attended his funeral that it remains one of the largest popular expressions of sorrow the city has ever seen.

Bibliography

Katra, William H., trans. María Teresa La Valle. *La Generación de 1837. Los Hombres que Hicieron el País*. Buenos Aires: Emecé, 2000.

Marco, Miguel Angel de. *Bartolomé Mitre*. Buenos Aires: Emecé, 2004.

Pasquali, Patricia. *La Instauración Liberal: Urquiza, Mitre y un Estadista Olvidado, Nicasio Oroño*. Buenos Aires: Planeta, 2003.

Robinson, John L. *Bartolomé Mitre, Historian of the Americas*. Washington, DC: University Press of America, 1982.

Vázquez, Germán, and Martínez Díaz, Nelson. *Historia de América Latina*. Madrid: Ediproyectos, SA, 1990.

Mario J. Molina

A Hole in the Air   Research Chemist

- ❖ Born in México City, México.
- ❖ Birth date: March 19, 1943.

Career Highlights

- Received his PhD in chemistry from the University of California, Berkeley, in 1972.
- Appointed to Jet Propulsion Laboratory in 1982.
- Began teaching at MIT in 1989.
- Awarded the Nobel Prize in Chemistry in 1995.

Important Contributions

Molina's research on the impact of chlorofluorocarbons in the atmosphere led to the 1987 worldwide ban on the use of Freon.

Career Path

In addition to being professor of Earth, Atmospheric, and Planetary Sciences at the Massachusetts Institute of Technology (MIT), Mario Molina won the Nobel Prize in Chemistry in 1995.

Molina was born into a well-respected family. His father, Roberto, was a lawyer, college professor, and ambassador. From a very early age, Molina knew he wanted to be a chemist. His interest in the science was aroused by a toy chemistry set he got as a child. The young scientist converted a seldom-used bathroom into his laboratory and spent hours playing with his set. An aunt, Esther Molina, who was a chemist, encouraged and tutored him, and became the most influential person in his career. She helped him conduct experiments that were beyond his ability.

Once he finished his early education in his hometown of México City, his father, presuming that a future chemist needed to learn German, and observing a family custom of studying overseas, sent Molina to study in Switzerland. By then, Molina had decided to become a research chemist.

In 1960 he enrolled at the *Universidad Nacional Autónoma de México* (the National Autonomous University of México) to study chemical engineering. Realizing he had an incomplete knowledge of mathematics and physics to get a PhD in physical chemistry, Molina registered at the University of Freiburg in Germany. He studied there for two years and then moved to Paris, where he studied mathematics on his own. When he returned to México he taught at the National University and in 1968 was accepted in graduate school at the University of California at Berkeley. During his first year at Berkeley, Molina took the required courses in physical chemistry, extra classes in mathematics and physics, joined a research group experimenting with chemical lasers and molecular dynamics, and met Luisa Tan, who would later become his wife and research partner.

He married Luisa in July 1973, the year after he received his doctorate from Berkeley, and moved to Irvine, California, to join a group investigating atoms formed by radioactivity. It was about this time he became interested in the accumulation of chlorofluorocarbon gasses (CFCs) in the earth's atmosphere, which at the time was believed to cause no harm. Through this research, Molina, joined by F. Sherwood Rowland, the research group leader, discovered that when CFCs rose high enough, sunlight turned them into chlorine. If left unchecked, the chlorine would eventually destroy the ozone layer that protects the earth from the sun's harmful ultraviolet rays. They made their findings public in the June 28, 1974, issue of the professional publication *Nature*. To this day, many people criticize their work. However, in 1985, just as Molina had predicted, a hole was found in the ozone layer over Antarctica.

Molina taught at the University of California, Irvine, and later worked at the Jet Propulsion Laboratory in Pasadena. From Pasadena, Molina went to MIT, where he was appointed to the faculty. He continued to investigate the impact on climate caused by the relationship between the atmosphere and the biosphere.

Molina and Rowland shared two-thirds of the Nobel Prize in Chemistry. Molina donated $200,000 of his $333,333 prize to aid developing nations' environmental researchers doing their work at MIT, where he still teaches.

Bibliography

Chuang, Shang-Lin. "Mario Molina Wins Nobel Prize in Chemistry." The Tech. http://www-tech.mit.edu/V115/N48/nobel.48n.html. (February 10, 2005).

Howe, Peter J. "Chemist Donates Nobel Winnings. Part of Prize to Fund Ecology Work at MIT." *Boston Globe* Online. http://www.boston.com/globe/search/stories/nobel/1996/1996d.html. (February 10, 2005).

Kurian, George Thomas. *The Nobel Scientists: A Biographical Encyclopedia.* Amherst, NY: Prometheus Books, 2002.

Sherby, Louise S., ed. *The Who's Who of Nobel Prize Winners 1901–2000.* Westport, CT: Oryx Press, 2002.

Ricardo Montalbán

Not Just a Latin Lover   Actor

❖ Born in México City, México.
❖ Birth date: November 25, 1920.

Career Highlights

- Founded *Nosostros* (Us) in 1973 to promote better roles and image for Hispanics in films.
- Won an Emmy Award for Best Supporting Actor in a Comedy or Drama Series in 1977.
- Received Screen Actors Guild Lifetime Achievement Award in 1993.
- Awarded the title of Knight Commander of Saint Gregory the Great by the Vatican in 1998.

Important Contributions

From early in his acting career Ricardo Montalbán was an outspoken critic of the way Hollywood portrayed Hispanics, so much so that in 1973 he founded the organization *Nosotros* (Us) to promote better roles and image for Hispanics in films.

Career Path

Known to today's audiences as the grandfather in the Spy Kids movies, the enigmatic Mr. Roarke of television's *Fantasy Island*, or even the villainous Khan of *Star Trek II: The Wrath of Khan*, Ricardo Gonzalo Pedro Montalbán y Merino has a long history in Hollywood, and not just as an actor. Almost from his very first day, Montalbán was an outspoken critic of the way Hollywood portrayed Hispanics.

Montalbán had a five-year career in his native México before coming to the United States in the early 1940s. His talents were obscured by his career at Metro-Goldwyn-Mayer, where he played Latin-lover types opposite the likes of Cyd Charisse and Esther Williams. One of the songs he performed with Williams, "Baby It's Cold Outside" has become one of the better known American standards. He won rave reviews for his role in *Battleground*, a 1949 World War II film by director William Wellman in which a unit of paratroopers is trapped in the city of Bastogne, Belgium, during the Battle of the Bulge.

But he couldn't shake the Latin-lover stereotype, so in the 1950s Montalbán sought other roles. Again he won accolades for his role as a snooty Japanese actor in 1957's *Sayonara*. In other movies and television shows he played people of different ethnic backgrounds and won an Emmy for playing a Sioux chief in the television miniseries *How the West Was Won*. He was one of the first bilingual actors to do commericals, pushing Bulova watches in Spanish and the Chrysler Cordoba automobile in English.

In the 1970s he founded *Nosotros* (Us). In numerous interviews, Montalbán was critical of the way the English-speaking media portrayed Hispanics. His outspokenness never gained him sympathy with the media establishment, but he was always grateful for television, which gave him the chance to move away from Latin stereotypes. The 1970s and 1980s saw him as the mystifying Mr. Roarke, the owner of Fantasy Island, and also as a nasty piece of work, Khan in *Star Trek II: The Wrath of Khan*, the 1982 movie in which he kills Mr. Spock. Montalbán had originally portrayed the character in a 1967 episode of the legendary television series.

In 1998 Pope John Paul II awarded Montalbán the highest charitable honor the Catholic Church bestows, that of Knight Commander of Saint Gregory the Great. In his 2002 comeback as Grandpa Cortex in *Spy Kids 2: The Island of Lost Dreams*, Montalbán demonstrated that he had lost none of the geniality, allure, and talent that made him a star to begin with.

Bibliography

Cierco, Salvador Clotas, et al, eds. *Enciclopedia Ilustrada del Cine*. Barcelona: Editorial Labor S.A., 1970.

Montalbán, Ricardo. *Reflections: A Life in Two Worlds*. Garden City, NY: Doubleday, 1980.

Reyes, Luís, and Rubie, Peter. *Los Hispanos en Hollywood*. New York: Random House Español, 2002.

Rodríguez, Clara E. *Heroes, Lovers, and Others: The Story of Latinos in Hollywood*. Washington, DC: Smithsonian Books, 2004.

Mario Moreno (Cantinflas)

Raggedy Man   Actor

- ❖ Born in México City, México.
- ❖ Birth date: August 12, 1911.
- ❖ Death date: April 20, 1993.

Career Highlights

- First starring role in *Hay Está el Detalle* (*That's Where the Detail Is*) in 1940.
- Filmed his first American movie in 1955.
- Won Golden Globe for Best Actor in a Musical or Comedy in 1956.
- Latin American countries granted him honorary membership in professions he played in his movies.

Important Contributions

Cantinflas made generations of Spanish speakers laugh. He was a social critic and a philanthropist. He was the most beloved comedian in Mexican movies.

Career Path

Except for a brief span between 1956 and 1960, American audiences never encountered Mario Moreno (Cantinflas); however, he was one of the best-known and most recognizable movie stars in the Spanish-speaking world. His movies were full of humor and tenderness but were not among the best produced. The scripts were usually weak and the productions unimpressive, but Moreno's natural comic ability, human warmth, and ad-lib capabilities always saved the day.

Moreno was born in a poor neighborhood in México City, México. Not much is known of his early education but it is widely assumed that he went to public schools. His father, a mail carrier, wanted his son to be a medical doctor and somehow managed to get him into the *Universidad Nacional Autónoma de México* (the National Autonomous University of México). But he was a poor student, preferring to spend time doing imitations and dancing. School did not last long and afterward Moreno worked as a professional dancer, boxer, and circus clown. He had small parts in radio shows, theatrical productions, and even a few early films.

In the late 1920s the character of Cantinflas, a poor, goodhearted, dowdy, nonsense-talker, took form. It is said that the character's fractured manner of speaking evolved when Moreno was forced to calm a rowdy crowd during a performance gone awry. He was so panic stricken that he did not make much sense. The audience thought he was funny, and that became Cantinflas' trademark. Later on he would add a ragged, long-sleeved T-shirt and drooping pants tied around his hips with a piece of fabric. This became his uniform.

In 1934 Moreno met and married Valentina Subarev, an actress of Russian ancestry who would have his only son, Mario Arturo.

Moreno first played the character Cantinflas in the movie *No Te Engañes Corazón* (*Don't be Fooled My Heart*) in 1936, but did not star in a picture until four years later. The great Charlie Chaplin was an early fan and wanted to bring Cantinflas to the United States. But he would not go north until he had made some twenty films in his homeland and had become a household name in the Spanish-speaking world. In 1955 producer Michael Todd got Cantinflas to play Passepartout, the cool-as-a-cucumber butler, in *Around the World in 80 Days*, the biggest, most expensive movie of its time. More than forty famous Hollywood stars had cameo roles in the film, and even though David Niven headed the cast as Phileas Fogg, Cantinflas was the star. The Mexican actor won a Golden Globe for his performance. The film went on to win five Academy Awards, including best picture. Cantinflas would not be seen again in an English-speaking role until 1960, when he made *Pepe* for director George Sidney. The film flopped and Cantinflas stuck to Spanish language movies after that.

Cantinflas was not only a comedian. In some of his later films such as *El Analfabeto* (*Illiterate*) in 1960, *El Señor Doctor* (*Mister Doctor*) in 1965, and *Su Excelencia* (*Your Excellency*) in 1966, he mixed stinging social and political commentaries into his material. Cantinflas was also a philanthropist. To this day, the various charitable foundations he established continue to provide relief for the needy in his native México and many other Latin American nations. He was honored the world over. His characterization of an illiterate who wants to learn won him honorary teacher awards from the Mexican and Venezuelan governments. Colombia and Guatemala made him an honorary policeman for his portrayal of officers in *El Gendarme Desconocido* (*The Unknown Gendarme*) in 1941 and *El Patrullero 777* (*Patrolman 777*) in 1977. Cantinflas addressed the General Assembly of the United Nations and Michigan University granted Cantinflas a *doctor honoris causa*.

Shattered by family problems and lung cancer, Cantinflas lived the last years of his life at his ranch, where he died at eighty-one. Today the name of Cantinflas and the various adjectives derived from it have been officially accepted as part of the Spanish vernacular by the Royal Academy of the Spanish Language.

Bibliography

Elizalde y Gallegos, Guadalupe. *Mario Moreno y Cantinflas...Rompen el Silencio*. México City: Fundación Mario Moreno Reyes, 1994.

Hershfield, Joanne, and Maciel, David R., eds. *Mexico's Cinema: A Century of Film and Filmmakers*. Wilmington, DE: Scholarly Resources, Inc., 1999.

Pilcher, Jeffrey M. *Cantinflas and the Chaos of Mexican Modernity*. Wilmington, DE: Scholarly Resources, Inc., 2001.

Reyes, Luís, and Rubie, Peter. *Los Hispanos en Hollywood*. New York: Random House Español, 2002.

Stavans, Ilan. *The Riddle of Cantinflas*. Albuquerque, NM: University of New México Press, 1998.

Rita Moreno

"I Like to be in America"   Actress

❖ Born in Humacao, Puerto Rico.
❖ Birth date: December 11, 1931.

Career Highlights

- Won Academy Award and Golden Globe for Best Supporting Actress in 1962.
- Won Grammy in 1972.
- Awarded Tony in 1975.
- Won two Emmys.

Important Contributions

Rita Moreno was and is a valuable pioneer in the struggle of Spanish actors against typecasting. She once said "I'm a star, I can do anything." And she has, blazing new trails in the entertainment industry for Hispanic actors.

Career Path

Rita Moreno is the only woman alive who has won an Oscar, an Emmy, a Grammy, and a Tony. If not for her talent and a steel will that would not let her quit, she might never have made it.

When she was five Rosa Dolores Alverío and her mother moved to New York, where her mother worked as a seamstress for very low wages. Even then, Rosa showed a talent for entertaining at family gatherings. The next year, young Rosa began dancing classes under Paco Cansino, an uncle of Rita Hayworth, and soon she was performing in shows at Macy's department store. Rosa took the stage name of Rita Moreno, and in 1944 made her Broadway debut in *Skydrift*. Four years later, when she was only seventeen, Metro-Goldwyn-Mayer gave her a contract.

Like many Hispanic actresses of the time, Moreno was typecast, playing Mexican shrews and Indian squaws in movies such as *Seven Cities of Gold, Jivaro*, and *The Yellow Tomahawk*. She complained at the time that she had always wanted to do Shakespeare and Chekhov, but was stuck playing only ragged, shoeless characters.

A brief flash of recognition came in 1952 when she danced opposite Gene Kelly in the classic *Singing in the Rain*. Another came in 1956 when she played Tuptim in *The King and I*. She would have to wait five more years to become a star. Her portrayal of Anita in *West Side Story* won her the both an Oscar and a Golden Globe for Best Supporting Actress. On Broadway Rita Moreno starred in such plays as *The Last of the Red Hot Lovers, Wally's Café*, and *Sunset Boulevard*. She won a Best Supporting Actress Tony in 1975 for her characterization of Googie Gómez in *The Ritz*.

In the 1970s Moreno was in such movies as *Popi* and *Carnal Knowledge*. She won a Grammy for *The Electric Company Album* (1972), and two Emmys for *The Muppet Show* (1977) and *The Rockford Files* (1978), which led to a television career in the 1980s. She returned to feature films in the 1990s, appearing in *The Slums of Beverly Hills* in 1998. Rita Moreno is still active in the theater, films, and television, as well as with many charitable causes.

Bibliography

Ada, Alma Flor, and Campoy, F. Isabel. *Pasos*. Miami: Santillana USA Publishing, 2000.

Cierco, Salvador Clotas, et al, eds. *Enciclopedia Ilustrada del Cine*. Barcelona: Editorial Labor S.A., 1970.

Reyes, Luís, and Rubie, Peter. *Los Hispanos en Hollywood*. New York: Random House Español, 2002.

Rodríguez, Clara E. *Heroes, Lovers, and Others: The Story of Latinos in Hollywood*. Washington, DC: Smithsonian Books, 2004.

Telgen, Diane, and Kamp, Jim, eds. *Latinas! Women of Achievement*. Detroit: Visible Ink Press, 1996.

Luís Muñoz Marín

There Can be Only One   Statesman

❖ Born in San Juan, Puerto Rico.
❖ Birth date: February 18, 1898.
❖ Death date: April 30, 1980.

Career Highlights

- Elected to the Puerto Rican Senate in 1932.

- Founded the *Partido Popular Democrático* (Popular Democratic Party) in 1938.

- Became first democratically elected governor of Puerto Rico in 1948.

- Presided over the writing of the Puerto Rican Constitution ratified in 1952.

- Presented the Presidential Medal of Freedom in 1963.

Important Contributions

In his sixteen years as governor of Puerto Rico, Muñoz Marín took the economy of his home island to unprecedented heights, expanded the industrial base, secularized the government, modernized agriculture, and gave his people a brighter future.

Career Path

Like his father before him, Luís Muñoz Marín was a journalist, poet, politician, and one of the most influential men in the modern history of Puerto Rico. Unlike his father, Luís Muñoz Rivera, the driving force for autonomy and a well known journalist, he became the first democratically elected governor in the history of the island.

190

José Luís Alberto Muñoz Marín was born just two months before the beginning of the Spanish-American War, which transferred Puerto Rico from Spanish rule to that of the United States. In his early years, José's family traveled regularly between Puerto Rico and New York, and when he turned thirteen years old, Muñoz Marín was enrolled at Washington, D.C.'s Georgetown Preparatory School. Afterward, he attended Georgetown University for a year, having to abandon his studies due to his father's death. By then he was more at ease with the English language and the American way of life than with Spanish and the traditions of his native island, but because of his father, he easily took to Puerto Rican politics.

Muñoz Marín began his political career in 1920 when, because of his advocacy of Puerto Rican independence and proletariat sympathies, he joined the *Partido Socialista Puertorriqueño* (Puerto Rican Socialist Party). However, a dozen years later, Muñoz Marín moved to the *Partido Liberal* (Liberal Party), took over the editorship of the party's newspaper, and was elected to the Puerto Rican Senate. By the time he completed his first term in 1937, he was at odds with the liberal leadership and moved on to form the *Partido Liberal Neto, Auténtico y Completo* (True, Clear, and Complete Liberal Party). The following year Muñoz Marín founded the *Partido Popular Democratico* (the Popular Democratic Party), known by its Spanish initials of PPD. He had not forgotten his sympathy for the poorer classes, and campaigned heavily in the countryside. That same year he met Inés María Mendoza, whom he would later marry.

To everybody's surprise, in 1940 the PPD won a majority of seats in the senate, and Muñoz Marín became that body's president. The PPD again won control of the senate in 1944. During both terms Muñoz Marín championed industrialization and agrarian reform for the island, both popular issues.

When the U.S. government finally allowed Puerto Ricans to elect their own governor, Muñoz Marín was the people's choice, becoming the first elected governor of Puerto Rico in 1948. He was re-elected in 1952, 1956, and 1960. During his second term, the Puerto Rico Constitution was drafted and approved by the U.S. Congress. It gave the island the status of a U.S. commonwealth. Even though that move was a far cry from his advocacy of independence and made many Puerto Ricans unhappy, he secured new investments in the island, developed new industries such as textiles and petrochemicals, and promoted music and the arts.

But not everything was going well for Muñoz Marín. He fiercely cracked down on pro-independence groups after gunmen attacked his residence on November 1, 1950, and U.S. President Harry Truman did not help him politically. In 1960 the PPD's policies on birth control and exclusion of religious classes in public schools led to opposition from the Catholic Church. Neither hampered his popularity. Muñoz Marín was an admired and respected man even on the mainland. On December 6, 1963, President Lyndon Baines Johnson decorated him with the Presidential Medal of Freedom.

Muñoz Marín declined to run for governor again in 1964, but was elected once more to the senate, where he served until 1968. Muñoz Marín remained a powerful force in his homeland politics until complications from a stroke took his life at the age of eighty-two.

Bibliography

Chrisman, Abbott. *Luís Muñoz Marín*. Austin, TX: Raintree Steck-Vaughn, 1993.

García Passalacqua, Manuel, ed. *Vate, de la Cuna a la Cripta: El Nacionalismo Cultural de Luís Muñoz Marín*. San Juan, PR: Editorial LEA, 1998.

Lluch Vélez, Amalia. *Luís Muñoz Marín: Poesía, Periodismo y Revolución*. San Juan, PR: Fundación Luís Muñoz Marín, 1999.

Muñoz Marín, Luís. *Discursos*. San Juan, PR: Fundación Luís Muñoz Marín, 1999.

Natal, Carmelo Rosario. *Luís Muñoz Marín: Juicios Sobre su Significado Histórico*. San Juan, PR: Fundación Luís Muñoz Marín, 1990.

Scarano, Francisco A. *Puerto Rico: Cinco Siglos de Historia*. San Juan, PR: McGraw-Hill, 1993.

Luís Muñoz Rivera

Dreams of Independence

Statesman, Journalist

- ❖ Born in Barranquitas, Puerto Rico.
- ❖ Birth date: July 17, 1859.
- ❖ Death date: November 15, 1916.

Career Highlights

- One of the founders of the Autonomist Party in 1887.
- Established three newspapers.
- Led Puerto Rico's struggle for autonomy against Spain and the United States.
- Led legislative battle that won U.S. Congressional approval of Puerto Rican autonomy in 1916.

Important Contributions

No other man is more responsible for Puerto Rico's independence than Luís Muñoz Rivera.

Career Path

Although he didn't live to see the fruits of his labor, Luís Muñoz Rivera was the driving force behind Puerto Rico's advance to self-rule. He was also the father of Puerto Rico's first elected governor, Luís Muñoz Marín.

Like many Puerto Ricans before and after, Rivera spent a good part of his life away from his homeland, but never forgot where he came from and the needs of his people.

Muñoz Rivera was born in a small town in the central part of Puerto Rico. After attending school in his hometown, he worked at his father's store. The poor economic conditions on the island, detrimental to political and social development, soon concerned the young man. His restlessness led him into politics and journalism.

Many Puerto Ricans saw self-rule as the first step toward a brighter future and Muñoz Rivera was an enthusiastic supporter. As one of the founders of the party that sought independence, Rivera established the newspaper, *La Democracia* (*Democracy*), where he made his case in 1890. Somewhat a poet, Muñoz Rivera also published two anthologies of verses, the first one, *Retamas* (*Bitterness*), in 1891.

Two years later he traveled to Spain. Upon his return to Puerto Rico, Muñoz Rivera collaborated in the Plan of Ponce, calling for self-rule while providing a national identity. Back in Spain in 1895, Muñoz Rivera and other members of the Puerto Rican delegation won the backing of the Liberal Party. True to their word, the Spanish liberals granted Puerto Rico its self-rule when they took power in 1898, and Muñoz Rivera became secretary of state and cabinet chief. But autonomy did not last long; the Spanish-American War broke out and U.S. forces landed on the island and set up military rule.

The occupying American forces rapidly established a trade ban that hurt Puerto Rican businessmen and landowners. To voice their complaints, in 1899 Muñoz Rivera established another newspaper, *El Territorio* (*The Territory*). He also went to the United States in an attempt to open commerce with Puerto Rico. He was unsuccessful but not defeated. He moved to New York to continue his work from there. As he did in Puerto Rico, Muñoz Rivera founded a newspaper, the *Puerto Rican Herald*, to advance his ideas. The publication was in English and Spanish. While in New York, he published his second volume of poems, *Tropicales* (*Tropical*), in 1902.

Eventually, he went back to the island and helped establish the Unionist Party. He was elected to the House of Delegates in 1906 and later was voted resident commissioner to the U.S. House of Representatives. The position was a kind of an observer congressman, but that was all he needed. Muñoz Rivera harangued, cajoled, and negotiated with the president and the U.S. Congress until legislation was passed on May 23, 1916, giving Puerto Ricans U.S. citizenship, political autonomy, and the right to pass their own laws. The piece of legislation is known as the Jones Act.

Fate would not let Muñoz Rivera revel in his triumph. Suffering from cancer, he went back to Puerto Rico in September 1916. Two months later he died in San Juan. On March 2, 1917, President Woodrow Wilson signed the Jones Act into law.

Bibliography

Arana Soto, Salvador. *La Ceiba de la Libertad y Otros Artículos sobre Luís Muñoz Rivera*. San Juan, PR: Arana-Soto, 1975.

Delgado Pasapera, Germán. *Puerto Rico: Sus Luchas Emancipadoras*. Rio Piedras, PR: Editorial Cultural, 1984.

Díaz Soler, Luís M. *Puerto Rico: Desde sus Orígenes Hasta el Cese de la Dominación Española*. Rio Piedras, PR: Editorial de la Universidad de Puerto Rico, 1994.

Fernández Méndez, Eugenio. *Luís Muñoz Rivera, Hombre Visible*. San Juan, PR: Biblioteca de Autores Puertorriqueños, 1982.

Picó, Fernando. *Historia General de Puerto Rico*. Rio Piedras, PR: Ediciones Huracán, 1986.

Scarano, Francisco A. *Puerto Rico: Cinco Siglos de Historia*. San Juan, PR: McGraw-Hill, 1993.

Pablo Neruda

Poems and Politics

Poet

❖ Born in Parral, Chile.
❖ Birth date: July 12, 1904.
❖ Death date: September 23, 1973.

Career Highlights

- Elected to the Chilean Senate in 1945.
- Published the enormous poetry collection *Canto General* (*General Song*) in 1950.
- Awarded the Nobel Prize in Literature in 1971.
- Served Chile in various diplomatic posts.

Important Contributions

A poetic visionary, Neruda was always ahead of other writers in embracing new forms of his art. From one collection of poems to another, he was a different kind of writer, always producing fresh and interesting work.

Career Path

If Pablo Neruda's life could be defined in two words they would be poems and politics. He was a passionate writer and a Communist zealot, so much so that he was one of the last leftist Latin American writers to break with Moscow over Joseph Stalin's crimes.

Born Neftalí Ricardo Reyes Basoalto to a family of modest means, he grew up in Temuco, where his family moved after his mother died.

Neruda wrote his first poem at age ten. Two years later he met poet Gabriela Mistral, who encouraged his writing aspirations. In 1917, when Neruda was thirteen, he published his first poem, *"Entusiasmo y Perseverancia"* ("Enthusiasm and Perseverance") in the daily newspaper *La Mañana* (*The Morning*). Three years later he became a regular contributor to the literary periodical *Selva Austral* (*Austral Jungle*). It was then that he took the pen name Pablo Neruda in honor of Czechoslovakian poet Jan Neruda, and also to avert family conflicts since the family objected to his literary goals. At seventeen he entered the University of Chile in Santiago to study French and pedagogy. While there Neruda wrote his best-known work, *Veinte Poemas de Amor y Una Canción* (*Twenty Love Poems and a Song*), which was published in 1924 and made him internationally famous.

From 1927 to 1935 Neruda held various consular positions in Europe and Asia. He never got used to life in Asia, and suffered from upsetting nightmares and depression while there. His work *Residencia en la Tierra* (*Residence on the Earth*) was published during this period.

The rise of Fascism during this time had a tremendous influence on Neruda's political views, so much so that in 1936 he resigned as Chilean consul in Spain because of his sympathies with the Republican government. The death of his friend Federico García Lorca at the hands of Nationalist forces caused him to move even farther to the left. Back in Chile, his poems became more political. In 1937 *España en el Corazón* (*Spain in the Heart*) was published, and he became involved in national politics. When leftist Pedro Aguirre Cerda was elected president in 1938, Neruda was appointed consul in Paris. He used his post to help settle Spanish refugees in Chile.

In 1942 one of his daughters died. Neruda traveled to Cuba, where he publicly read a poem called *"Canto de Amor A Stalingrado"* ("A Love Song to Stalingrad") praising the Red Army's tenacious resistance in that city during the German invasion of World War II. He returned to Chile in 1943, and two years later joined the Communist Party and was elected senator. His fiery opposition to President Gabriel González Videla made him a marked man. Neruda was forced underground for two years and fled to México. From there he went to the Soviet Union and then to Italy, where he lived for a time. While in exile he wrote the 340 poems that formed *General Song*, an assessment of Latin American history from a Marxist perspective.

Neruda was allowed to return to Chile in 1952. Unlike many other Marxists of his time, he remained faithful to Moscow during that time. Not until 1958 did he start to examine his beliefs. For the next few years Neruda continued to write and travel. He was appointed ambassador to France in 1970. While serving in France he was honored with the Nobel Prize in Literature in 1971.

Neruda died in Santiago of leukemia on September 23, 1973. He is regarded as one of the greatest poets of the twentieth century.

Bibliography

Bloom, Harold, ed. *Pablo Neruda*. New York: Chelsea House, 1989.

Díaz Granados, José Luís. *El otro Pablo Neruda*. Bogotá: Planeta, 2003.

Duran, Manuel, and Margery Safir. *Earth Tones: The Poetry of Pablo Neruda*. Bloomington, IN: Indiana University Press, 1981.

Flores, Angel. *Spanish American Authors: The Twentieth Century*. New York: H.W. Wilson, 1992.

Longo, Teresa, ed. *Pablo Neruda and the U.S. Culture Industry*. New York: Routledge, 2002.

Magill, Frank N., ed. *The Nobel Prize Winners: Literature*. Englewood Cliffs, NJ: Salem Press, 1989.

Skármeta, Antonio. *Neruda por Skármeta*. Buenos Aires: Seix Barral, 2004.

Carlos I. Noriega

Better Than the Next Guy   Astronaut

❖ Born in Lima, Perú.
❖ Birth date: October 8, 1959.

Career Highlights

- Selected as an astronaut by NASA in 1994.
- Retired lieutenant colonel of the U.S. Marine Corps.
- Held first-ever Spanish-language interactive online chat from space in 2000.
- Awarded numerous military and NASA honors including the Navy Achievement Medal and NASA Space Flight Medal.

Important Contributions

Noriega is a shining example to all immigrants in the United States. From a kid who spoke no English, Noriega went on to earn two master's degrees from the Naval Postgraduate School in 1990, one in computer science and the other in space systems operations. He served in the U.S. Marine Corps and eventually became an astronaut.

Career Path

From Perú to the United States and into space is Carlos Noriega's story in a nutshell.

Noriega was born in the Peruvian capital, and his family moved to Santa Clara, California when he was five. He was nine years old when Neil Armstrong walked on the moon. He thought it was amazing but beyond the reach of a boy who was still learning to speak English. To young Noriega, astronauts were special, almost mythological beings. It would be a long time before he thought he could actually join their ranks.

After graduating from Wilcox High School in Santa Clara, he attended the University of Southern California, where he joined the Navy Reserve Officer Training Corps (ROTC) program. He felt it was his patriotic duty. The ROTC helped pay for his education in return for his service. He earned his bachelor's degree in computer science from USC.

Noriega got a taste of active deployment as a helicopter pilot in operations supporting the Multi-National Peacekeeping Force in Beirut, Lebanon in 1985. Afterward, he served as Base Operation Officer, for Marine Air Base Squadron 24, in Hawaii. In 1996, he was an instructor pilot and an aviation safety officer at Tustin, California. Two years later he was selected for the Master of Science program at the Naval Postgraduate School in Monterey. After graduation in 1990, Noriega was assigned to the U.S. Space Command Center in Colorado Springs, Colorado. While serving at the U.S. Space Command Center in Colorado Springs, Colorado, he applied for the astronaut program. A friend was applying, and Noriega thought that he was as good as the next guy. As it turned out, he was better—the friend did not make it. Noriega started the grueling one-year training in 1995. By 1997 he was aboard the Space Shuttle *Atlantis* on his first shuttle mission, rendezvousing with the Russian Mir Space Station. Noriega tells the story that just before blastoff he had to pinch himself to make sure he was really going into space.

He went on one more space adventure. On the last one, on the Space Shuttle *Endeavour,* from November 30 to December 11, 2000, the crew assembled the International Space Station. Noriega walked in space twice and held the first Spanish-language online chat from space.

Noriega has five children and particularly enjoys talking to young people. He feels they should be steered toward hard work, service, and patriotism. He has visited many high schools and colleges in the United States and in Perú. He feels that he has come a long way, and it's true: He has logged more than eight million miles in space.

Bibliography

"Biographical Data." NASA. http://www.jsc.nasa.gov/Bios/htmlbios/noriega.html (March 29, 2004).

"Noriega, Carlos Ismael. USA." Spacefacts. http://www.spacefacts.de/bios/astronauts/english/noriega_carlos.htm (April 13, 2005).

Rhem, Staff Sgt. Kathleen T. (USA). "Hispanic Officer Flies Into Space." Defenselink. http://www.defenselink.mil/specials/Hispanic2001/space.html (March 29, 2004).

"Space: Jerry Linenger and Carlos Noriega" Alumni News. *USC Trojan Family Magazine*, Spring 1997. www.usc.edu/dept/pubrel/trojan_family/spring97/alumninews/AP_space.html (April, 2005).

Antonia Novello

For Healthy Children　　　Medical Doctor

❖ Born in Fajardo, Puerto Rico.
❖ Birth date: August 23, 1944.

Career Highlights

- First woman to be named Intern of the Year in the pediatric department at the University of Michigan Medical Center.
- Appointed US. General Surgeon in 1990.
- Received 1995 Ronald McDonald House Charities Award for improving lives of children.

Important Contributions

Not only was Antonia Novello the first Hispanic and first woman to serve as surgeon general of the United States, but she also left a legacy of caring for the young. Her crusade to inform teenagers about the specific health risks of smoking, drinking, and drug use has been unrivaled by any other surgeon general.

Career Path

Possibly because she suffered from a congenital medical condition until she was twenty, Antonia Novello has a soft spot for young people.

She was born Antonia Coello in the village of Fajardo, and was promptly diagnosed with an anomalous colon. She needed remedial surgery immediately, but it was unavailable. To make matters worse, her father died when she was eight years old. The young girl excelled in her studies due to the prodding of her mother. Such was her brilliance that she graduated from high school at the age of fifteen.

Antonia Coello finally received her first corrective operation when she was eighteen, but the procedure, which would have solved her problem if done sooner, was only partially successful. By then she was attending the University of Puerto Pico at Rio Piedras. Her health troubles motivated her to study medicine. She suffered complications from her first operation and in 1964 traveled to Rochester, Minnesota's famous Mayo Clinic for treatment and a second, successful surgery.

In 1970 she received her medical degree from the University of Puerto Rico at San Juán and married Joseph R. Novello, a U.S. Army flight surgeon. The couple moved to Ann Arbor, Michigan, where Novello studied at the University of Michigan Medical Center. There she was an intern, a resident, and completed a fellowship in pediatric nephrology. Later they moved to Washington, D.C., where Novello had a fellowship at Georgetown University Hospital. In 1978 she went to work for the National Institutes of Health (NIH) in Bethesda, Maryland, ultimately rising to deputy director of the National Institute of Child Health and Human Development (NICHD) in 1981.

While at the NIH, Novello earned a master's degree in public health at Johns Hopkins University. During this time pediatric AIDS attracted her interest. The administration of President George Herbert Walker Bush was aware of her work, and the president appointed her surgeon general in 1990. Novello served for three years, during which she campaigned for more AIDS education, as well as health care for minorities, women, and children.

Hispanic groups presented a problem for Novello's campaign. The diversity of the groups living in the United States made it difficult to ascertain the specific health issues each faced and how to go about solving them. A study conducted during her term found that some kinds of cancers and kidney illnesses are more common and more fatal to Hispanics than the rest of the population. The study also revealed that AIDS is a growing problem among Spanish women and children, and that the number of Hispanics immunized against measles is much lower than for other Americans. The hazards of teenage drinking and smoking were foremost on her agenda as well.

In 1993 she left her position as surgeon general and assumed new duties with the United Nations Children's Fund (UNICEF) as a special representative for health and nutrition. In 1999 she was appointed commissioner of health for the state of New York.

❖   ❖   ❖

Vasco Núñez de Balboa

In and Out of Favor   Explorer

- ❖ Born in either Badajoz or Jerez de los Caballeros, Spain.
- ❖ Birth date: Around 1475.
- ❖ Death date: January 21, 1519.

Career Highlights

- Sailed for Hispaniola in either 1500 or 1501.
- Traveled to the New World's mainland in 1510.
- First European to see the Pacific Ocean, in 1513.
- Appointed *Adelantado* (Commander) of the South Sea and Governor of Coyba by King Ferdinand.

Important Contributions

While the significance of his explorations—whether he "discovered" the Pacific Ocean or was just the first European to view it from its eastern shore—is still hotly debated among historians, there is no doubt that Balboa was a first-rate explorer who added much to the European knowledge of Central America and the true dimensions of the New World.

Career Path

Vasco Núñez de Balboa's family might have been aristocratic, but lacked influence and wealth. As a youth Balboa (really Núñez in the Spanish tradition, but he is known as Balboa) was probably a servant in a rich household in Palos de Moguer, today's Palos de la Frontera, the port from which Christopher Columbus departed on his first voyage to the Americas. Balboa caught the New World bug and went on an expedition to the north coast of South America. The voyagers lacked resources, causing them to shorten the trip. They landed in Hispaniola, the foremost Spanish base in the New World. While there, Balboa became a farmer or a pig herder. He did poorly and when he tried to join the first Spanish expedition to colonize the mainland in 1509, his creditors would not let him leave the island. Undeterred, the following year he stowed away on an expedition to take supplies to San Sebastian, a colony on the eastern shore of the Gulf of Urabá. During this trip, Balboa became one of the main lieutenants of Martín Fernández de Enciso, the expedition's leader. The leader of the colony was none other than Francisco Pizarro, the future conqueror of Perú. He told them that Indians had overrun the village. Balboa convinced Fernández de Enciso to go to the region of Darién. Once on the mainland, the Spaniards subdued the Indians and established a village. In 1511, Balboa was feeling confident and he not only vanquished Fernández de Enciso, but also Diego de Nicuesa, who had been appointed governor by King Ferdinand. Enciso, he forced to go back to Spain. Nicuesa was obliged to take an un-seaworthy ship with his supporters. They drowned on the way to Hispaniola. Balboa declared himself governor of Darién.

Concerned that King Ferdinand wanted him back in Spain to put him on trial for rebelling against Enciso and Nicuesa, Balboa decided to go on a mission for more land and treasures in order to mollify the king. He sailed to San Blas, on the North Coast of Panama, in early September 1513, and from there moved south through the Isthmus of Panama. It was a wise move as that is the narrowest strip of land between the Atlantic and Pacific oceans. As had been his policy, Balboa befriended most Indians, but thrashed those who were hostile, seizing considerable booty on the way. Finally, on September 25, 1513, he saw the Pacific Ocean. The next day Balboa waded into what he called *Mar del Sur* (South Sea), claiming it and all its bordering territories for Spain.

When Balboa returned to Darién, Pedro Aria de Ávila (better known as Pedrarias) had taken over the governorship. They did not clash, but political enmity and personal differences soon led to trouble. Balboa was generous, happy-go-lucky, and amiable, while Pedrarias was cunning, rancorous, and politically savvy. Even though King Ferdinand showered Balboa with honors and gave Balboa one of his daughters in marriage, Pedrarias knew how to undermine the explorer. He wrote to the Spanish monarch that there was doubt that Balboa had indeed discovered the South Sea. Ultimately Pedrarias accused Balboa of high treason, claiming that Balboa had tried to establish a separate government. Balboa was beheaded in Darién on January 21, 1519. While there are no records of where Balboa was buried, there is a tomb with his name on it in Havana, Cuba.

❖   ❖   ❖

Bibliography

Fritz, Jean. *Around the World in a Hundred Years: From Henry the Navigator to Magellan.* New York: Putnam, 1994.

Garrison, Omar V. *Balboa el Conquistador: La Odisea de Vasco Núñez, Descubridor del Pacífico.* Barcelona: Ediciones Grijalbo, 1977.

Herrera, Juan Ignacio. *Vasco Núñez de Balboa.* Madrid: Susaeta Ediciones, 1981.

Marcovitz, Hal. *Vasco Núñez de Balboa: Explorer of the Pacific.* Philadelphia: Chelsea House Publishers, 2002.

Martínez Rivas, J.R. *Vasco Núñez de Balboa.* Madrid: Quorum, 1997.

Oftinoski, Steven. *Vasco Núñez de Balboa and the Discovery of the South Sea.* New York: Benchmark Books, 2005.

Ellen Ochoa

The Sky's Not the Limit

Astronaut, Inventor

❖ Born in Los Angeles, California.
❖ Birth date: May 10, 1958.

Career Highlights

- Received PhD in electrical engineering in 1985.
- Became an astronaut in 1991.
- Blasted off into space for the first time in 1993.
- Co-invented three optical devices to find objects in space.
- Awarded the 1995 NASA Outstanding Leadership Medal and four NASA Space Flight Medals.

Important Contributions

Ellen Ochoa holds a doctoral degree in electrical engineering, and is an inventor and an astronaut. She has made a career of breaking new ground not just for Hispanic women, but for all women.

Career Path

The first Hispanic female astronaut, Ellen Ochoa almost became a professional musician, but at her mother's insistence she went to graduate school, had a successful career as a researcher, and eventually became an astronaut. Today, Ochoa uses her celebrity status to encourage young people, particularly Hispanics, to stay in school and work in their chosen field.

Ochoa graduated from Grossmont High School in La Mesa, California, in 1975. During her youth, music was a passion, but so were math and science. In 1980 she received a bachelor's degree in physics from San Diego State University. At the time, she was thinking of becoming a classical flutist or going into business. Enter her mother, Rosanne Ochoa. The elder Ms. Ochoa had always insisted on an education. Ochoa went to graduate school at Stanford University, earning her master's and doctorate in electrical engineering. She decided to become an astronaut.

While at Stanford she dedicated herself to designing optical systems for information processing. She continued these efforts after graduation at Sandia National Laboratories in Albuquerque, New Mexico. Ochoa then worked at the NASA Ames Research Center in Mountain View, California, as chief of the Intelligence Systems Technology Branch. In January 1990 Ochoa joined NASA and became an astronaut in July 1991. Her first space mission took place on April 4, 1993, aboard the Space Shuttle *Discovery*. During a nine-day mission the crew studied the sun's impact on the earth's weather systems. She took part in two more space missions; on her final mission in April 2002, the Space Shuttle *Discovery* docked for the first time with the International Space Station.

Today Ochoa is deputy director of Flight Crew Operations at the Johnson Space Flight Center in Houston. She has earned many honors and awards, including the Women in Aerospace Outstanding Achievement Award, the Hispanic Heritage Leadership Award, and the San Diego State Alumna of the Year. She is married and has two children.

Bibliography

"Ellen Ochoa." Las Mujeres. http://www.lasmujeres.com/ellenochoa/biography.shtml (March 28, 2004).

Morey, Janet, and Dunn, Wendy. *Famous Hispanic Americans.* New York: Cobblehill Books, 1996.

Romero, Maritza. *Ellen Ochoa: The First Hispanic Woman Astronaut.* New York: PowerKids Press, 1997.

Stille, Darlene R. *Extraordinary Women Scientists.* Chicago: Children's Press, 1995.

Telgen, Diane, and Kamp, Jim, eds. *Latinas! Women of Achievement.* Detroit: Visible Ink Press, 1996.

Bernardo O'Higgins

Noble Patriot   Statesman

❖ Born in Chillán, Chile.
❖ Birth date: August 20, 1778.
❖ Death date: October 24, 1842.

Career Highlights

- Elected to first Chilean Congress in 1810.
- Appointed head of Chilean government in 1817.
- Oversaw the writing of constitutions in 1818 and 1822.
- Resigned his post as head of government in 1823.

Important Contributions

Bernardo O'Higgins was one of the most important figures in Chile's struggle for independence from Spain. He was a brilliant strategist, a man of honor, and had a profound love for his homeland. Although helped by Argentina's José de San Martín, Chileans consider Bernardo O'Higgins the true liberator of Chile.

Career Path

Bernardo O'Higgins Riquelme was the illegitimate son of Ambrosio O'Higgins, an Irishman in the service of Spain who became governor of Chile and viceroy of Perú. The elder O'Higgins placed his son in the care of a Portuguese entrepreneur and later enrolled young Bernardo at the best schools in Chillán and Lima, Perú. At seventeen, O'Higgins was sent to study in Spain and England. When his father died in 1801, O'Higgins returned home to manage the family's land holdings, becoming a prosperous landowner.

When Napoleon conquered Spain in 1808 many South American colonies took advantage of the situation and declared their independence. Chile was no different. First a *junta* (a government of high-ranking military officers) was established to replace the Spanish governor in 1810, then a congress was elected. O'Higgins served as a representative from Los Angles, a town some 500 miles south of Santiago. Perú's viceroy invaded Chile, forcing all republicans to flee. O'Higgins went to Argentina, where he planned the independence of his country and waited for a time to strike.

In 1813 he returned to Chile and joined the revolutionary army. He was a gifted strategist and gallant warrior, characteristics that propelled him up the ranks until he became the commander in chief. A brilliant Spanish general, Mariano Osorio, as well as bickering among the revolutionaries, led to the failure of this second attempt to free Chile. Thousands of soldiers and civilians, among them O'Higgins' mother and sister, joined him to escape through the Andes into Argentina. There he met the noble Argentinian patriot José de San Martín. The two established the Army of the Andes, and soon after made their move. On February 12, 1817, they defeated the Spaniards at Chacabuco, and later entered Santiago. O'Higgins, as commander in chief, convened a meeting of powerful citizens to decide how to rule Chile. The government was offered to San Martín, who declined, and then to O'Higgins, who accepted. His title was supreme director and his powers dictatorial.

To ensure Chile's independence the Spaniards had to be driven from Perú. O'Higgins began a naval buildup, but the Spaniards struck first. General Osorio defeated the Chileans at Cancha Rayada. Even though he had been wounded at Cancha Rayada on April 5, 1818, O'Higgins was with San Martín at the Battle of Maipú that sealed Chile's independence. Perú was liberated two years later and its independence proclaimed on July 28, 1821.

O'Higgins was an unpopular ruler. He executed many independent-minded individuals, crossed aristocrats by prohibiting the use of noble titles and coats of arms, and infuriated conservatives by trying to establish a republic. In order to avoid a civil war, O'Higgins stepped down in January 1823 and went into exile in Perú, never to return to his country. He died in Lima on October 24, 1842, and his remains were transferred to Chile in 1868.

❖ ❖ ❖

Bibliography

Díaz-Trechuelo Sínola, María Lourdes. *Bolívar, Miranda, O'Higgins, San Martín: Cuatro Vidas Cruzadas.* Madrid: Ediciones Encuentro, 1999.

Fernández Larraín, Sergio. *O'Higgins.* Santiago: Editorial Orbe, 1974.

Harvey, Robert. *Liberators: Latin America's Struggle for Independence, 1810–1830.* London: John Murray, 2000.

Robinovitch, Rosa. *Bernardo O'Higgins: El difícil Camino del Hombre Prócer.* Santiago: Publicaciones Peldaño, 1973.

Rodríguez S., Juan Agustín. *La Vida Militar de O'Higgins, Síntesis de la Historia de la Independencia.* Santiago: Gabriela Mistral, 1975.

Vicuña Mackenna, Benjamín. *Vida del Capitán General don Bernardo O'Higgins.* Santiago: Editorial del Pacífico, 1976.

José Ortega y Gasset

Not Part of the Masses　　　Philosopher

- ❖ Born in Madrid, Spain.
- ❖ Birth date: May 9, 1883.
- ❖ Death date: October 18, 1955.

Career Highlights

- Began teaching metaphysics at the *Universidad Central de Madrid* (Madrid's Central University) in 1910.
- Elected to the Royal Spanish Academy of Moral and Political Sciences in 1915.
- Published his most important book, *La Rebelión de las Masas* (*The Revolt of the Masses*), in 1930.
- Elected to the Spanish parliament in 1931.

Important Contributions

Gasset was an important proponent of the theory that the self cannot be separated from the environment and the circumstances in which one lives. He also proposed the theory of the "mass man" who does not think or care, but who dominates modern-day politics.

Career Path

Practically unknown in the English-speaking world, José Ortega y Gasset was one of the momentous thinkers of the twentieth century. But few have seen their work put to such disparate use. Ortega's most famous work, *The Revolt of the Masses*, was published in 1930. In it

Ortega argues that even though the masses dominate the political and social agenda, it is the educated minority that should rule. The mass man, he says, knows and wants nothing. Fascism and Communism are extreme examples of mass-man rule. Extremists of all brands like to name Ortega as one of their philosophical ancestors.

The great philosopher, essayist, and college professor was born into a well-to-do family of newspaper owners. After completing elementary school in Madrid, Ortega was sent to Málaga to study at the Jesuit school of Miraflores. He graduated in 1897 and enrolled at the University of Deusto, in Bilbao. After attending that institution for only a year, he enrolled at the University of Madrid, where he received a PhD in philosophy in 1904. For the next two years, Ortega continued studying at various German universities and later taught philosophy, logic, and ethics. In 1910 he was appointed chair of metaphysics at Madrid's Central University, where he developed a captivating, well-structured style of public speaking that made his lectures enjoyable for students and general public. The talks were so interesting that many of them were later compiled in a book. Four years later, Ortega published his first book, *Meditaciones del Quijote* (*Meditations of Quixote*), a treatise on the old and new politic in Spain.

Ortega was a liberal and as such he opposed military dictator Primo de Rivera who ruled under King Alfonso XIII from 1923 to 1930. In protest, he resigned his post at the central university, but continued to write his philosophy about the essence of knowledge and Spain, all subjects typical of the *Generación del 98* (Generation of '98), a group of Spanish intellectuals. Ortega was deeply concerned with the political, social, economic, and philosophical changes caused by the loss of the last vestiges of the empire during the Spanish-American War.

In 1931 de Rivera fell and King Alfonso abdicated. Convinced that his country needed a democratic government, Ortega participated in the constituent assembly for the second republic that met for the next two years. This foray into politics was not a particular happy one for Ortega. The reality of government was too tedious and trying for him. After one year in parliament, he withdrew and kept silent about Spanish politics. Such was his disgust that when the Spanish civil war broke out in 1936, Ortega took no side. He went into voluntary exile, traveling to Europe and South America, finally settling in Lima, Perú, in 1941. There he taught philosophy at the University of San Marcos.

At the end of World War II, Ortega returned to Spain, but refused to take an academic assignment while Francisco Franco remained in power. From 1945 on Ortega would spend little time in Spain, lecturing often in Germany, Switzerland, and the United States.

Like a good *madrileño* (a resident or native of Madrid), Ortega died in his hometown. Many of his works were published posthumously, including *Goya, Velázquez*, and anthologies of his writings. Ortega's powerful philosophical influence continues to this day.

Bibliography

Aguilar, Enrique, et al. *Ortega y Gasset en la Cátedra Americana*. Buenos Aires: Nuevohacer, Grupo Editor Latinoamericano, 2004.

Fernández, Ana María. *Teoría de la Novela en Unamuno*, Ortega y Cortázar. Madrid: Ediciones Pliegos, 1991.

Fernández, Pelayo Hipólito. *La Paradoja en Ortega y Gasset*. Madrid: J. Porrúa Turanzas, 1985.

Graham, John T. *A Pragmatist Philosophy of Life in Ortega y Gasset*. Columbia, MO: University of Missouri Press, 1994.

Gray, Rockwell. *José Ortega y Gasset: El Imperativo de la Modernidad*. Madrid: Espasa Calpe, 1994.

Ouimette, Victor. *José Ortega y Gasset*. Boston: Twayne Publishers, 1982.

Romualdo Pacheco

Californio for California

Statesman,
Soldier

- ❖ Born in Santa Barbara, California.
- ❖ Birth date: October 31, 1831.
- ❖ Death date: January 23, 1899.

Career Highlights

- Appointed brigadier general of a California force of the Union army in 1862.
- Elected to office for the first time in 1863.
- Became governor of California in 1875.
- Served three terms in the U.S. House of Representatives.
- Appointed U.S. chief diplomat in Central America in 1890.

Important Contributions

Elected as lieutenant governor, then assuming the governorship of California when the governor was elected to the U.S. Senate, Romualdo Pacheco's feat is not diminished. No other Hispanic before or after has served as governor of California. Pacheco is an example of what bilingual, bicultural, and hard-working people can accomplish.

Career Path

José Antonio Romualdo Pacheco, Jr., was born into a notable, well-to-do *Californio* (old Spanish for native Californians of Hispanic origin) family. His father died when Pacheco was five years old, and his mother married Captain John D. Wilson, a Scot. Soon, under the pretext of furthering the boy's education, his stepfather sent Pacheco to Honolulu, Hawaii. Pacheco returned home when he was twelve years old and became an apprentice for the agent of a trading vessel. Eventually he worked as a ship's skipper and later turned to ranching and gold prospecting.

During the early 1850s he became interested in politics. Moving with equal ease among the traditional Californios and Anglo-American settlers, Pacheco earned the support of both and was elected to the San Luis Obispo Superior Court. Before long he joined the Democratic Party and was elected to the state senate. Returning to California in 1861 after a long trip to Europe, Pacheco ran again for the state senate and won. This time, however, he did so as a Republican, the party he had joined because of his strong anti-slavery sentiments. He wasn't destined to serve this term. The American Civil War had begun. California's governor chose Pacheco to lead the First Brigade of California's Native Cavalry, with the rank of brigadier general. The unit's main contribution to the war effort came in May 1862, when it was sent to Los Angeles County and confiscated all weapons not in the hands of Union faithful. Pacheco was again elected to the state senate later that year.

In 1863 he won the post of state treasurer. Five years later he was elected Republican lieutenant governor, under Newton Booth. When Booth was elected to the U.S Senate in 1875, Pacheco took over as governor and served out the remainder of the term.

In 1876 Pacheco ran for the U.S. House of Representatives and won by one vote. Opponent Peter D. Wigginton disputed the results and the House Committee on Elections sided with him despite appeals from the House Republican leader and future president James A. Garfield. Undaunted, Pacheco ran again in 1879 and won a second term, during which he became the first Hispanic to chair a standing committee in Congress.

While managing a ranch in northern México in 1890, Pacheco was picked to serve as Envoy Extraordinary and Minister Plenipotentiary to the Central American States. The task proved too much for one man and he was reappointed as Minister Plenipotentiary to Honduras and Guatemala the following year. When his tour of duty ended, Pacheco returned to California, where he lived quietly the rest of his days. He died in Oakland, California, on January 23, 1899.

❖　❖　❖

Bibliography

Conmy, Peter Thomas. *Romualdo Pacheco: Distinguished Californian of the Mexican and American Periods.* San Francisco: Grand Parlor, Native Sons of the Golden West, 1957.

Genini, Ronald. *Romualdo Pacheco: A Californio in Two Eras.* San Francisco: Book Club of California, 1985.

"Governor José Antonio Romualdo Pacheco, Jr." The California State Military Museum. http://www.military museum.org/Pacheco.html (February 1, 2005).

Nicholson, Loren. *Romualdo Pacheco's California: The Mexican-American Who Won.* San Luis Obispo, CA: California Heritage Publishing Associates, 1990.

"Romualdo Pacheco." Hispanic Americans in Congress, 1822–1995. http://www.loc.gov/rr/hispanic/congress/pacheco.html (February 1, 2005).

Octavio Paz

Pestering the Totalitarians   Writer

❖ Born in México City, México.
❖ Birth date: March 31, 1914.
❖ Death date: April 19, 1998.

Career Highlights

- Published first collection of works, *Luna Silvestre* (*Sylvan Moon*), in 1933.
- Published his masterpiece *El Laberinto de la Soledad* (*The Labyrinth of Solitude*) in 1950.
- Awarded the 1984 German Booksellers Peace Prize.
- Received the Nobel Prize in Literature in 1990.

Important Contributions

Octavio Paz understood and wrote about Mexican culture like no one else. His exalted status in the world of literature helped transmit his ideas of political and personal freedom the world over.

Career Path

Mexican writer and winner of the 1990 Nobel Prize in Literature, Octavio Paz must have done something right. During his lifetime he managed to displease extremists on both the left and the right.

Paz was born to be in the middle of political turmoil. His father provided legal counsel to agrarian revolutionary Emiliano Zapata and played a part in agrarian reform plans. His grandfather fought against Mexican strongman Porfirio Díaz.

Paz was an insatiable reader from an early age. The huge library his grandfather owned increased his thirst for the written word. After Zapata was assassinated in 1919, the family moved to the United States for a while. After returning to México in late 1919, Paz attended the National University where he studied law and literature but did not receive a degree. Paz published his first collection of poems, *Sylvan Moon*, when he was only nineteen years old.

In 1937 he traveled to Valencia, the Republican's provisional capital during the Spanish civil war, to take part in the Second International Congress of Anti-Fascist Writers. There is evidence he also saw combat there. He even found time to publish *Bajo tu Clara Sombra y Otros Poemas* (*Under Your Light Shadow and Other Poems*), another poetry anthology.

Back in México, he was one of the founders of *El Popular* (*The Popular One*), a leftist magazine, and of the literary publication *Taller* (*Workshop*), which helped develop new writers. During the next twenty years, he spent little time in México. First he received a Guggenheim scholarship to study in the United States. After joining the Mexican diplomatic corps, he was sent to Paris in 1944. There he wrote his masterpiece *The Labyrinth of Solitude*, a pithy study of Mexican characteristics. He brought upon himself the wrath of the powerful French Communist Party and other Soviet partisans by publicly denouncing Russian dictator Joseph Stalin's atrocities. In 1962 he was appointed ambassador to India. Indian philosophy influenced his criticism of Western materialism that appeared under the title of *Corriente Alterna* (*Alternate Current*) in 1967.

When the Mexican government violently suppressed student protests during the Olympic Games, Paz resigned his post to India in protest. He earned a living by teaching at Cambridge and Harvard. Ending his self-imposed exile in 1972, he founded *Plural* magazine in México. It was an intellectual publication that soon got him into trouble with the Mexican government. He published another of his great essays, *Los Hijos de Limo* (*Children of the Mire*), a chronicle of avant garde poetry from the 1790s to the 1960s.

In the 1970s Paz received honorary degrees from Boston University and the University of New Mexico. Harvard and New York University honored him similarly in the following decade. In 1990 the Nobel Foundation awarded him the Nobel Prize in Literature. His last published work was 1995's *Vislumbres de la India,* (Glimpses of India).

Paz died in México City on April 19, 1998. Freedom-loving people around the world mourned his passing. Political extremists of all stripes did not.

Bibliography

Bloom, Harold, ed. *Octavio Paz.* Philadelphia: Chelsea House Publishers, 2002.

Gallardo Muñoz, Juan. *Octavio Paz.* Las Rozas, Madrid: Dastin, 2003.

Grenier, Yvon. *From Art to Politics: Octavio Paz and the Pursuit of Freedom.* Lanham, MD: Rowman & Littlefield, 2001.

Poniatowska, Elena. *Octavio Paz: Las Palabras del Arbol.* Barcelona: Plaza Janes, 1998.

Quiroga, José. *Understanding Octavio Paz.* Columbia, SC: University of South Carolina Press, 1999.

Santí, Enrico Mario. *El Acto de las Palabras: Estudios y Diálogos con Octavio Paz.* México City: Fondo de Cultura Económica, 1997.

Benito Pérez Galdós

The Best Since Cervantes

Writer, Playwright

❖ Born in Las Palmas de Gran Canaria, Spain.
❖ Birth date: May 10, 1843.
❖ Death date: January 3, 1920.

Career Highlights

- His four-volume masterpiece, *Fortunata y Jacinta*, became available in 1886 or 1887.
- Published his series about the inquisitor Tomás de Torquemada between 1889 and 1895.
- Selected to the Royal Spanish Academy in 1907.
- Elected to the Spanish Chamber of Deputies in 1910.

Important Contributions

Extremely anticlerical and liberal, Pérez Galdós gathered around him a group of writers who would be known as the *Generación del 98* (Generation of '98). His novels, full of realism, historical perspective, and naturalist allegories, had such impact that he is considered the finest Spanish novelist since Miguel de Cervantes.

Career Path

The son of a career soldier, Benito Pérez Galdós grew up to be a great writer and the forerunner and teacher of the Generation of '98.

After attending elementary and secondary school in his hometown of Las Palmas, Pérez Galdós moved to Madrid in 1863 and lived there most of his adult life. Like many ambitious youngsters he planned to be a lawyer. His contacts with the intellectuals and authors who flocked to the Spanish capital at the time caused him to lose interest in his studies and he began to write. In 1865 he wrote for the daily *La Nación* (*The Nation*) and *La Revista Intelectual de Europa* (*Europe's Intellectual Magazine*). His journalistic activities demanded an ever-increasing amount of time, and because he missed so many classes the University of Madrid School of Law expelled him in 1868.

Galdós would write forty-five novels about the history of Spain from 1805 to 1899. *La Fontana de Oro* (*The Gold Fountain*), his first published novel, hit bookstores in 1870. Soon after, the first of his *Episodios Nacionales* (*National Episodes*) was published. A somewhat light, anticlerical novel *Doña Perfecta* (*Mrs. Perfect*), published in 1876, was his next great work. Two years later, the didactic novel *La Casa de León Roch* (*Leon Roch's House*) appeared. It would be eight years until the publication of the first volume of *Fortunata y Jacinta*, his tour de force about the lives of two very different women. In 1901, just three years after Spain lost the Spanish-American War, his great anticlerical play *Electra* (*Elektra*), opened to rave reviews. Future members of the Generation of '98—Miguel de Unamuno, Pio Baroja, Jacinto Benavente, and others—rallied around him.

Pérez Galdós became militantly pro-republic and anti-monarchic early in the twentieth century. He was elected as Madrid's delegate to the Chamber of Deputies. In 1912 he won another term in the Chamber, but this time representing his hometown of Las Palmas. At about that time, he lost his eyesight and he had to dictate all his works from then on. *La Razón de la Sinrazón* (*The Reason of the Unreason*), his final novel, was published in 1915, the same year his essays about World War I revealed him to be an Allied sympathizer. Efforts to nominate him for the Nobel Prize in Literature in 1916 failed as too much time had passed. His final play, *Santa Juana de Castilla* (*Saint Joan of Castile*), debuted in 1918 and was well received.

The day Benito Pérez Galdós passed away, Madrid's businesses closed their doors. All of Spain mourned his death.

Bibliography

Bly, Peter. *The Wisdom of Eccentric Old Men: A Study of Type and Secondary Character in Galdós' Social Novels*. Montreal: McGill-Queen's University Press, 2004.

McGovern, Timothy Michael. *Galdós Beyond Realism: Reading and the Creation of Magical Worlds*. Newark, DE: Juan de la Cuesta, 2004.

Montero-Paulson, Daria Jaroslava. *La Figura de Don Juan en Los Episodios Nacionales de Benito Pérez Galdós*. Miami: Ediciones Universal, 2005.

Navarrete-Galiano, Ramón. *Galdós en el Cine Español*. Madrid: T & B Editores, 2003.

Peñate Rivero, E. Julio. *Benito Pérez Galdós y el cuento Literario como Sistema*. Zaragoza: Libros Pórtico, 2001.

Willem, Linda M. *Galdós Segunda Manera: Rhetorical Strategies and Effective Response*. Chapel Hill, NC: UNC Department of Romance Languages, 1998.

Pablo Picasso

- ❖ Born in Málaga, Spain.
- ❖ Birth date: October 25, 1881.
- ❖ Death date: April 8, 1973.

Career Highlights

- Painted first canvas in 1891.
- Experienced the Blue Period between 1900 and 1904.
- Went through the Rose Period from 1905 to 1906.
- Unveiled *Guernica* in 1937.

Important Contributions

One of the great artists of the twentieth century, Pablo Picasso was unique. He was an innovator, originator, and trendsetter in the world of art as well as one of the most productive artists the world has known.

Career Path

Pablo Picasso, the gold standard of twentieth-century art, was not a likable man. He was misogynistic, superstitious, acerbic, cowardly, and cruel. Of course, he was such a genius that art lovers conveniently forget his faults.

In true Spanish fashion Picasso was given a first name, nine middle names, and four last names at birth. He was baptized Pablo Diego José Santiago Francisco de Paula Juan Nepumuceno Crispín Crispiano de los Remedios Cipriano de la Santísima Trinidad Ruiz Blanco y Picasso

López. His father, José, was a painter and professor of art. Under his father's tutelage Picasso was a precocious artist. He painted his first work at age ten and at fifteen dazzled his future instructors at the Barcelona School of Fine Arts with a virtuoso entry test. He continued studying art and eventually attended the Royal Academy of San Fernando in Madrid.

He was at the Royal Academy for less than a year, but by then he'd had enough training. In 1900 Picasso moved to Paris, which proved to be a turning point in his life and career. The cruel Paris winter depressed him. The suicide of his friend and fellow artist, Carlos Casagenas, over a failed love affair, added to his sorrow. This was the beginning of his Blue Period, a post-impressionist stage in which blue was the dominant color in his works. The blues and grays he used revealed his sadness. Many of his harlequins and circus scenes are from this period. He also stopped signing his works as Ruiz Blasco, changing his signature to Picasso, his mother's last name.

Depressed, Picasso returned to Spain for a while, and when he felt better settled in Paris again in 1904. This was the beginning of his Rose Period, when happier pinks and reds ruled his palette. However, his identification with the harlequin, the sad misfit, continued. *Acrobat and Young Harlequin* is one of his better-known works from this period.

Back in Spain by the end of 1906, Picasso painted *Les Demoiselles d'Avignon*, a work of such sweeping change that it is considered the forerunner to cubism. Two years later, Picasso and fellow artist Georges Braque began painting in a style critics said looked like little cubes, called cubism. About this time Picasso also began working as a sculptor. His sculptures were as singular as his paintings. He used paper, wire, rocks, trash, and anything that caught his eye, to mold into works of art.

At the beginning of World War I, Picasso, then living in France, declared himself a pacifist. He refused to fight the Germans and remained a pacifist throughout his life. Many of his contemporaries and scholars believe that Picasso was a coward, not an idealist.

Between wars, Picasso was greatly influenced by surrealism, a movement that maintained that art should express the unconscious mind. The large, distorted, hard-hitting figures that populate Picasso's paintings of the time brought about what is called his Monster Period. *Figures by the Sea*, an oil painting from 1931, is an impressive example of his work during this period.

The German bombing of the Basque town of Guernica on April 26, 1937, inspired his most famous work, *Guernica*. To this day it is one of the most powerful images ever created of the horrors of war.

His work made him a millionaire many times over and an international celebrity. Picasso was a born self-promoter, and often made up stories about himself. He became such a fanciful chronicler of his own life that in many cases it is difficult to ascertain what is true and what is made up. Picasso simply enjoyed seeing his name in print. Picasso was so self-assured that he even mocked himself publicly. He was fond of saying: "My mother said to me, 'If you are a soldier, you will become a general. If you are a monk, you will become the Pope.' Instead, I was a painter, and became Picasso."

In 1954 he met Jacqueline Roque, who later became his last wife. Jacqueline, however, was no pushover. She controlled his life to the point of not allowing his children from previous marriages to visit him. Picasso's creativity appeared to dissipate around the same time. His works from the 1960s and 1970s did not meet the critics' approval, but as usual, he was ahead of his time. Picasso's style of that era is today called neo-expressionism.

The great master, who produced more than 20,000 works, died at Mougins, France on April 8, 1973.

Bibliography

Bonet Correa, Antonio, et al. *Picasso, 1881-1981*. Madrid: Taurus, 1981.

Caws, Mary Ann. *Pablo Picasso*. London: Reaktion, 2005.

Karmel, Pepe. *Picasso and the Invention of Cubism*. New Haven: Yale University Press, 2003.

Krull, Kathleen. *Lives of the Artists*. New York: Harcourt Brace, 1995.

Utley, Gertje. *Picasso: The Communist Years*. New Haven: Yale University Press, 2000.

Widmaier Picasso, Olivier. *Picasso: The Real Family Story*. London: Prestel, 2004.

Francisco Pizarro

From Obscurity to Fame   Explorer

❖ Born in Trujillo, Spain.
❖ Birth date: Between 1475 and 1478.
❖ Death date: June 26, 1541.

Career Highlights

- Arrived in the New World in 1509.
- Was part of the expedition that discovered the Pacific Ocean in 1513.
- Became mayor of Panama City in 1519.
- Led a failed expedition to Perú in 1524.
- Conquered Perú in the period between 1526 and 1528.

Important Contributions

Pizarro's subjugation of the Incan empire, including present-day Perú and parts of Ecuador, Bolivia, and Chile, added vast land holdings and immense riches to Spain's colonial empire, increasing Madrid's influence upon world affairs.

Career Path

Francisco Pizarro, the conqueror of Perú, was illegitimate and illiterate. Born in one of Spain's poorest areas, he was raised by his grandparents, and spent his early years in absolute poverty. As an adult, he became a soldier and fought in Italy.

Fascinated by the stories of Diego Velázquez's conquest of Cuba and Hernán Cortés' subjugation of México's Aztec Empire, Pizarro left for the New World. He became one of the main lieutenants of Alonzo de Ojeda and was with the explorer during the discovery of the areas that are today Venezuela and Colombia. Ojeda left him as governor of the settlement of San Sebastián, in Colombia, but troubles soon arose in the form of food shortages and unfriendly natives, among others. Pizarro was forced to flee to Cartagena where he attached himself to a fleet that was bringing supplies to the now-abandoned colony.

Pizarro's desire for conquest and wealth brought him to the forefront of Spanish exploration in the New World. After eleven years of minor military duty in South America, he surfaced again in Panama accompanying Vasco Nuñez de Balboa when he discovered the *Mar del Sur* (South Sea), the Pacific Ocean. During the next six years, Pizarro was a small landowner, entered local politics, and became mayor of Panama City. While mayor, he heard of a rich and large empire to the south in the Andes Mountains. He resigned his post to organize an expedition. His first trip failed. The second, after many difficulties, explored the coast of Perú. Pizarro then returned to Spain where he obtained King Charles V's consent to conquer Perú. In addition, the king granted him the title of *Adelantado* (governor general and military leader) of the new lands.

On January 19, 1530, Pizarro sailed for Panama and a year later to South America. His legion consisted of three ships, forty horses, and more than 150 men. The Incas' superb roads proved a blessing to the conquerors, who made excellent time. Of course, Incan spies were able to report to Atahualpa, the emperor, every move the Spaniards made. When the Spaniards reached the inland city of Cajamarca, they resorted to treachery to bypass the superior Incan army and invited Atahualpa to visit them. The Spaniards hid in city buildings while a Catholic priest waited for the emperor at the plaza. Atahualpa showed up with a huge retinue of servants and soldiers; however, they were unarmed. When the Inca rejected Christianity and the sovereignty of the Spanish monarch, Pizarro and his men emerged from their hiding places and massacred more than 2,000 Indians. Atahualpa was taken prisoner and held for ransom. The ransom was paid, but the Incan emperor was executed anyway. The Incan Empire ceased to exist.

Pizarro continued his conquest of Perú and in 1535 he founded *Ciudad de los Reyes* (City of the Kings, today's Lima). The conquistador also chose Atahualpa's brother, Manco, as a puppet emperor. Manco decided to rule by himself and led a revolt against the Spaniards, but he failed. Pizarro and his men continued their domination. Quarrels eventually broke out among the Spaniards over control of the territory. In 1541 Pizarro's opponents ambushed and killed him in Lima. By then, the addition of Incan gold to that already taken from the Aztecs in México, facilitated Spain's emergence as the most affluent and dominant country in the world.

Bibliography

Díaz-Trechuelo Spínola, María Lourdes. *Francisco Pizarro: El Conquistador del fabuloso Perú*. Madrid: Anay, 1988.

Chrisp, Peter. *The Spanish Conquest of the New World*. New York: Thomson Learning, 1993.

González Ochoa, José Ma. *Francisco Pizarro (Trujillo, 1478–Lima, 1541)*. Madrid: Acento Editorial, 2002.

Jaramillo, Mario. *Perfiles de Conquista: La Aventura de España en América*.

Bogotá: Universidad Sergio Arboleda, Fondo de Publicaciones, 2003.

Prescott, William Hickling. *Historia de la Conquista del Perú*. Madrid: Colegio Universitario, Ediciones Istmo, 1986.

Varón Gabai, Rafael, trans. Javier Flores Espinoza. *Francisco Pizarro and his Brothers: The Illusion of Power in Sixteenth-Century Perú*. Norman, OK: University of Oklahoma Press, 1997.

Wood, Michael. *Conquistadors*. Berkeley, CA: University of California Press, 2000.

Anthony Quinn

A Man of the World   Actor

- ❖ Born in Chihuahua, México.
- ❖ Birth date: April 21, 1915.
- ❖ Death date: June 3, 2001.

Career Highlights

- Won first Oscar for Best Supporting Actor in 1952.
- Won second Oscar for Best Supporting Actor in 1956.
- Nominated for, but did not win, Oscar for Best Actor in 1964.
- Received the 1987 Golden Globes' Cecil B. DeMille Award for Career Achievements.

Important Contributions

Anthony Quinn's flair for convincingly playing any character was his greatest contribution as an actor. It was his way of proving that people are basically the same all over the world.

Career Path

A Greek partisan, a French painter, an Indian chief, an Arab sheik, a Filipino guerilla—Anthony Quinn had a knack for playing all sort of nationalities. He considered himself a citizen of the world, but the Academy Award-winning actor was Mexican.

He was born Antonio Rodolfo Oaxaca Quiñones to a half-Irish father and a *mestizo* (mixed Indian and Spanish) mother. Like other emigrants looking for a better life, his family moved to the United States when he was about four months old. In time, the Quiñones ended up in East Los Angeles and young Antonio grew up in the *barrio*. He was not very committed to a formal education, and tried to pursue a career in the arts. But times were tough, and by adulthood he had worked as a street corner preacher, a taxicab driver, a butcher, and a boxer, among other jobs. Quinn's artistic talents won him a scholarship to study with Frank Lloyd Wright. The famous architect took a liking to the young man and paid for surgery to remedy a speech impediment. Wright recommended acting lessons to help Quinn's recovery. Quinn enjoyed acting and got his first break in 1936. That year he made four movies: *Parole*, *Sworn Enemy*, *Night Waitress*, and *The Plainsman*, the last for legendary director Cecil B. DeMille. Quinn worked for Paramount until 1940, and then spent the next six years working for Warner Brothers and Twentieth Century Fox. His most noteworthy roles of that era were in 1941's *They Died With Their Boots On*, in which he played Indian chief Crazy Horse, 1943's *Guadalcanal Diary*, and 1945's *Back to Bataan*, in which he portrayed a Filipino guerrilla.

The 1950s were good to Quinn. He made *Against All Flags* with Errol Flynn and *Viva Zapata* with Marlon Brando, which won Quinn his first Oscar for Best Supporting Actor. In 1956 he was in Italian director Federico Fellini's *La Strada* and in *Lust for Life* with Kirk Douglas. Quinn won a second supporting actor Oscar for his portrayal of Paul Gauguin opposite Douglas's Vincent Van Gogh.

In 1961 Quinn appeared in *The Guns of Navarrone* as a Greek freedom fighter and played a Bedouin chief in David Lean's masterpiece, *Lawrence of Arabia*. In 1964 he made the movie most people associate him with, *Zorba the Greek*.

By then, he could afford to indulge his passion for art. He became a well-known collector of sculptures and painting, including a work by Picasso. Quinn even tried his own hand at art. Some critics considered him a quality painter and sculptor, but others derided his talent, asserting that he should stick to acting.

During the next thirty years Quinn would create some of his most unforgettable characters, such as the Russian-born Pope in 1968's *The Shoes of the Fisherman*, and Italo Bombolini, the inept World War II-era mayor of a Italian town in 1969's *The Secret of Santa Vittoria*.

Quinn's career sank when he started overacting, and the roles he coveted stopped coming his way. Upset by this, he went to work in Italy. His state of mind at the time is revealed by a comment he made to the media: "What could I play here? They only think of me as a Mexican, an Indian, or a Mafia don." This seemed an unfair charge by the man who had played so many characters of different ethnic backgrounds in countless Hollywood films. His self-imposed exile did not last long. Quinn returned to the United States to star in such films as

The Greek Tycoon, The Last Action Hero, and *A Walk in the Clouds.* His last film was *Avenging Angelo* in 2001. He died that year in a Boston hospital of respiratory failure at the age of eighty-six.

Bibliography

Marill, Alvin H. *The Films of Anthony Quinn.* Secaucus, NJ: Citadel Press, 1975.

Quinn, Anthony. *The Original Sin: A Self-Portrait.* Boston: Little, Brown & Co., 1972.

Quinn, Anthony, with Daniel Paisner. *One Man Tango.* New York: HarperCollins, 1995.

Reyes, Luis, and Rubie, Peter. *Los Hispanos en Hollywood.* New York: Random House Español, 2002.

Rosenfeld, Richard, ed. *Star Profiles.* New York: Gallery Books, 1984.

José A. Quintero

A Cuban Confederate Spy   Secret Agent

- ❖ Born in Havana, Cuba.
- ❖ Birth date: May 6, 1829.
- ❖ Death date: September 8, 1885.

Career Highlights

- Participated in unsuccessful attempt to annex Cuba to the U.S. in 1851.
- Named editor of New York's Spanish-language *Leslie's Illustrated Newspaper* in 1859.
- Enlisted in San Antonio's Quitman Rifles, a Confederate unit, in 1861.
- Selected for the Confederate Secret Service in 1861.
- Fought in México against the French in 1862.
- Edited Havana's *Boletín Comercial* (*Business Gazette*) in 1868.

Important Contributions

The appointing of Quintero to work with Mexican authorities to keep the port of Matamoros open to Confederate ships might have been one of the best decisions Confederate President Jefferson Davis made in the American Civil War. Matamoros enabled the South to export cotton and import arms, munitions, and other war materials, keeping the Confederacy alive much longer than expected.

Career Path

As unlikely as it may sound, the most valuable agent the South had during the Civil War was a Cuban.

José Agustín Quintero's father was Cuban and his mother English. He was bilingual from the time he learned to speak. His early education took place at *Colegio de San Cristóbal* (Saint Christopher School). He was sent to the United States at an early age to complete his education. Quintero attended Harvard, but due to his father's death, he had to give up his studies and earn a living giving Spanish lessons. He was quite gregarious and became a favorite of New England's cultured society, becoming friendly with Ralph Waldo Emerson and Henry Wadsworth Longfellow.

Around 1848 he returned to Cuba and earned a law degree from the University of Havana. During that period he also became involved in the cause of Cuban independence from Spain, and turned to journalism to express his views. His articles got him in hot water with Spanish authorities and he was arrested three times. Quintero was also involved in the disastrous attempt by Narciso López to overthrow the Spanish government and annex Cuba to the United States. He was detained a fourth time and condemned to death in 1851 for his participation in López's last attempt. While awaiting execution at Havana's Morro Castle he managed to escape and returned to the United States.

Quintero went to San Antonio and in 1856 became editor of *El Ranchero* (*The Rancher*), the Democratic Spanish-language newspaper that at the time had great influence in San Antonio. He also traveled extensively on both sides of the border and made friends with many influential people. In 1857 Quintero went to New Orleans where he was admitted to the bar and practiced law. In 1859 he went to New York City and became editor of the Spanish-language *Leslie's Illustrated Newspaper*.

When the Civil War broke out in April 1861, Quintero, a believer in states' rights and a supporter of slavery, decided to cast his lot with the Confederacy. He joined the Quitman Guards in Texas and went to Virginia with the unit. There he met Confederate President Jefferson Davis. Davis chose him as a confidential agent of the Confederacy in México on September 4, 1861. Quintero promptly established headquarters in Brownsville, Texas, and instituted what is known as the Matamoros Trade. Just across the border from Brownsville, México's port of Matamoros served as the outlet to ship overseas the cotton produced by the Confederacy, whose ports were blockaded by the Union Navy. Using his contacts in the city and on the other side of the border, Quintero smuggled more than 320,000 bales of cotton from the South. It was shipped to European ports to pay for essential war equipment. Quintero managed to smuggle some 20 percent of all the cotton exported by the Confederacy. When Union troops took Brownsville in November 1863, Quintero simply moved to Matamoros and continued his work. In the middle of all this, Quintero still found time to help Mexican President Benito Juárez fight the French troops occupying the country.

At the end of the Civil War, Quintero returned to New Orleans and earned his law degree. Eventually, he edged back into journalism in Havana, and in 1868 he edited a business journal, the *Boletín Comercial*. However, when the *Guerra de los 10 Años* (the Ten Years' War) broke out, Quintero decided to leave Cuba. Spanish authorities distrusted him because of his former insurrectionist activities. He returned to the United States, joining the *New Orleans Daily Picayune*. Quintero also served as consul for Costa Rica and Belgium in New Orleans. His health began deteriorating at about that time and he died eight years later, on September 8, 1885.

Bibliography

Báez, Vicente, ed. *La Enciclopedia de Cuba*. San Juan PR: Enciclopedia y Clásicos Cubanos, Inc., 1973.

Marbán, Jorge A. *José Agustín Quintero: Un Enigma Histórico en el Exilio Cubano del Ochocientos*. Miami: Ediciones Universal, 2001.

Perkins, Robert. "Diplomacy and Intrigue: Confederate Relations with the Republic of México, 1861–1862." Tripod.com. http://members.tripod.com/~azrebel/page//.html (March 17, 2005).

Santiago Ramón y Cajal

Inside the Human Brain   Medical Doctor

❖ Born in Petilla de Aragón, Spain.
❖ Birth date: May 17, 1852.
❖ Death date: October 18, 1934.

Career Highlights

- Selected to the Madrid Royal Academy of Sciences in 1895.

- Appointed director of Spain's *Instituto Nacional de Higiene* (National Hygiene Institute) in 1900.

- Elected to the Spanish Royal Academy in 1905.

- Received Heimholts Medal from the Berlin Royal Academy of Science in 1906.

- Awarded the Nobel Prize in Medicine in 1906.

Important Contributions

Without the work of Santiago Ramón y Cajal, we still might not know that our brains are composed of separate cells called neurons that communicate among themselves. Before his work, scientists believed that brain filaments were combined in an uninterrupted mesh. His research was the foundation of contemporary neuroscience, and has enabled scientists to find cures for many mental illnesses.

Career Path

While Santiago Ramón y Cajal won a Nobel Prize in medicine, his fame is partly due to his artistic talents.

Little is known of Cajal's first twelve years, except that the family moved many times, ending up in the city of Jaca, where he started secondary school in 1861. He demonstrated a talent for draftsmanship. Cajal admitted to having "an irresistible mania" for doodling and drawing as a young man. Yet he trained as a barber and a cobbler. His father, who was a professor of anatomy at the University of Saragossa, persuaded him to study medicine. Cajal enrolled in 1870 and three years later received his *licentiate*, the equivalent of a master's degree, in medicine. He then joined the Spanish Army Health Corps.

Almost immediately Cajal was shipped to Cuba, where he caught malaria and tuberculosis. He returned to Spain in 1875 and was appointed temporary assistant professor at Saragossa's School of Anatomy. In 1877 Cajal received his doctorate degree in medicine and published his first scientific paper three years later. Indefatigable and determined, he taught, wrote, and researched for the next seven years. In 1888 he discovered that the nervous system is not one great association of strands, but is made up of individual cells. He polished his findings over the next four years.

The next year, the German Anatomical Society requested that he present his findings at its annual congress in Berlin. Cajal spoke no German and only broken French; however, his exact, colorful drawings more than made up for his language deficit. He got his ideas across thanks to his art training.

Afterward, he began to publish some of his most important works, including *Manual de Histología Normal y Técnica Micrográfica* (*Manual of Normal Histology and Micrographic Technique*), *Manual de Anatomía Patológica General* (*Manual of General Pathological Anatomy*), and *Textura del Sistema Nervioso del Hombre y de los Vertebrados* (*Structure of the Nervous System of Man and Vertebrates*). He also received many honors, including doctor *honoris causa* degrees from Cambridge University and Worcester University in 1905. The next year he declined the post of Spain's minister of public education, and on December 10th received the Nobel Prize.

Another book, *Degeneración y Regeneración del Sistema Nervioso* (*Degeneration and Regeneration of the Nervous System*), was published in 1914. By 1922 Ramón had retired for all practical purposes. Santiago Ramón y Cajal died in Madrid a few months after his last book, *El Mundo Visto a los Ochenta Años* (*An Eighty-Year-Old Looks at the World*) was published. On April 17, 1998, original glass microscope slides prepared by Cajal became the first scientific historical objects to go into space as part of the Neurolab project aboard the Space Shuttle *Columbia*.

❖   ❖   ❖

Bibliography

Albarracín Reuló, Agustín. *Santiago Ramón y Cajal: La Pasión de España*. Barcelona: Editores Labor, 1982.

Aragón, Juan. *Figuras Estelares*. Barcelona: Bruguera, 1974.

Calvo Roy, Antonio. *Cajal: Triunfar a Toda Costa*. Madrid: Alianza, 1999.

Ibarz Serrat, Virgilio. *La Psicología en la Obra de Santiago Ramón y Cajal*. Zaragoza. Instituto "Fernando el Católico," 1994.

Leiros, Waldo. *Santiago Ramón y Cajal: Texto Biográfico*. Madrid: Editorial Hernando D.L., 1977.

López Piñero, José María. *Cajal*. Madrid: Debate, 2000.

Pérez-Embid, Florentino, ed. *Forjadores del Mundo Contemporáneo*. Barcelona: Editorial Planeta, 1960.

Diego Rivera

Of Murals and Aztecs   Muralist

❖ Born in Guanajuato, México.
❖ Birth date: December 8, 1886.
❖ Death date: November 24, 1957.

Career Highlights

- Held first one-man show in Paris in 1914.

- Began transition from European to Mexican themes in 1924.

- Held one-man show at New York's Museum of Modern Art in 1931.

Important Contributions

His combination of Italian Renaissance-style frescoes with Aztecs and revolutionaries as subjects made him one of the co-founders of the movement known as *Sindicato de Pintores* (Painters' Union). This movement revolutionized Mexican art, especially mural painting. Rivera's art is among the most recognizable in the world.

Career Path

Wherever brilliant Mexican muralist Diego Rivera went, trouble soon followed. Diego María Concepción Juan Nepumoceno Estanislao de la Rivera y Barrientos Acosta y Rodríguez had a twin brother, Carlos María, but he died two months after the twins' first birthday. From the time Rivera could hold a pencil, it is said, he was painting on walls, furniture, and everywhere else he could. At an early age, his father, a freemason, exposed him to progressive ideas. Eventually, the town conservative majority declared the elder Rivera persona non grata and the family was forced to move to México City. Diego Rivera would find himself in the same position many times.

The family arrived in the Mexican capital in 1893, where the boy contracted scarlet fever and typhoid. Rivera learned to read and write while recovering, and was then sent to Catholic school, from which he was promptly expelled for expressing sacrilegious views. Studying art at the *Academia de Bellas Artes de San Carlos* (San Carlos' Fine Art Academy) proved to be no more stable. He started at San Carlos in 1898 and in 1902 was kicked out for partaking in student uprisings.

Four years later an exposition of his work earned him a scholarship to study art in Paris. Dazzled by the City of Light's artsy environment and European liberalism, Rivera decided to live there. In 1920 the Mexican government funded his studies in Italy. He moved to Rome and discovered wall frescoes. The next year he was back in his homeland and painted his first mural, at the National Preparatory School in México City. The frescoes technique began to pay off.

Increased radicalism in his political views led Rivera to join the Communist Party. His political activism, however, did not preclude him from accepting appointments to paint murals for the Ministry of Education. In 1927 he finished his *Agricultural School* mural at Chapingo and began the mural *History of México*, full of pre-Columbian imaginary, at the *Palacio Nacional* (National Palace). He went to the Soviet Union to celebrate the anniversary of the October Revolution, but controversy followed him there. Two years later, the Soviets kicked him out of the country because he criticized the government. Returning to México in 1929, he married painter Frida Kahlo, a Communist like him. But the party, unhappy with Rivera working for the government, barred him.

His marriage to Kahlo was tempestuous, full of infidelities and scandals. During their first marriage, they traveled to the United States where he painted *Allegory on California* at the Pacific Stock Exchange in 1931; the walls of the Detroit Institute of Arts between 1932 and 1934; and, finally, *Man at the Crossroads Looking with Hope and High Vision to the Choosing of a New and Better Future* in the RCA Building at Rockefeller Center, which he never finished due to political controversy. He had included an image of the Russian Communist leader Vladimir I. Lenin, and the mural was eventually destroyed.

Back in México, Rivera and Kahlo divorced and then remarried. When Soviet leader Leon Trotsky was assassinated in México 1940, both were suspects, but were exonerated. Later that year he divorced Kahlo for good.

In 1947 Rivera was commissioned to paint a history of México, which he entitled "Dream of a Sunday Afternoon in Alameda Park." The next year, the work was covered and kept from the public because he had written on it *Dios no existe* (God does not exist) and would not remove the phrase.

When Kahlo died in 1954 under mysterious circumstances that have suggested a possible suicide, Rivera was overcome by grief. But more bad news soon followed. In 1955 doctors diagnosed him with cancer. He went back to the Alameda Park mural in 1956, painted over "God does not exist," and proclaimed himself a Catholic. The next year Rivera succumbed to cancer at his México City home.

During his lifetime he almost single-handedly changed the history not only of art, but also of his country.

Bibliography

Arquin, Florence. *Diego Rivera: The Shaping of an Artist*. Norman, OK: University of Oklahoma Press, 1971.

Gallardo Muñoz, Juan. *Diego Rivera*. Madrid: Dastin, 2003.

Hamill, Pete. *Diego Rivera*. New York: Harry N. Abrams, Inc., 1969.

Krull, Kathleen. *Lives of the Artists*. New York: Harcourt Brace, 1995.

Morales, Dionisio. *Diego Rivera: Luz de Guanajuato*. México City: Ediciones La Rana, 2000.

West, Rebecca, Dame. *Survivors in México*. New Haven: Yale University Press, 2003.

Winter, Jonah. *Diego*. New York: Dragonfly, 1994.

Gilbert Roland

Unknown Actor Actor

- ❖ Born in Ciudad Juárez, México.
- ❖ Birth date: December 11, 1905.
- ❖ Death date: May 15, 1994.

Career Highlights

- Only Mexican actor to portray the Cisco Kid (in eleven movies).
- Nominated for Golden Globe as Best Supporting Actor in 1952.
- Nominated for Golden Globe as Best Supporting Actor in 1964.

Important Contributions

Despite his relative anonymity, Gilbert Roland's durability, talent, and versatility speak for him. His happy-go-lucky, macho image endeared him to movie lovers, mainly in Latin America.

Career Path

Gilbert Roland might just be the most unknown actor who ever made more than 100 films and television appearances. Roland began his career in silent films of the 1920s, playing his final role in 1981.

Born Luís Antonio Dámaso de Alonso, he was between five and six years old when the instability created by the Mexican revolution forced his family to move to California. His father, a bullfighter, wanted Roland to stick to the same career path, but once north of the border, young Luís made other plans. He wanted to be an actor. Roland was thirteen when he got his first part in silent movies. He decided on his stage name by combining the name to his two favorite movie stars: action hero John Gilbert and serial star and damsel in distress Ruth Roland. At nineteen Roland got one of his first screen credits opposite Clara Bow in *The Plastic Age*. During that time he became friends with Rudolph Valentino, whose contacts in the industry helped to launch Roland's career.

While many actors' careers ended when movies went from silent to talkies, Roland's voice was admirably apt for the new technology, and he made the transition. The change also brought a small detour in his career. Roland went from playing leads to character parts. His voice might have been good, but his accent wasn't. In most of Roland's early films he was typecast as a Latin lover, but his talent enabled him to move beyond the stereotype. Even though he had quite a flair for comedy, Roland preferred portraying strong and unwavering characters. Among his best-known films are 1940's *The Sea Hawk* starring Errol Flynn and 1945's *Captain Kidd* starring Charles Laughton. In the 1950s he appeared in *The Miracle of Our Lady of Fatima* and *The Racers,* and was one of the more than forty stars to make cameo appearances in *Around the World in 80 Days.* He was nominated for two Golden Globe Awards for best supporting actor. However he turned down the 1964 nomination for *Cheyenne Autumn.*

Roland made numerous appearances on *Gunsmoke, Bonanza, The High Chaparral, The Fugitive, Kung Fu,* and *Zorro.*

Roland died in Beverly Hills at the age of eighty-eight. He was one of the 500 stars (250 men) nominated by the American Film Institute for its list of the 100 (fifty men) greatest American screen legends of the movies' first century.

Bibliography

Cierco, Salvador Clotas, et al, eds. *Enciclopedia Ilustrada del Cine.* Barcelona: Editorial Labor S.A., 1970.

Halliwell, Leslie. *Halliwell's Filmgoer's Companion.* New York: Charles Scribner's Sons, 1988.

Liebman, Roy. *From Silent to Sound: A Biographical Encyclopedia of Performers who Made the Transition to Talking Pictures.* Jefferson, NC: MacFarland & Company, Inc., 1998.

Parish, James Robert, and Leonard, William T. *Hollywood Players: The Thirties.* New Rochelle, NY: Arlington House Publishers, 1976.

Reyes, Luís, and Rubie, Peter. *Los Hispanos en Hollywood.* New York: Random House Español, 2002.

César Romero

- ❖ Born in New York City.
- ❖ Birth date: February 15, 1907.
- ❖ Death date: January 1, 1994.

Career Highlights

- First Broadway role in 1927.
- Movie debut in 1933.
- Nominated for a Golden Globe as Best Supporting Actor in 1962.
- Awarded the 1984 Nosotros Golden Eagle Award for his success as a Hispanic in the entertainment industry.
- Received the Imagen Foundation's Lifetime Achievement Award in 1991.

Important Contributions

Romero had two stages in his career. From the 1930s to the 1950s, he played a Latin lover better than any other actor. His second incarnation, and the one most baby boomers remember him for, was in the role of the Joker in the 1960s *Batman* television series. Romero is one of the most beloved and revered Hispanics ever to appear on film.

Career Path

As one of the first New York-born Hispanics to gain fame in Hollywood, he earned the nickname, "Latin from Manhattan." César Romero was a grandson of José Martí, Cuba's beloved founding father and poet. The tall, good-looking César Julio Romero, Jr., studied dramatic art at New York's Collegiate and Riverdale Country schools, and began his show-business career as a ballroom dancer. He made his Broadway debut when he was twenty years old in a production of *Lady Do*. He later caught the eye of Hollywood producers with his role in *Strictly Dishonorable*. In 1933, two more plays followed: *Spring in Autumn* and *Ten-Minute Alibi*.

That same year, he made his first film, *The Shadow Laughs*. The following year he was in the William Powell production, *The Thin Man*. Romero played a naïve ladies man, a part that he would repeat again and again. He also portrayed many characters of undetermined ethnicity and national origin.

Romero was an expert comedian and acted in many of the lighthearted comedies that were popular in the 1940s and 1950s. Most notable among his 115 movies are *The Story of Mankind* (1957), *Around the World in 80 Days* (1956), *The Racers* (1955), *Vera Cruz* (1954), and *The Lost Continent* (1951). In 1939 and 1940 Romero played the role of the Cisco Kid in six low-budget westerns. Many critics agree that his best role was that of Hernán Cortez in the 1947 film *Captain From Castile* starring Tyrone Power.

In the early 1960s critics finally began to take notice of his work. The Hollywood Foreign Press Association nominated Romero for a 1962 Golden Globe for Best Supporting Actor for his part in *If a Man Answers*. After that, the entertainment industry changed, and Romero found fewer parts in movies. Two of his best roles at the time were in the Frank Sinatra vehicle *Oceans Eleven* and in *The Castilian*. Romero took to television, starring in six series. His most famous television role was that of the Joker in the absurd *Batman* series of the 1960s. Even though the Joker is clean-shaven, Romero refused to shave his mustache and wore white makeup over it, adding to his character's ridiculous appearance.

Romero once said that Hispanics make "splendid older men." He was one of them. Even at the age of seventy-eight in 1985, his good looks won him the part of Peter Stavros, the husband of matriarch Angela Channing, played by Jane Wyman, in the series *Falcon Crest*. He played the part for two seasons. His last appearances were on cable television's American Movie Classics channel, where he hosted romantic films.

Romero was a secret philanthropist who contributed to many causes, particularly that of the homeless. He was known to serve Thanksgiving dinner at the Los Angeles Mission.

He was one of the 500 stars (250 men) nominated by the American Film Institute for its list of the 100 (fifty men) greatest American screen legends of the twentieth century. This veteran of almost sixty years in show business died in Santa Monica, California, of complications from a blood clot. César Romero was eighty-six years old.

Bibliography

"Cesar Romero." StreetSwing. http://www. streetswing.com/histmai2/d2cesar1.htm (March 25, 2004).

Cierco, Salvador Clotas, et al, eds. *Enci-clopedia Ilustrada del Cine*. Barcelona: Editorial Labor S.A., 1970.

Maltin, Leonard, ed. *Leonard Maltin's Movie Encyclopedia*. New York: Penguin Books, 1994.

Parish, James Robert, and Leonard, William T. *Hollywood Players: The Thirties*. New Rochelle, NY: Arlington House Publishers, 1976.

Reyes, Luís, and Rubie, Peter. *Los Hispa-nos en Hollywood*. New York: Random House Español, 2002.

Carlos Saavedra Lamas

He Could Solve Anything　　　Statesman, Diplomat

❖ Born in Buenos Aires, Argentina.
❖ Birth date: November 1, 1878.
❖ Death date: May 5, 1959.

Career Highlights

- First elected to the Argentine Chamber of Deputies in 1908.
- Appointed Argentina's foreign minister in 1932.
- Selected as president of the Assembly of the League of Nations in 1936.
- Awarded the Nobel Peace Prize in 1936.

Important Contributions

With his talent, charm, and perseverance, aided by his nation's powerful push toward industrialization, Saavedra Lamas made Argentina the leading South American country during the 1930s and 1940s. His most important achievement was brokering a peace treaty between Paraguay and Bolivia. Both countries were involved in the Chaco War over the oil-rich border region of el Chaco.

Career Path

Carlos Saavedra Lamas' passion for problem-solving earned him a Nobel Peace Prize. Born to a patrician *porteño* (residents of Buenos Aires) family, Saavedra attended some of the best schools in Argentina. He was an eminent student at the University of Buenos Aires, receiving his law degree *magna cum laude* in 1903. A well-dressed man, rumored to wear the highest dress collars in the Argentine capital, Saavedra then studied in Paris and traveled widely. Returning to his country, he was selected to the chair of law and constitutional history at the University of La Plata. Later he taught constitutional law and political economy at his alma mater.

In 1906 the sober Saavedra was thrust into the world of politics when he was appointed director of public credit. Afterward, he would serve as secretary general (a kind of city manager and clerk) for the municipality of Buenos Aires. Saavedra's leadership of the Chamber of Deputies, in which he served two consecutive terms, was key in salvaging an important arbitration treaty with Italy. He presented projects on immigration, expansion to the interior of the country, water rights, and irrigation, many of which were adopted as law.

When he took over the Ministry of Justice and Education in 1915, Saavedra streamlined the public education system. Concerned about the industrial future of his country, he fleshed out a new program of study for middle-level vocational and technical students.

Although he was considered an aristocrat, his interest in the rights of workers was demonstrated when he advocated the creation of the International Labor Organization in 1919. Nine years later he led his country's delegation to the organization's 1928 Geneva conference and presided over it. The year before the conference he published *Centro de Legislación Social y del Trabajo* (*Center for Social and Labor Legislation*), a treatise on labor. General Agustín P. Justo took office as president of Argentina and made Saavedra his foreign minister. Saavedra promptly took Argentina back to the League of Nations. He helped his homeland become a leader of Latin America during the 1930s and personally participated in many important global conferences. While at this post, Saavedra found time to write the three-volume *Código Nacional del Trabajo* (*National Code of Labor Law*), which was published in 1933.

The Chaco War between Paraguay and Bolivia broke out in 1932, and for the next three years, Saavedra would work to end it. He drew up a series of declarations and treaties in which Latin American nations refused to accept territorial alterations that resulted from the war. Furthermore, he promoted nonaggression, reconciliation, and mediation as ways to solve the major differences. The Chaco region was divided among the two nations and the war ended in 1935.

Saavedra was elected president of the Assembly of the League of Nations the next year. The organization was suffering because the major powers ignored the organization's rule and he could do nothing to save it. But the Nobel Foundation was aware of the Argentinian diplomat's work and awarded him the Peace Prize in 1936.

Saavedra retired from the foreign ministry two years later and went back into academia. He was president of the University of Buenos Aires from 1941 to 1943 and taught there from 1943 to 1946.

Saavedra was eighty years old when he died of a brain hemorrhage in Buenos Aires on May 5, 1959.

Bibliography

Alboukrek, Aarón, and Cayuela, Nuria, eds. *Chaco (Guerra del)*. El Pequeño Larousse. Barcelona, México, Paris, Buenos Aires: Ediciones Larousse, 2003.

"Carlos Saavedra Lamas." Hispanos Famosos. http://coloquio.com/famosos/ saalamas.html (February 15, 2005).

"Carlos Saavedra Lamas—Biography." The Official Web Site of The Nobel Foundation. http://nobelprize.org/peace/ laureates/1936/lamas-bio.html (February 15, 2005).

Schilling, Warner R. "The League of Nations." *World Book Encyclopedia*, 1990 edition. Chicago: World Book Inc., 1990.

Wilkie, Richard W. "Argentina." *World Book Encyclopedia*, 1990 edition. Chicago: World Book Inc., 1990.

José de San Martín

The Gentleman Patriot

Revolutionary, Statesman

- ❖ Born in Yapeyú, Argentina.
- ❖ Birth date: February 25, 1778.
- ❖ Death date: August 17, 1850.

Career Highlights

- Won his first victory as the head of Argentina's Mounted Grenadiers in 1813.
- Forced the Assembly of Delegates of the provinces to declare independence in 1816.
- Defeated Spaniards at the Battle of Chacabuco and liberated Chile in 1817.
- Victorious at the Battle of Maipú in 1818.

Important Contributions

Not as well known in the United States as Simón Bolívar, José de San Martín holds the same moniker, *El Libertador*, in the southern portion of South America as Bolívar does throughout the rest of the continent.

San Martín is just as famous for what he didn't do as for what he did. When confronted by Simón Bolívar over the kind of government the new independent nations should have, he decided to step down rather than divide the liberating forces. He felt that the freedom of the South American countries was more important than personal glory, and averted a possible war between independence-minded factions.

Career Path

Argentina's great hero, José Francisco de San Martín, was born in a Spanish household in the northeastern province of Corrientes. In recent times, serious discussions have taken place about San Martín's legitimacy and his race. Many historians argue that there is enough evidence to prove he was the illegitimate son of Juan de San Martín and an Indian woman. This would mean that the great hero was not a *criollo* (descendant of Europeans), but a *mestizo* (of mixed Indian and European ancestry). This is considered serious revisionism in Argentina, a nation where the native population was totally eradicated and there are no Africans to speak of.

The San Martín family moved to Spain when José was seven or eight years old. He attended military school in Madrid and in 1789 became a cadet in the Murcia Regiment. He served as an officer in the Spanish Army for twenty-two years and battled Napoleon when the French emperor's forces invaded Spain. After three years of fighting the French, San Martín became obsessed with freeing his own homeland and resigned his commission. From Spain he went to England and from there to Buenos Aires, where he arrived on March 9, 1812. Once home, San Martín became a co-founder of the Lautaro Lodge, an important Masonic-style group for those in favor in self-government. After offering his services to the independent government of the city, he was appointed a lieutenant colonel in the revolutionary forces, the same rank he had in the Spanish army.

San Martín then established a regiment of mounted grenadiers. A year later, he won his first victory at the Battle of San Lorenzo. His troops defeated a Spanish expeditionary force which had arrived from Montevideo on the north bank of the River Plate. In 1814 San Martín was appointed commander of the Army of the North and began to plan the independence of Chile and Perú, the stronghold of Spanish power in the region. He later resigned for health reasons. He was subsequently appointed governor of the province of Cuyo. Two years later he sent a provincial delegation to the constitutional convention meeting in the northwestern city of Tucumán. He gave the delegates explicit orders to make a case for the declaration of independence for the United Provinces of the River Plate, what is today Argentina. He succeeded, and the congress declared independence from Spain on July 9, 1816.

In January of the following year, in a feat of sheer strategic brilliance, boldness, and organization, he crossed the Andes with the Army of the Andes, defeated the Spaniards at Chacabuco, and on February 12, entered Chile's capital, Santiago. The citizens of Santiago wanted

San Martín to lead their country, but in a display of modesty, he declined in favor of Chilean general Bernardo O'Higgins. The Spanish army counterattacked, defeating and wounding O'Higgins, but on April 5, 1818, under the command of San Martín, the independent forces won the Battle of Maipú, ending all Spanish threat to Chile. San Martín sailed to Perú, entering Lima on July 21. He was again offered the leadership of an independent nation. He accepted the offer, but would serve only as protector (a temporary ruler to guarantee the new nation's independence). On July 25, 1822, he met Bolívar at the city of Guayaquil, Ecuador. A disagreement broke out over the kind of government that the newly independent nations were to have. To avoid dividing the independence movement, San Martín resigned his position in Perú and returned to Argentina. From there he traveled to France and then went back to Buenos Aires in 1829. However, due to chaos reigning in his country, he did not disembark. He returned to France and died in obscurity in Boulogne-sur-mer on August 17, 1850.

Bibliography

Chumbita, Hugo. *El Secreto de Yapeyú: El Origin Mestizo de San Martín.* Buenos Aires: Emecé Editores, 2001.

Galasso, Norberto. *Seamos Libres y lo Demás no Importa nada: Vida de San Martín.* Buenos Aires: Ediciones Colihue, 2000.

García Hamilton, and Ignacio, José. *Don José la Vida de San Martín.* Buenos Aires: Editorial Sudamericana, 2000.

Lemos Quiroga, Jorge O. *San Martín, el Mar y el Perú.* Capital Federal: Ediciones Pardo, 2001.

Pasquali, Patricia. *San Martín: La Fuerza de la Misión y la Soledad de la Gloria: Biografía.* Buenos Aires: Planeta, 1999.

Ramos Pérez, Demetrio. *San Martín: El Libertador del Sur.* Madrid: Anaya, 1988.

Uzal, Franciso Hipólito. *San Martín Contraataca.* Buenos Aires: Ediciones Theoría, 2002.

Francisco de Paula Santander

From Friend to Foe

Revolutionary,
Statesman

- ❖ Born in Cúcuta, Colombia.
- ❖ Birth date: April 12, 1792.
- ❖ Death date: May 5, 1840.

Career Highlights

- Joined struggle for independence from Spain in 1810.

- Commanded guerrilla troops in the decisive Battle of Boyacá in 1819.

- Appointed vice president of *Nueva Granada* (New Granada) in 1821.

- Became leader of opposition to Simón Bolívar's dictatorship in 1828.

- Appointed, and later elected, first constitutional president of Colombia in 1832.

Important Contributions

Nicknamed by Simón Bolívar "a man of laws," Santander was intrinsically just that. After following *El Libertador* in the battle against Spanish colonialism, Santander's belief in the rule of law moved him to oppose his former commander in chief. He was one of the first Hispanic American leaders to fight the region's tendency to follow *caudillos* (military strongmen) and install them as heads of governments.

Career Path

After liberating *Gran Colombia* (Greater Colombia) from Spain, Francisco de Paula Santander, Simon Bolívar's chief of staff, became one of his former commander's most bitter enemies. Santander believed in democracy and the rule of law; Bolívar in autocracy and the rule of the *caudillo*.

Santander was born near the Venezuelan border into a well-to-do family of cacao planters. In his early teens he moved to Bogotá to study political science and law. He would never graduate, but what he learned there would forever guide his political life.

When Santander was just seventeen years old and about to get his law degree, Greater Colombia—the Spanish colony known as New Granada, that encompassed today's Venezuela, Colombia, Ecuador, and Panama—first declared its independence. The endeavor failed. In 1813, when Bolívar landed in Venezuela, Santander joined him. He fought in many battles and was promoted many times until he reached the rank of general.

Perhaps Santander's greatest contribution as military leader took place during the Battle of Boyacá on August 7, 1819. Appointed commander of the *llaneros* (rangers), a troop of mobile, horse-riding, guerilla fighters who harassed the colonial troops, Santander engaged a number of enemy soldiers, preventing them from joining the main battle. At Boyacá, Spanish power in northern South America was forever broken. With independence won, Bolívar took over the government of Greater Colombia, and appointed Santander vice president. In reality Santander was more of an acting president since Bolívar continued to lead attacks on the royalist Spanish forces in other places.

By 1821 the three countries of Greater Colombia—Venezuela, Colombia, and Ecuador—wanted secession. One of them was led by Venezuelan general José Antonio Páez. Santander favored a unified nation. The two clashed on numerous occasions, but Páez won, and a federal government was established. At the same time, Bolívar continued to amass dictatorial powers. Santander also opposed this, and on September 24, 1828, Bolívar removed him from office That night there was an attempt on Bolívar's life. While it appears that Santander wasn't involved, he was found guilty and sentenced to death. Intervention from respected revolutionary heroes saved Santander's life, but he was sent into exile. Santander first went to Europe and then to the United States.

With Bolívar's death on December 17, 1830, the disintegration of Greater Colombia began. Santander lost no time in returning to his homeland. He took part in the fighting that ended with an independent, separate Colombia and was elected its first constitutional president in 1832. Once in power, Santander developed progressive policies for his country, especially in the development of its educational system. However, he also embarked on a bloody hunt against opponents, especially after an unsuccessful attempt on his life. It was this cruelty that cost him the elections of 1837.

Down, but not out, Santander was elected to the chamber of deputies, where he served until his death. He died in Bogotá on May 5, 1840.

Bibliography

Camacho Roldán, Salvador. *Santander.* Bogotá: Universidad Externado de Colombia, 1993.

Gómez Aristizábal, Horacio. *Santander y el Estado de Derecho.* Bogotá: Universidad Central, 1990.

Harvey, Robert. *Liberators: Latin America's Struggle for Independence.* New York: The Overlook Press, 2000.

Moreno de Angel, Pilar. *Santander.* Bogotá: Planeta, 1989.

Reales Orozco, Antonio. *Santander, Fundador del Estado Colombiano.* Santa Fé de Bogotá: Tercer Mundo Editores, 1994.

Riaño Cano, Germán. *El Gran Calumniado: Réplica a la Leyenda Negra de Santander.* Bogotá: Planeta, 2001.

Domingo Faustino Sarmiento

Education Promoter

Writer,
Statesman

- ❖ Born in San Juan, Argentina.
- ❖ Birth date: February 15, 1811.
- ❖ Death date: September 11, 1888.

Career Highlights

- Established his first school, an adult education center, in 1826.
- Became governor of San Juan province in 1862.
- Appointed ambassador to the United States in 1864.
- Elected president of Argentina in 1868.
- His writing encompasses fifty-two volumes.

Important Contributions

As president of Argentina, Sarmiento promoted education and democracy. He was a staunch enemy of *caudillismo,* the idea that only the strongman on horseback or military leader could rule. This notion hampered the development of democracy not only in Argentina, but also in most of the South American nations.

As a writer, his work clearly expressed his opposition to ignorance and intolerance, which he saw as the two main enemies of social and political development.

Career Path

Domingo Faustino Sarmiento was a versatile man. He was a statesman, writer, educator, and promoter of science. Like many other democratic founding fathers of Latin American countries, he had to confront military leaders who wanted to turn the newly independent territories into their personal fiefdom.

The family of the future president of Argentina was poor but well educated and Sarmiento followed in that tradition. By the time he was four years old, he knew how to write and entered the *Escuela de la Patria* (the Motherland School) in 1816. Ten years later Sarmiento established his first school in a small town in the San Luís province. His pupils were much older than he was.

He traveled throughout the United States and Europe to study their educational systems. Around 1828 his opposition to the rule of the *caudillo* Juan Facundo Quiroga forced Sarmiento's first exile to Chile. Within eight years, Quiroga had been murdered, and Sarmiento returned to his hometown, where he joined a literary society and established a girls' boarding school. He also started a newspaper, *El Zonda*, named after a wind that blows from the Andes into eastern Argentina. However, a series of *caudillos* succeeded each other for leadership of Buenos Aires, and Sarmiento's opposition to them all brought about his second exile to Chile, from 1840 to 1852. In 1845 he published *Facundo*, his scorching biography of Quiroga, and *De la Educación Popular* (*About Public Education*) in 1849.

He tried to return to Argentina in 1854, but was taken prisoner in the province of Mendoza, accused of conspiracy, and sent back to Chile. He was elected to congress but refused the position. Within the year he returned to his country and began working for the union of all the Argentinian provinces. He also wrote for *El Nacional* (*The National*), one of the country's foremost newspapers. From 1856 to 1862 he was director of the newly established Ministry of Education and was a member of the constitutional assembly of 1860.

When the governor of Buenos Aires, Bartolomé Mitre, defeated the forces of the Unified Provinces in 1862, and became the first president of Argentina, Sarmiento became governor of San Juan. He promoted public education, mining, and European immigration. He also reformed public administration and the court system, continued to support democratic processes, and fought provincial insurgents.

Sarmiento was appointed ambassador to the United States, where he traveled and published *Vida de Abraham Lincoln* (*Life of Abraham Lincoln*) in 1866. In 1868 the University of Michigan granted him an honorary doctorate degree. While in the United States, Sarmiento was elected president of Argentina. He took his post in October 1868, and true to his beliefs, supported public education and immigration. Under his presidency military and naval schools were established; a teachers school at Paraná and the University of Cordoba's School of Science and Mathematics opened their doors; and the number of students in Argentina rose from 30,000 to 120,000. Sarmiento also reinforced federal controls over the provinces and put down a rebellion.

After his term was over, Sarmiento served in many posts, working as minster of the interior and the superintendent of national education, among others. Failing health forced him to give up work, and seeking a better climate, Sarmiento moved to Asunción, Paraguay, where he died. During its 1943 meeting in Panama, the Inter-American Education Conference proclaimed September 11, the day of Sarmiento's demise, as the official teacher's day in the western hemisphere.

Bibliography

Alonso Piñeiro, Armando. *Sarmiento y el Periodismo: Con la Reproducción de Cuartro Artículos Periodísticos de Domingo Faustino Sarmiento.* Buenos Aires: Academia Nacional de Periodismo, 2001.

Bellota, Araceli. *Sarmiento, Maestro del éxito.* Buenos Aires, Grupo Norma: 2000.

Botana, Natalio R. *Domingo Faustino Sarmiento: Una Aventura Republicana.* Buenos Aires: Fondo de Cultura Económica, 1996.

Criscenti, Joseph T., ed. *Sarmiento and his Argentina.* Boulder, CO: Lynne Rienner Publishers, 1993.

Halperin Donghi, Tulio, et al. *Sarmiento: Author of a Nation.* Berkeley, CA: University of California Press, 1994.

Katra, William H. *Sarmiento de Frente y Perfil.* New York: P. Lang, 1993.

Sorensen, Diana. *Facundo and the Construction of Argentine Culture.* Austin, TX: University of Texas Press, 1996.

Andrés Segovia

To Elevate the Guitar

Musician

❖ Born in Linares, Spain.
❖ Birth date: February 21, 1893.
❖ Death date: June 2, 1987.

Career Highlights

- Began learning the guitar in 1908.
- First toured the United States in 1928.
- Received honorary degree from Florida State University in 1969.
- Awarded a doctorate *honoris causa* from California State University in 1983.

Important Contributions

Before Segovia, the guitar was a second-class instrument, played only in taverns and private performances. After Segovia, it was the kind of instrument that soloist could, and would want to, play in great concert halls.

Career Path

His father wished that Andrés Segovia would become a lawyer. Instead Segovia became one of the greatest classical guitar players the world has ever known.

Andrés Segovia Torres was born in the Spanish province of Andalucía. Even though Segovia's father wanted his son to follow in his footsteps, he also made sure the young man had a broad cultural education that included music lessons. In the classical tradition, Segovia was first exposed to piano and violin, but neither appealed to him. Once he heard the guitar, Segovia was hooked. Neither his family nor his instructors wanted the boy to learn such an inferior instrument, played only by low-class entertainers and gypsies.

Having nobody to teach him the guitar, Segovia taught himself. He did such a great job that at the age of fifteen he gave his first recital in Granada. More performances followed over the next few years, most notably in Madrid in 1912 and in Barcelona in 1916. After painful years of learning, practicing, and adapting music to the guitar—for there was almost no classical guitar music available at the time—Segovia was ready to play beyond Spanish borders. He toured South America in 1919 and then went on his first European tour. He delighted listeners and critics in London, won over an audience full of celebrities in Paris, and cemented his star status in Berlin. Even though he continued touring, Segovia soon discovered that he could reach a much larger audience through recordings. His first record appeared in 1927.

Segovia then set out to conquer the United States. His initial performances did not reflect the impact he would have on the nation. The first took place in a small house in Proctor, Massachusetts, in front of fewer than thirty spectators. His next venue would be Town Hall in New York City, again in front of a small audience. This time, however, one of those present was a *New York Times* reporter. Once the *Times* published a review of Segovia's playing, all of his other New York concerts sold out. Segovia and his guitar became stars in the United States. But his newly found fame would not last. Like many others, Segovia exiled himself from his homeland when the Spanish civil war began in 1936. He moved to Montevideo, Uruguay, and for the next six years performed only in Central and South America.

By 1943 Segovia was ready to return to the United States, where he had been mostly forgotten. His talent, though, won audiences all over again. Segovia, who always wanted to enjoy the finest things in life, could do so. He became a wine connoisseur, gourmet, art collector, and enjoyed luxurious accommodations wherever he went. He performed in just about every nation outside of what was then the Communist Block. The Japanese firm Yamaha contracted him to design a guitar, and he did, recommending the finest woods and polishes. The instrument was originally priced at $10,000. Segovia also taught a generation of classical guitar players in Italy, Spain, and the United States, and supported the establishment of many guitar schools at universities.

During the later years of the Francisco Franco regime, Segovia returned to Spain to live in Madrid. There he died of unspecified causes on June 2, 1987.

Bibliography

Casares Rodicio, Emilio. *Diccionario de la Música Española e Hispano Americana*. Madrid: Sociedad General de Autores y Editores, 2000.

Duarte, John. *Andres Segovia: As I Knew Him*. Pacific, MO: Mel Bay Publications, Inc., 1999.

Kenneson, Claude. *Musical Prodigies: Perilous Journeys, Remarkable Lives*. Portland, OR: Amadeus Press, 1998.

Segovia, Andrés. *Andrés Segovia: An Autobiography of the Years 1893–1920*. New York: Macmillan, 1976.

Wade, Graham. *A New Look at Segovia, His Life, His Music*. Pacific, MO: Mel Bay Publications, Inc., 1997.

Junípero Serra

The Father of California   Missionary

- ❖ Born in Petra (Island of Mallorca), Spain.
- ❖ Birth date: November 24, 1713.
- ❖ Death date: August 28, 1784.

Career Highlights

- Ordained a Franciscan priest in 1738.
- Traveled to New Spain, today's México, in 1749.
- Founded nine missions in California between 1769 and 1782.

Important Contributions

Father Serra was the most influential Spaniard, indeed European, in the colonization of California by Spain. Many of the missions he founded, such as San Diego de Alcalá, San Luis Obispo de Tolosa, San Francisco de Asís, and San Juan Capistrano, grew into some of present-day California's largest and best-known cities.

Career Path

If California has a father, it is Junípero Serra. He was born Miguel José Serra to a humble family that nevertheless managed to send him to a Franciscan school at Palma, Mallorca's main city. He was either fifteen or sixteen at the time. In 1729 he became a novice priest and nine years later was ordained. It was then that he changed his first name to that of St. Francis, most beloved companion.

Junípero Serra's intelligence, determination, obedience, humility, and kindness were already so well known within the order that he became a professor of theology right around the time of his ordination. In 1743 he was appointed full professor at the influential Lullian University at Palma. But academic life was not for him. Serra had a genuine desire to spread the Gospel, so six years later he traveled to México. After landing at the port of Veracruz, he walked 250 miles to México City to offer his work in the New World to the shrine of Our Lady of Guadalupe. Near México City was the Franciscan convent of San Fernando, where Serra and the other missionaries learned how to live in the wilderness and were taught the Indians' ways.

For the next eight years Father Serra traveled around México, always preaching and defending the rights of the indigenous people. In 1767 missions in remote Baja, California, came under the Franciscan order's auspices and Father Serra became the chief administrator. Two years later the Spanish government, afraid of the Russian expansion south from today's Alaska, decided to colonize *Alta* (Upper) California. By then, Father Serra was forty-six years old and suffered from asthma and an ever-present leg lesion, which made him limp noticeably. On July 16, 1769, Father Serra established San Diego de Alcalá, the first of his many missions at Presidio Hill, where the Spaniards had a small fort. The site is today in San Diego's Old Town area. In rapid succession, Father Serra founded eight other missions: San Carlos Borromeo (1770), San Antonio de Padua and San Miguel Arcángel (1771), San Luis Obispo de Tolosa (1772), San Francisco de Asís and San Juan Capistrano (1776), Santa Clara de Asís (1777), and San Buenaventura (1782).

The road connecting Father Serra's string of missions and fortified towns spanned 700 miles from San Diego in the south to Sonoma in the north. It became what is known as *El Camino Real* (the Royal Road, a fairly common name for important roads in all the Spanish colonies), and was the backbone of European settlement and civilization in California.

Father Serra not only established missions but also converted many Native Americans to Christianity. His love for the California natives usually put him at odds with Spanish settlers and authorities. He also introduced agriculture and irrigation systems to the area. Today more than half of the population of the state of California lives near missions he founded and those established by others under his supervision.

Father Serra was laid to rest under the chapel at San Carlos Borromeo mission, in present-day Carmel, where he died.

Today the Catholic Church calls him Blessed, the first step to sainthood. The state of California calls him Father.

Bibliography

Anderson, Dale. *The California Missions.* Milwaukee, WI: World Almanac Library, 2002.

Couve de Murville, M.N.L. *The Man Who Founded California: The Life of Blessed Junípero Serra.* San Francisco: Ignatius Press, 2000.

Gleiter, Jan, and Thompson, Kathleen. *Junípero Serra.* Austin, TX: Raintree Steck-Vaughn, 1993.

Hilton, Sylvia L. *Junípero Serra.* Madrid: Historia 16–Quorum, 1987.

Morgado, Martin J. *Junípero Serra's Legacy.* Pacific Grove, CA: Mount Carmel, 1987.

Palóu, Francisco. *Junípero Serra y las Misiones de California.* Madrid: Dastin, 2002.

Rolle, Andrew F. *California: A History.* Wheeling, IL: Harlan Davidson, 1998.

Hernando de Soto

To Reach the Mississippi   Explorer

- ❖ Born in Villanueva de la Serena, Spain.
- ❖ Birth date: 1496 or 1500.
- ❖ Death date: May 21, 1542.

Career Highlights

- Participated in the conquest of Nicaragua in 1524–1527.
- Joined Francisco Pizarro's expedition to Perú in 1531.
- Appointed governor of Cuba in 1537.
- Reached Tampa Bay in 1539.
- Discovered the Mississippi River in 1541.

Important Contributions

De Soto was the first European to explore northwest Florida, Georgia, North and South Carolina, Alabama, Mississippi, Arkansas, and most of Louisiana. He is also credited with discovering the Mississippi River.

Career Path

After being second to other Spanish *conquistadores* (conquistadors), Hernando de Soto got his big chance when King Charles V granted him the right to explore Florida.

De Soto was born in southwestern Spain. Thanks to Pedro Arias de Ávila (also known as Pedrarias) the poor young nobleman was able to obtain a higher education. By the time Pedrarias was appointed governor of Darién in 1519, de Soto was ready to go with him. He supported Pedrarias against Vasco Nuñez de Balboa and Francisco de Córdoba. The governor rewarded him by giving him a cut of the profitable slave trade. Later de Soto took part on expeditions to Nicaragua and Venezuela. In 1532 he was with Francisco Pizarro in the conquest of Perú. De Soto disapproved of the killing of the Incan emperor, Atahualpa, and decided to leave Perú. He took with him a considerable fortune of more than 18,000 ounces of gold.

He returned to Spain and due to his wealth, charm, and looks, became a fixture at court. De Soto married Pedrarias's daughter, Isabella de Bobadilla, adding her family's considerable influence to his own. The Bobadillas were a wealthy family, well connected to the Spanish crown and the Catholic Church.

De Soto wanted to be greater than Hernán Cortez or Pizarro, so he pestered King Charles V to approve a voyage of exploration. Concerned that there were too many explorers in South America, the king decided to send de Soto north to Florida. In addition, the king named de Soto governor of Cuba. The island would be used as a forward base from which to launch the voyage of exploration.

The region the Spaniards called Florida was much larger than today's state of the same name. It stretched west as far as the Rio Grande and north to the Carolinas. Such was de Soto's reputation that his expedition was composed mostly of young noblemen from Spain and Portugal. The nine ships that de Soto purchased left Spain with some 650 men. The fleet reached Havana on May 18, 1539. He was in Cuba just long enough to leave all of the wives on the island, his own as provisional governor. On May 30 the expedition laid anchor in Tampa Bay and de Soto began his exploration of Florida.

On one of the early treks into the mainland, the Spaniards ran into one Juan Ortiz, a survivor of a previous expedition who lived among the natives. Ortiz became de Soto's interpreter and one of his main lieutenants. However, the dashing de Soto proved to be no smarter than other European conquerors and was soon fighting hostile Indians. He pillaged, lied, cheated, and murdered as he advanced from Florida to today's Alabama. He made enemies of the Creeks, Choctaws, Chickasaws, Timucuan, Tuskegees, and Seminoles. Continually harassed by the natives, de Soto turned west, eventually reaching the Mississippi. He would go down in history as the discoverer of the great river.

Tired and disappointed in not finding gold and richess to take back to Spain, de Soto and his men, by now reduced to half of the original strength, built a small fort on the banks of the river and decided to stay there to recover. But the Indians would not let them rest. The Spaniards were almost under constant attack.

By then de Soto was not as arrogant and flamboyant as when the expedition started, and he asked for forgiveness from his men. He felt he had led them to their deaths. Finally, after enduring various injuries, and probably suffering from malaria, de Soto died on May 21, 1542. To prevent the Indians from finding out that the great leader was dead, his men wrapped his body and submerged it into the mighty river. His wife, Isabella, died in Havana three days after being notified of her husband's death.

Bibliography

Duncan, David Ewing. *Hernando de Soto: A Savage Quest in the Americas.* New York: Crown Publishers, 1995.

Ewen, Charles Robin. *Hernando de Soto Among the Apalachee: The Archeology of the First Winter Encampment.* Gainesville, FL: University Press of Florida, 1998.

Hudson, Charles M. *Knights of Spain, Warriors of the Sun: Hernando de Soto and the South's Ancient Chiefdoms.* Athens, GA: University of Georgia Press, 1997.

Manning, Ruth. *Hernando de Soto.* Chicago: Heinemann Library, 2001.

Milavich, Jerald T., and Hudson, Charles. *Hernando de Soto and the Indians of Florida.* Gainesville, FL: University Press of Florida/Florida Museum of Natural History, 1993.

Thompson, Kathleen. *Hernando de Soto.* Milwaukee, WI: Raintree Publishers, 1989.

Whitman, Sylvia. *Hernando de Soto and the Explorers of the American South.* New York: Chelsea House Publishers, 1991.

John Philip Sousa

Marching into History

Composer, Band Leader

❖ Born in Washington, D.C.
❖ Birth date: November 6, 1854.
❖ Death date: March 6, 1932.

Career Highlights

- Enlisted in the U.S. Marines in 1867.
- Published first composition, "Moonlight on the Potomac Waltzes," in 1872.
- Became director of the U.S. Marine Band in 1880.
- The Sousa Band first performed in 1892.
- Wrote the patriotic American march, "The Stars and Stripes Forever," in 1896.

Important Contributions

Military marches before Sousa were just that, marches. Sousa imbued the plain musical genre with his own brand of rhythm and harmonious energy, creating a new kind of music, a more robust and rhythmic style of march.

Career Path

John Philip Souza is not a classic American name. Sousa—or Souza—is a somewhat widespread Spanish last name, and John Philip is not as common a combination in English as Juan Felipe is in

Spanish. But the man who made the name famous could not be more of an American icon. Sousa's father, a trombone player in the U.S. Marine Band, was a Spaniard of Portuguese ancestry, and his mother was Bavarian. Music was part of the lives of their ten children (John Philip was the oldest). From the time he could hold an instrument, John Philip Sousa studied the harp, trombone, piano, flute, cornet, and the alto horn. He also took voice lessons.

By age eleven he played the violin in a local band. When a circus came to town in 1867, he tried to join its band. Sousa's father was not amused and enlisted him in the U.S. Marine Band. While in the Marines, he published "Moonlight on the Potomac Waltzes." It should be pointed out that Sousa used no musical instrument to write his pieces, as most composers do. He simply wrote down the notes inspiration provided him.

He was released from service in 1875 and toured as a violinist and conductor. He even directed the Gilbert and Sullivan musical *H.M.S. Pinafore* in Philadelphia. When the U.S. Marine Band needed a new conductor, Sousa was asked to take over and did. He immediately began improving it. He was disenchanted when he first met the band. Morale was poor, its repertoire was dull, the uniforms old, and most of the players wanted out. Sousa retained new musicians, pestered his superiors until he got new uniforms, and made bandmembers practice, practice, practice. As a result, the U.S. Marine Band became one of the nation's best bands. Sousa directed it for the next twelve years. The band played for presidents Rutherford B. Hayes, Grover Cleveland, Chester A. Arthur, and Benjamin Harrison. But the band's limited touring schedule bothered him, so he left the Marines again and formed his own band.

Nothing but the best would do for the Sousa Band: the best musicians, the best instruments, and the best venues. The ensemble became immensely popular, drawing large crowds wherever it went. Twice a year the band toured the United States from coast to coast, playing in many remote locales. In many of America's small towns, a concert by the Sousa Band was the most exciting event of the year.

In 1895 his famous operetta *El Capitan* debuted. The following year he wrote the songs "King Cotton" and "The Stars and Stripes Forever." "Semper Fidelis" was released in 1898 and "The Washington Post March" in 1889.

From 1900 to 1910 Sousa toured Europe three times. In 1910 the band played in Australia, New Zealand, Fiji, Hawaii, Great Britain, Canada, Spain's Canary Islands, and South Africa, becoming the first American orchestra to tour the world.

When the United States entered World War I, Sousa was already sixty-two years old; however, he volunteered and was accepted as a lieutenant in the naval reserves. His job was leading the Marine Band. After World War I ended, Sousa returned to touring and composing. He also advocated for music education in public schools and for song royalties to be paid to composers.

Sousa died of a heart attack in Reading, Pennsylvania, on March 6, 1932. His last concert had ended with "The Stars and Stripes Forever." He left the world 135 marches, eleven operettas, various minor works, and a new instrument, the sousaphone, a kind of tuba without which his marches cannot be played.

Bibliography

Bierley, Paul E. *John Philip Sousa: American Phenomenon.* New York: Appleton-Century-Crofts, 1973.

Bierley, Paul E. *The Works of John Philip Sousa.* Columbus, OH: Integrity Press, 1984.

Bredeson, Carmen, and Thibodean, Ralph. *Ten Great American Composers.* Berkeley Heights, NJ: Enslow Publishers, Inc., 2002.

Ewen, David. *American Songwriters: An HW Wilson Biographical Dictionary.* New York: HW Wilson, 1987.

Greene, Carol. *John Philip Sousa: The March King.* Chicago: Children's Press, 1992.

Zannos, Susan. *The Life and Times of John Philip Sousa.* Hockessin, DE: Mitchell Lane Publishers, 2003.

Antonio José de Sucre

Self-effacing Hero

Soldier,
Revolutionary

❖ Born in Cumaná, Venezuela.
❖ Birth date: February 3, 1795.
❖ Death date: June 4, 1840.

Career Highlights

- Joined anti-Spanish forces in 1811.
- Annihilated the Spaniards at Pichincha in 1822.
- Won seminal battles at Junín and Ayacucho in 1824.
- Proclaimed first president of Bolivia in 1825.

Important Contributions

The great Venezuelan patriot Simón Bolívar was the charismatic leader who rallied independence forces to fight for South America's secession from the Spain. But the military genius behind Bolívar was Antonio José de Sucre. He was the strategist who made independence possible.

Career Path

The chief field lieutenant for Simón Bolívar, Antonio José de Sucre Alcalá was the perfect complement to his chief. Sucre was quiet, meticulous, efficient, and even-tempered. Bolívar was the opposite.

Sucre was born into a wealthy Venezuelan family of noble Spanish blood. By the time he was thirteen years old he was studying engineering in Caracas. There he studied mathematics, fortification, artillery, and surveying. At seventeen he quit school and joined independentist forces in his native country as a lieutenant in the corps of engineers. A modest, self-effacing, individual, Sucre nevertheless made a name for himself as an accomplished strategist by his early twenties. Sucre was just twenty-one when Bolívar promoted him to lieutenant colonel and assigned him to general staff of the *Ejército de Oriente* (Eastern Army).

He was one of the high-ranking officers that remained loyal to Bolívar during political infighting among the insurgents in 1817. Bolívar then sent him to the West Indies to obtain weapons. As usual, Sucre performed brilliantly, returning with close to 10,000 rifles, twelve field guns, and ample ammunition. Bolívar appointed Sucre second chief of the general staff, a job he carried out with such zeal and efficiency that *El Libertador* considered him the "soul of the army."

Sucre's brilliant military mind was demonstrated on May 24, 1822, when forces under his command routed the Spanish army, gaining autonomy for Ecuador. Two years later Sucre's genius was forever engraved in the annals of military history when he distinguished himself in battle against Spanish forces at Junín, Perú, on August 6, 1824. On December 9, 1824, Sucre defeated Spanish forces in the Battle of Ayacucho, resulting in 3,000 casualties and 2,000 prisoners from a force of 10,000 Spanish loyalists, mostly Indians and *mestizos*. His troops, just under 7,000, suffered only 500 dead and 600 wounded. At Ayacucho, the Spanish domination over South America ended. For his victory, the Peruvian Congress granted him the title of Great Marshall of Ayacucho.

The following year, Sucre entered La Paz, proclaimed the independence of Bolivia, and became the first president of the newly established republic. His term was for life, but after an assassination attempt, Sucre resigned in 1828. He spent his last years trying to prevent the separation of Venezuela from Greater Colombia. On his way to Quito to prevent the separation of Ecuador, Sucre died during an ambush in the mountains of Berruecos, near Pasto, southern Colombia. While there are many theories of who was responsible for the crime, the identities and motives of his assailants remain unknown.

Arnaldo Tamayo

A Double First   Cosmonaut

❖ Born in Guantánamo, Cuba.
❖ Birth date: January 29, 1942.

Career Highlights

- Traveled to the Soviet Union for training on the MiG-15 in 1961.
- Promoted to lieutenant in 1963.
- Selected as a cosmonaut in 1978.
- Blasted into space for the first and only time in 1980.
- Received the first ever Hero of the Republic of Cuba medal.

Important Contributions

Outside of Cuba, Arnaldo Tamayo is almost unknown. Race and politics have kept him out of the spotlight, but his presence aboard *Soyuz* 38 confirmed that space is not just the domain of powerful industrial nations, but that it belongs to mankind.

Career Path

Although the Cuban government widely publicized Arnaldo Tamayo's one-week spaceflight that began on September 18, 1980, he has fallen into obscurity. His space suit and return capsule are exhibited in Cuba's space museum in his native Guantánamo, but he hardly ever appears at public functions or is mentioned by the official press.

Colonel Arnaldo Tamayo Méndez was not only the first Hispanic to go into space, but also the first person of African ancestry to do so. He was born to a poor family. After his father died in 1955, he worked as a shoe shiner. By the time Fidel Castro's revolution took power in

Cuba, Tamayo was a carpenter's apprentice. An early member of the *Asociación de Jóvenes Rebeldes* (the Rebel Youth Association, a young Communists group), he attended the *Ejército Rebelde* (Rebel Army) technological school and then joined the Cuban air force.

In 1961 Tamayo was trained as a MiG-15 pilot in the former Soviet Union and in 1962, during the Cuban Missile Crisis, flew patrol sorties around Cuba. The following year he was promoted to lieutenant. In 1967 Tamayo was a squadron commander and traveled to Vietnam to study military tactics, to be used mainly against the United States. From 1971 to 1975 he was chief of staff of an air brigade and was promoted to lieutenant colonel in 1976.

As part of the *Intercosmos* program for cosmonauts from other Marxist nations, the Soviets selected two Cuban trainees, of which Tamayo was one. He traveled to the USSR for training, and was able to finish, while the other failed. In two years his preparation was complete. With veteran cosmonaut Yuri Romanenko, Tamayo boarded *Soyuz* 38 and launched from the spaceport at Baikonur in today's Kazakhstan. Imitating Yuri Gagarin, the first man in space, Tamayo shouted "*Poeijali*," the Russian equivalent of "Let's go!" They rendezvoused with the *Salyut* 6 space station.

Tamayo used his time aboard the *Salyut* 6 space station to perform chemical experiments, to do research on organic mono-crystals from Cuban sugar, and to map his homeland from high altitude. Upon his return to the USSR he received the Order of Lenin and the Hero of the USSR Gold Star medal, two of the highest honorary titles in the Soviet Union. Once back in Cuba, he was awarded the Hero of the Republic of Cuba medal. The Cuban government issued a commemorative stamp bearing his likeness.

He is now a brigadier general in Cuba's Revolutionary Air Force.

Bibliography

Alboukrek, Aarón, and Cayuela, Nuria, eds. "Tamayo-Médez (Arnaldo)" El Pequeño Larousse. Barcelona: Ediciones Larousse, 2003.

"Arnaldo Tamayo-Méndez." Astroinfoservice. http://www.astroinfoservice.co/uk/html/tamayo-mendez.html (January 20, 2005).

"Arnaldo Tamayo Méndez." Tayabeixo.org. http://www.tayabeixo.org/biografias/tamayo.htm (March 7, 2005).

Ianiszewski, Jorge. "Latinoamericanos en el espacio orbital." Circuloastro. http://circuloastro.freewebpage.org/chile.html (January 20, 2005).

Teresa of Ávila

God's Friend

Writer,
Nun

- ❖ Born in Ávila, Spain
- ❖ Birth date: March 28, 1515.
- ❖ Death date: October 4, 1582.

Career Highlights

- Became a Carmelite nun in 1536.
- Mystic visions began in 1540.
- Opened first convent of the order that would become known as Discalced Carmelites in 1562.
- Finished *Camino de Perfección* (*Way of Perfection*) in 1567.
- Her mystic masterpiece *Castillo Interior* (*The Interior Castle*) appeared in 1577.

Important Contributions

Teresa's mystical theology and her emphasis on prayer, virtue, and solitude earned her the respect of all Christendom. She was able to express her visions and beliefs in a rich metaphorical style that was also simple and direct. She was also the first woman to be honored as a Doctor (Teacher) of the Catholic Church.

Career Path

A saint of the Catholic Church, Teresa Sánchez Cepeda Dávila y Ahumada, who was born just two years after Martin Luther launched the Protestant Reformation, was something of reformer herself. At a time when many nuns wore jewelry and fancy veils, received friends at the convent, and threw parties, Teresa turned to prayer, writing, and a true spiritual life.

The daughter of a well-to-do merchant of old Castile and his second wife, Teresa was drawn into religious life from an early age. The problem was that she was attractive and flirty. Her mother died in 1528 and Teresa was placed in the local Augustinian convent to continue her education. Four years later, ill health forced her to leave, but she still found religion very appealing. In 1534 she convinced one of her brothers to run away so they both could enter religious life. That ended when a relative picked them up as they were leaving town. Afterward, the lure of worldly affairs distracted her from joining the Church until she entered the Carmelite monastery in her hometown on November 2, 1535. She professed the following year even though she felt no vocation.

Acutely ill with malaria, Teresa would be forced to abandon the convent once again. Her health took a turn for the worse, and on August 15, 1539, she fell into a four-day coma. Her illness eventually subsided and she began to recover, although she would not be able to use her legs for three years. During these challenging times she began to have visions and hear voices. Many believers of the time thought that manifestations were evil and Teresa kept them to herself.

By 1540 she was strong enough to return to the convent and the revelations became more intense. Thanks to her spiritual directors, first Francis Borgia and then Peter of Alcántara, Teresa began to accept the manifestations as the work of God.

Unhappy with the casual lifestyle of the convents at that time, Teresa decided to establish her own order, which, following ancient rules, required its members to go barefoot. Amid much opposition from lay and church authorities, she opened her convent at Ávila on August 24, 1562. She took the name Teresa of Jesus and spent the next five years writing *Way of Perfection*, which advised members of the order on solitude, virtue, and the habit of praying. It was not published until 1583.

Carmelite General Giovanni Battista Rossi, known as Father Rubeo, allowed Teresa to establish various other convents, but when the traditional Calced Carmelites complained, he ordered her to stop. Many nasty incidents took place between the Discalced (Shoeless) Carmelites and the Calced Carmelites. Eventually Spain's King Phillip II, who apparently had sided with Teresa, prevailed upon Pope Gregory XIII to recognize the Discalced Carmelites as a separate order. Legend has it that during this time, Teresa was traveling by horsedrawn cart along one of Spain's dusty old roads. Rain had turned the road into mud. The vehicle got stuck and Teresa had to get out to push. During the effort, Teresa slipped, falling on her face. As the story goes she looked up to heaven and, exasperated, shouted: "Hey, I'm doing Your work." A thunderous voice from heaven replied: "Teresa, that's how I treat My friends." To that she responded: "Yes! That's why You have so many!"

In the course of working with her order and convents, Teresa found time to write her masterpiece, *The Interior Castle*. In this large-scale work of mystical insight, Teresa expresses in clear, concise language her vision of true Christianity, which includes prayer, preaching, and service. The interior castle is the soul.

Teresa of Ávila, or Teresa of Jesus, died at Alba de Tormes in the present province of Salamanca. Many miracles have been attributed to her. She was canonized in 1622 and declared a Doctor of the Church in 1970. Her feast day is October 15.

Bibliography

Ahlgren, Gillian T. W. *Teresa of Ávila and the Politics of Sanctity*. Ithaca, NY: Cornell University Press, 1996.

Butler, Albqn. *Vidas de los Santos*. Madrid: Editorial LIBSA, 1998.

Chorpenning, Joseph F. *The Divine Romance: Teresa of Ávila's Narrative Theology*. Chicago: Loyola University Press, 1992.

Delaney, John J. *Dictionary of Saints*. New York: Doubleday, 1980.

García Valdés, Olvido. *Teresa de Jesús*. Barcelona: Ediciones Omega, 2001.

Gross, Francis L. *The Making of a Mystic: Seasons in the Life of Teresa of Ávila*. Albany, NY: State University of New York Press, 1993.

Slade, Carole. *Teresa of Ávila: Author of a Heroic Life*. Berkeley, CA: University of California Press, 1995.

Miguel de Unamuno

An Enigma Inside a Puzzle   Philosopher, Writer

- ❖ Born in Bilbao, Spain.
- ❖ Birth date: September 29, 1864.
- ❖ Death date: December 31, 1936.

Career Highlights

- Obtained doctorate in philosophy in 1884.
- Suffered religious crisis around 1897.
- First chosen as president of the University of Salamanca in 1901.
- Elected a second time as president of the University of Salamanca in 1931.
- Appointed to the Spanish Royal Academy in 1932.

Important Contributions

It is hard to underestimate the impact Miguel de Unamuno had on Spain and the world. As president of the renowned University of Salamanca he influenced Spanish intellectual life, and as a philosopher he touched the world. His philosophy was not orderly, but rather an amalgam of beliefs that reaffirmed faith over rationalism, because faith gives hope. His most important philosophical concept was called *intrahistoria* (interhistory), which has been explained as history being the waves of the sea, which are what you see; *intrahistoria* is what lies beneath. For Unamuno, the waves were the big historical events—wars, inventions, conquests—what lay beneath were the lives of the common people, who, in the long run, were the real history.

Career Path

If anybody could have incorporated an enigma, that person would have been Miguel de Unamuno, who with many other eminent intellectuals formed Spain's famous *Generación del 98* (Generation of '98).

Miguel de Unamuno y Jugo was a Basque, and as such, was never totally accepted by mainstream Spanish society. His well-thought-out, lucid attacks on the political and cultural supremacy of Castile in the Iberian peninsula did not endear him to the rest of the populace either. The third of six children, Unamuno was taken in by an uncle when his father died.

His early education took place in Bilbao. He went to primary school at the *Colegio de San Nicolás* (Saint Nicolas School) and secondary school at the *Instituto Vizcaino* (Vizcaine Institute). The violence between conservatives and liberals taking place in his native city during this time shaped his future political ideals. He moved to Madrid in 1880 to study philosophy at the University of Madrid. Four years later he completed his PhD and moved back to Bilbao. For the next seven years he earned a living as a private tutor, and in 1891 was appointed to the chair of Greek studies at the University of Salamanca. Ten years later he became president of that university.

In 1895 Unamuno published *En Torno al Casticismo* (*About the Castilian Character*), essays on what it means to be Spanish. He was a sincere and devout Catholic as a young man, but he suffered a dreadful religious crisis. Unable to rationalize the existence of God and life's meaning, Unamuno struggled with his *fe de duda* (faith in doubt). This conflict would dominate the rest of his life and shape all of his thinking and writing. Unamuno's work, *Del Sentimiento Trágico de la Vida* (*About Life's Tragic Sense*), concerning his lost of confidence in an immortal afterlife, was published in 1913. His support of the Allies during World War I, and his opposition to dictator Miguel Primo de Rivera, forced him into exile in 1914. He first went to the Canary Islands and then to France. That same year that he wrote *Niebla* (*Fog*), a novel of tremendous stylistic influence.

Back in Spain, Unamuno wrote an article considered offensive by King Alfonso XIII and was again exiled from his homeland. At de Rivera's death in 1930, Unamuno returned to Spain and Salamanca. Almost immediately, he published the novel *San Manuel Bueno, Martir* (*Saint Manuel the Good, Martyr*), about a priest with no faith. He was chosen president of the University of Salamanca for a second time. He held the post until early 1936 when again he was removed from his position. Although the facts support the view that Unamuno lost his position over an argument with a nationalist general, some historians blame the Spanish Republic. These historians suggest that Unamuno supported General Francisco Franco's uprising. Others believe it was his opposition to Franco—whose forces controlled parts of Spain—that cost him his post. In reality, both points of view are correct. At the beginning of the conflict, Unamuno supported Franco's Nationalists, but his opinion soon changed because of the Nationalist's Fascist ideology.

Unamuno had an acrimonious disagreement with General José Millán Astray, a Franco supporter. Witnesses to the confrontation reported that Unamuno said to the general: "You will win because you have enough brute force. But you will not convince. For to convince you need to persuade. And in order to persuade you need what you lack: reason and right." Millán Astray answered with one of the most infamous phrases ever heard: "Long live death. Death to intelligence!" Whereupon he escorted Unamuno out of the building at gunpoint and placed him under house arrest. Unamuno died a few months later in Salamanca.

A man of polemic, incompatible ideas, Unamuno was one of the most prominent thinkers of the late nineteenth and early twentieth centuries. His influence can be seen in the works of French philosopher Jean-Paul Sartre, English author Graham Greene, Spanish Nobel laureate Juan Ramón Jiménez, and Spanish poet Antonio Machado.

Bibliography

Basdekis, Demetrios. *Miguel de Unamuno*. New York: Columbia University Press, 1969.

Ellis, Robert Richmond. *The Tragic Pursuit of Being: Unamuno and Sartre*. Tuscaloosa, AL: University of Alabama Press, 1988.

Ferreiro Villanueva, Cristin A. *Claves de San Manuel Bueno, Mártir, Miguel de Unamuno*. Madrid: Ciclo, 1990.

París, Carlos. *Unamuno: Estructura de su Mundo Intelectual*. Barcelona: Anthropos, 1989.

Ribas, Pedro. *Para Leer a Unamuno*. Madrid: Alianza Editorial, 2002.

Rudd, Margaret Thomas. *The Lone Heretic: A Biography of Miguel de Unamuno y Jugo*. Austin, TX: University of Texas Press, 1963.

Zambrano, María. *Unamuno*. Madrid: Debate, 2003.

Félix Varela

The First Cuban

Philosopher,
Priest

- ❖ Born in Havana, Cuba.
- ❖ Birth date: November 20, 1788.
- ❖ Death date: February 25, 1853.

Career Highlights

- Ordained a priest on December 21, 1811.
- Elected one of Cuba's representatives to the Spanish Cortes (legislative body) in 1821.
- Established *El Habanero*, one of the first Spanish-language newspapers in the United States, in 1824.
- Assigned to the diocese of New York in 1825.

Important Contributions

Through his activism and writing, Félix Varela was the first Cuban native to effectively foster within his people the spirit of a separate nation and independence from Spain.

Career Path

Father Félix Varela y Morales is regarded as the first true Cuban. He was also one of the first in the island nation to propose the abolition of slavery. In addition he was a brilliant, strong defender of the Roman Catholic faith.

The son of a Spanish father and a Cuban-born mother, Varela's mother died when he was only four and his father when he was six. Relatives sent him to live with his maternal grandfather, a brevet colonel commander of a regiment of Cubans in San Agustin, Florida, at that time a Spanish colony. He attended primary school there and also was an eyewitness to the selling of black slaves. That horrifying experience had a profound impact in his life.

In 1801 Varela's grandfather, who had wanted him to be a soldier, gave in to the boy's wishes and sent him back to Havana to become a priest. Varela was ordained at age twenty-three. Soon afterward he became a teacher at the prestigious *Colegio-Seminario San Carlos* (Saint Charles Seminary School), his alma mater. Varela fostered in his students love of God, neighbor, and motherland. He was also a patron of the arts and sciences.

When Varela left Cuba as one of the three island deputies to the Spanish Cortes, little did he know he would never return to his beloved homeland. While in the Cortes, Varela presented three projects: recognition of the newly independent Hispanic American states; autonomy (a kind of commonwealth status for Cuba, Puerto Rico, and the Philippines); and the emancipation of slaves in Cuba. None proved popular with the other deputies, most of whom were from Spain. In 1823 King Ferdinand VII broke up the Cortes and sentenced various delegates to death, Varela among them. He managed to escape to the British possession of Gibraltar and then to the United States.

On December 15, 1823, Varela arrived in New York City and moved to Philadelphia to wait for his canonical documentation. While in the City of Brotherly Love he began the publication *El Habanero,* a newspaper that campaigned for the independence of Cuba and the rest of Hispanic America. The publication caused such an uproar in Cuba and other Spanish colonies where the paper was smuggled that it was confiscated and banned in all Spanish territories. The last edition was published from New York in 1826.

Varela began his work as a priest in New York City, establishing schools, a nursery and an orphan shelter. He was active during a cholera epidemic, and became one of the Church's firmest defenders during a particularly vicious outbreak of anti-Catholicism. He was particularly beloved by the Irish immigrants of the time who, being Catholics, faced hardships and discrimination. He defended and helped them. In return they helped save his life. Due to Varela's fiery writing in *El Habanero,* the governor of Cuba paid an assassin a large sum of money to kill him. It appears that a combination of Varela's facing his killer with kindness, as well as arguments from many of the priest's Irish parishioners, convinced the man to go back to Cuba without completing his mission.

For the rest of his life Varela would be a well-known leader of the Catholic Church in the United States, and he was quoted in many publications of the time. In declining health, Varela moved to San Agustin in the winter of 1846. Seven years later he died peacefully. Like many of his countrymen before and after him, "the first Cuban" died in exile. His remains were buried in his homeland after Cuba won its independence. When the late Pope John Paul II visited Cuba in 1998, he prayed at Varela's grave at the University of Havana.

Bibliography

Báez, Vicente, ed. *La Enciclopedia de Cuba*. San Juan and Madrid: Enciclopedia y Clásicos Cubanos, Inc., 1973.

Cartaya Cotta, Perla. *El Legado del Padre Varela*. México City: Obra Nacional de la Buena Prensa, 2002.

Céspedes, Mons. Carlos Manuel de. *Pasión por Cuba y por la Iglesia: Aproximación Biográfica al P. Félix Varela*. Madrid: Biblioteca de Autores Cristianos, 1998.

Esquenazi-Mayo, Roberto, ed. *El Padre Varela: Pensador, Sacerdote, Patriota*. Washington, DC: Georgetown University Press, 1990.

Esteve, Juan P. *Félix Varela y Morales: Análisis de su ideas Políticas*. Miami: Ediciones Universal, 1992.

Hernádez Travieso, Antonio. *El Padre Varela: Biografía del Forjador de la Conciencia Cubana*. Miami: Ediciones Universal, 1984.

Varona, Frank de, ed. *Hispanic Presence in the United States*. Miami: Mnemosyne Publishing Company, 1993.

Félix Lope de Vega

Prolific Writer . . . and Lover   Playwright

❖ Born in Madrid, Spain.
❖ Birth date: November 25, 1525.
❖ Death date: August 26, 1635.

Career Highlights

- Wrote his first play in 1537.
- Joined the Spanish Armada in 1588.
- Wrote his most famous play, *Fuenteovejuna* (*The Sheep Well*), in 1613.
- Entered the seminary in 1614.
- Appointed a Knight of Malta by the pope in 1627.

Important Contributions

The sheer volume of his work, from 1,800 to 2,200 plays and minor works, makes Lope de Vega the most fruitful playwright in the history of Spain. His talent, passion, popularity, and numerous thematic styles—from cloak-and-dagger to bucolic, from mythological to biblical—have made Lope the greatest Spanish playwright of all time.

Career Path

Félix Lope de Vega y Carpio was born into a family of modest means. He displayed his genius at an early age, reading Latin and Spanish by the time he was five and writing his first play at twelve. His early schooling was with the Jesuits and at fourteen he was already attending Madrid's Imperial College. He ran away from school to enlist in an armed expedition against Portugal, but the Bishop of Ávila stopped him and took him back to Madrid.

After graduating from the University of Alcalá, Lope once again joined a military adventure, this time a naval action in the Azores. Afterward he returned to the Spanish capital and began his career as a playwright, only to be lured by another adventure. This time he joined the Spanish Armada. Alhough the expedition ended in disaster, his ship, the *San Juan*, returned in one piece. He had spent his six months at sea writing *La Hemosura de Angélica* (*The Beauty of Angelica*).

After returning to Spain in 1590, he moved to Valencia and worked for the Duke of Alba. Five years later Lope returned to Madrid where he found himself writing sonnets to an enigmatic lady he called Lucinda. Her real name was Michaela de Luxán, an actress. In 1598 Lope became a secretary to powerful nobles. That year he also wrote the bucolic fable *La Arcadia* (*Arcadia*).

Lope, although successful, was never wealthy. In 1612 his life took a turn for the worse. His son, Carlos Félix, died and his wife, Juana, passed away in 1613. It appears the pain stirred his creative juices, since after the death of Juana, he wrote *The Sheep Well*, about a peasant insurrection. The following year Lope joined the priesthood. Even though his work did not always sit well with the Church, Pope Urban VIII was a fan and granted him a doctorate of theology and other honors.

Money was always a problem since he had many children from various marriages. Broken and penniless, Lope turned more and more to his faith. He finally died in Madrid on August 26, 1635. He left uncountable descendants and plays, 500 of which are still in print.

Bibliography

Abad Nebot, Francisco. *Estudios Filológicos*. Valladolid: Universidad de Valladolid, Secretariado de Publicaciones, 1980.

Alin, José María, and Barrio Alonso Begonia María. *Cancionero Teatral de Lope de Vega*. Woodbridge, Suffolk, UK: Tamesis, 1997.

Canning, Elaine M. *Lope de Vega's Comedias de Temas Religiosos: Re-Creations and Re-Presentations*. Woodbridge, Suffolk, UK: Tamesis, 2004.

Leiberg, Germán, and Marías, Julián, eds. *Diccionario de Literatura Española*. Madrid: Ediciones de la Revista de Occidente, 1972.

Parker, Mary. *Spanish Dramatists of the Golden Age: A Bio-Bibliographical Sourcebook*. Westport, CT: Greenwood Press, 1998.

Sánchez Romeralo, Antonio, ed. *Lope de Vega, el Teatro*. Madrid: Taurus, 1989.

Diego Velázquez

The Court Painter

Painter

- ❖ Born in Seville, Spain.
- ❖ Birth date: 1599.
- ❖ Death date: February 10, 1660.

Career Highlights

- Appointed royal chamber artist in 1623.
- Began development of his magnificent use of colors in 1628.
- Painted *La Rendición de Breda* (*The Surrender of Breda or the Lances*), circa 1635.
- Painted *Las Meninas* (*The Maids of Honor*) between 1656 and 1657.

Important Contributions

Considered one of the greatest artists ever, Diego Velázquez's works are known for his magnificent composition and realism. His use of color, pigment, light, shadows continues to be studied by artists the world over.

Career Path

He was one of the greatest painters the world has ever known. His talent is beyond discussion, but Diego Rodríguez de Silva y Velázquez was not interested in art for art's sake. He wanted to make money. He wanted to be important. His paintings were just the way to getting what he desired.

The exact date of his birth is not known, but Velázquez was baptized on June 6, 1599. While still a boy, Velázquez received his first art lessons from Francisco de Herrera, *el Viejo* (the Elder), but by the age of eleven he was already under the tutelage of Francisco Pacheco, a renowned art instructor and artist in his own right. When he was nineteen Velázquez began to show a penchant for naturalism and his work from this period has a shadowy perspective. *El Aguador* (*The Water Vendor*) and *La Vieja Friendo Huevos* (*The Old Woman Frying Eggs*) are well-known creations from this time.

In 1622 Velázquez moved to Madrid and the following year an aristocratic friend arranged for him to paint a portrait of King Phillip IV. The Spanish monarch was so impressed with the young artist's work that he appointed him the position of royal chamber artist.

Five years later, after meeting the Flemish artist Peter Paul Rubens, Velázquez's paintings began to brighten. They became more stirring and clear. He produced his *Equestrian Portrait of Phillip IV* during this period. He also created *The Surrender of Breda or the Lances*, one of the world's great historical paintings, during this time. There was at least one more painting of the same event. The oil represents the capitulation of the Dutch city's governor, Justin of Nassau, to the Spanish forces led by General Ambrosio de Spínola in 1625. Velázquez, who was not present at the event, captured the moment in such a way that any other depiction of the moment has been forgotten.

In addition to his duties as court artist, Velázquez had other royal functions. He was in charge of buying works of art for the Spanish Crown and ultimately was appointed marshal of the royal household, a position in which he was in charge of the royal accommodations and ceremonies. He still found enough time to paint portraits of Pope Innocence X and Juan de Pareja, as well as landscapes. Between 1656 and 1658, Velázquez created *Las Hilanderas* (*The Spinners*) and *The Maids of Honor*, two of his greatest works.

Velázquez died in Madrid on February 10, 1660.

Bibliography

Brown, Jonathan, and Garrido, Carmen. *Velázquez: The Technique of Genius.* New Haven: Yale University Press, 1998.

Glubok, Shirley. *Painting—Great Lives.* New York: Charles Scribner's Sons, 1994.

Harris, Henriqueta. *Velázquez.* Oxford, UK: Phaidon, 1982.

Justi, Carl, trans. del Alemán, Pedro Marrades. *Velázquez y su siglo.* Madrid: Espasa Calpe, 1999.

Lafuente Ferrari, Enrique. *Velázquez.* New York: Skira/Rizzoli, 1988.

Moliner, José María. *Vida Ejemplar de Velázquez: Su Espiritualidad.* Burgos: Editorial Monte Carmelo, 1996.

Pancho Villa

Revolutionary Bandit   Revolutionary

❖ Born in San Juan del Río, México.
❖ Birth date: June 5, 1877, 1878, or 1879.
❖ Death date: July 23, 1923.

Career Highlights

- Joined revolution against strongman Porfirio Díaz in 1910.
- Won the Battle of Ojinaga in 1913.
- With Emiliano Zapata occupied México City in 1914.
- Lost battle of Celaya to Alvaro Obregón in 1915.

Important Contributions

Whatever his past and reasons for joining the revolutions against two dictators, Pancho Villa definitely is one of the figures that helped bring a more democratic form of government to México.

Career Path

Pancho Villa is one of the most colorful and famous, although some say infamous, characters to emerge from the succession of insurrections that rocked México in the 1910s. He was a bandit, a minor revolutionary leader, a major revolutionary leader, and, finally, a legend.

Nobody is really sure in what year Doroteo Arango, Villa's real name, was born. The only thing we know for sure is that he spent most of his early life in the western Mexican state of Durango. He had very little education, if any. When Doroteo Arango was about sixteen his sister was raped and he killed the supposedly guilty man. Trying to avoid punishment, he disappeared for the next four years, emerging with a new name, Francisco "Pancho" Villa. He surfaced in northern México in the state of Chihuahua, where he was known as a cattle rustler and a miner. He tried mining in a couple of towns, but that was not the life for him, so he turned to robbing banks.

From 1900 to 1909 he was known as a bandit in the northern area of México. Villa was all the rage among the poor farmers for adeptly eluding the *rurales* (rangers) of Dictator Porfirio Díaz. Part of the time Villa resided in El Paso, Texas, where he could move freely, away from the Mexican authorities. When Francisco Madero began his revolution to overthrow Díaz, Villa joined him. In one stroke, Villa had gone from bandit to respectable revolutionary. Villa recruited a great army whose exploits in northern México were among the main reasons for Madero's victory and his ascendancy to the presidency. The success, however, was short-lived. In February 1913, *caudillo* (military leader) Victoriano Huerta deposed and executed Madero. Mexicans rebelled again, and Villa, together with Alvaro Obregón and Venustiano Carranza, fought Huerta. That same year, at Ojinaga, Villa defeated Huerta's troops, bringing to an end Huerta's control of México in 1914.

During this time, Villa became the darling of U.S. reporters, cameramen, movie producers, and others. They went to his camp in droves to write about and photograph him and even to film a simulated skirmish. The 2003 television movie, *Starring Pancho Villa as Himself*, with Antonio Banderas as Villa, is a fictionalized account of the contract signed by Villa with the Mutual Film Company to tell his story on the screen.

When Carranza took power in 1914, Villa broke with him. Washington, D.C., eager for stability on its southern border, supported Carranza and made an enemy of Villa. Even though one of Carranza's lieutenants, Alvaro Obregón, defeated Villa in an important battle, Villa was far from finished. He began to attack American border towns. His most famous incursion was in Columbus, New Mexico, in 1916, when he burned the town and killed eighteen people. Not only were Carranza's men hounding Villa, but so was the U.S. Army under General John J. Pershing. But no one could capture him. In 1919 the U.S. Army went into México one more time looking for Villa. Again he eluded apprehension.

In 1920 Obregón overthrew Carranza, who had been elected in 1917, and attempted to appease Villa by giving him a land grant and a general's pension. It worked. Villa retired to the Canutillo ranch in Durango. There he lived the next three years in peace. He was ambushed and killed while returning from a business trip to Parral, Chihuahua, on July 23, 1923.

Contrary to his image, Villa was a teetotaler. However, contemporaries said he liked to party and claimed that he was married twenty-six times. Whether or not this is true, it only adds to the legend of Pancho Villa.

❖   ❖   ❖

Bibliography

Anderson, Mark Conlund. *Pancho Villa's Revolution by Headlines*. Norman, OK: University of Oklahoma Press, 2000.

Atkin, Ronald. *Revolution! México 1910–20*. New York: The John Day Company, 1970.

Katz, Friederich. *The Life and Times of Pancho Villa*. Sanford, CA: Stanford University Press, 1998.

McLynn, Frank. *Villa and Zapata: A History of the Mexican Revolution*. New York: Carroll & Graf Publishers, 2001.

Plana, Manuel, trans. Arthur Fligiola. *Pancho Villa and the Mexican Revolution*. New York: Interlink Books, 2002.

Vives Azancot, Pedro A. *Pancho Villa*. Madrid: Historia 16: Ediciones Quorum: Sociedad Estatal para la Ejecución Programas del Quinto Centenario, 1987.

Emiliano Zapata

"Viva Zapata!" Revolutionary

- ❖ Born in Anenecuilco, México.
- ❖ Birth date: August 8, 1879.
- ❖ Death date: April 10, 1919.

Career Highlights

- Elected town representative for land reform in 1909.
- Joined the revolution against Porfirio Díaz in 1911.
- Took Cuatula and entered Cuernavaca in 1911.
- First distributed land to peasants in 1912.
- Together with Pancho Villa occupied México City in 1914.
- Rebelled against Venustiano Carranza in 1919.

Important Contributions

Though not as colorful or as well known in the United States as Pancho Villa, Emiliano Zapata had a much greater impact on Mexican history than just about any of the revolutionaries of the 1910s. He coined the phrase *Tierra y Libetad* (Land and Freedom), which very much expressed his philosophy of agrarian reform. Zapata believed that the land belonged to those who worked it. To this day, this is an issue that evokes great passions in México. Unlike most of the other Mexican revolutionaries, he fought for an ideal rather than for personal gain.

Career Path

Zapata's *mestizo* father died when he was seventeen years old. The young man went to work to support his brothers and sisters. By 1897 he was already involved in the struggle for peasants to own the land they worked. Zapata's activities resulted in him serving various minor prison sentences. In 1908 the government forced him to join the army. The military draft was a common form of punishment under the dictatorship of Porfirio Díaz. Zapata was an excellent soldier and took to military strategy, which is why he was released from service before his tour of duty was completed.

When in 1910 Francisco Madero declared himself the rightful president of México in opposition to Díaz, Zapata joined the revolution. After ousting Díaz, Madero promptly sided with landowners, and Zapata took up arms against him. His ragtag army took Yatupec, Cuautla, and Cuernavaca. This time he refused to disperse his troops or lay down their weapons until land was given to the peasants. When Madero was murdered and Victoriano Huerta took power, Zapata joined Pancho Villa and Venustiano Carranza in forcing the fall of Huerta's government in August 1914. Carranza took the presidency but by September had parted ways with his allies. Zapata and Villa also had a disagreement in December of the same year.

By 1915 Villa had been defeated in northern México, and the armies of Carranza threw the bulk of their forces against Zapata. Zapata reorganized his army and in 1916 started an anti-Carranza offensive in southern México, transferring ownership of land, sugar mills, and other industries to peasants in areas under his command. He also established schools for children and adults. His opponent nicknamed him the *Atila del Sur* (Attila of the South). Many modern scholars consider Zapatism and Marxism equals. After all, Zapata exposed many of the ideas that Marxists propose, such as land reform and communally-owned farms. However, Zapata never said that all lands should be given to peasants or become communes. He saw the successful economic future of México as a collaboration between small farmers, wealthy landowners, professionals, and investors, in other words, a partnership of all the economic classes in the country.

Four months short of his fortieth birthday, a Carranza sympathizer shot Zapata at a farm near Cuautla. To this day Emiliano Zapata is a symbol of the struggles and dreams of Mexican *campesinos* (farm hands).

❖ ❖ ❖

Bibliography

Atkin, Ronald. *Revolution! México 1910–20*. New York: The John Day Company, 1970.

Brunk, Samuel. *Emiliano Zapata: Revolution and Betrayal in México*. Albuquerque, NM: University of New Mexico Press, 1995.

Gallardo Muñoz, Juan. *Emiliano Zapata*. Las Rozas, Madrid: Dastin, 2003.

Mejía Prieto, Jorge. *Zapata, el Caudillo del Sur*. México City: Editorial Diana, 1990.

Newell, Peter E. *Zapata of México*. Montréal, New York: Black Rose Books, 1997.

Pineda Gómez, Francisco. *La Irrupción Zapatista 1911*. México City: Ediciones Era, 1997.

Index

About the Author

IVÁN A. CASTRO is a former reporter for the Spanish-language edition of *The Miami Herald* and for the erstwhile *Miami News*. His freelance work has been published throughout much of Latin America. He was born in Cuba and is a graduate of the University of New Mexico, where he majored in political science and Spanish literature. Mr. Castro lives in Miami with his wife and three children.